TESTIMONIALS

If you are looking for a book that provides a simple description of the rise of Donald Trump, Trumpism, the Trump cult and their impact on America's mental health, this is not the book for you. On the other hand, if you want to gain a deeper understanding of the multi-dimensional nature of these factors, this book will serve you well. Dr. D'Andrea's new book represents the most researched and comprehensive analysis of the threats to our country's democracy and mental health. This book will not disappoint interested readers.

Kara Shea Pitt-D'Andrea

Executive Director of the Renaissance Child Care Center, Milwaukee, Wisconsin

Dr. Michael D'Andrea's exploration of the post-Trump era is an impressive showcase of meticulous research and a genuine dedication to unraveling the intricate complexities of our ever-evolving multicultural, multi-racial world. His new book deviates from the conventional, presenting readers with a distinctive perspective that captures attention to our nation's diverse and constantly shifting landscape. While steadfast in its commitment to upholding scholarly standards, this book explores a more varied tone and inclusive language, potentially fostering a deeper connection with the diverse readership it aims to engage. Dr. D'Andrea's work stands as a significant contribution, offering readers a thought-provoking exploration of the post-Trump era.

Retired Professor of Physics, Robert King

This book's commendable research offers invaluable insights. These reflections will aid others in evaluating and expanding their political preferences and interests.

Darlene Smith-Hall, Professional Nurse

The research in this book is truly impressive. The author, demonstrating clear knowledge and scholarly prowess, expertly guides readers through a profound exploration of the Trump era and beyond. The thoroughness of the research speaks volumes about the author's dedication to tackling the complicated issues of this critical period in our history.

Howard Jackson, retired video editor, photographer, author and community organizer

DR. MICHAEL D'ANDREA

BEYOND THE LIES

**PROMOTING OUR MULTIRACIAL/MULTICULTURAL
DEMOCRACY, ADDRESSING TRUMPISM, THE TRUMP
CULT, AND THE MENTAL HEALTH OF
THE UNITED STATES**

MINDSTIR MEDIA

Published by MindStir Media, LLC
45 Lafayette Rd | Suite 181| North Hampton, NH 03862 | USA
1.800.767.0531 | www.mindstirmedia.com

Printed in the United States of America.
ISBN-13: 978-1-961532-51-9

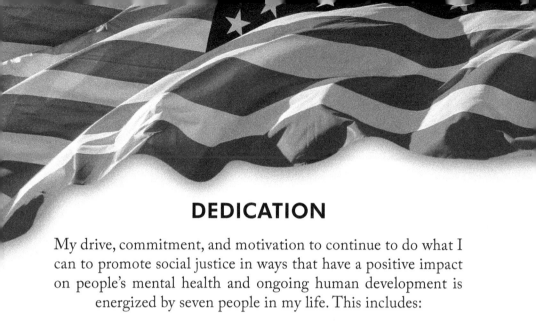

DEDICATION

My drive, commitment, and motivation to continue to do what I can to promote social justice in ways that have a positive impact on people's mental health and ongoing human development is energized by seven people in my life. This includes:

Shawn Michael, Irene, Kara Shea, Mahealani, Oscar, Charlette, and Alexius.

I dedicate this book in appreciation of the ways they continue to teach me about the importance of love when striving to build a more just and healthy society.

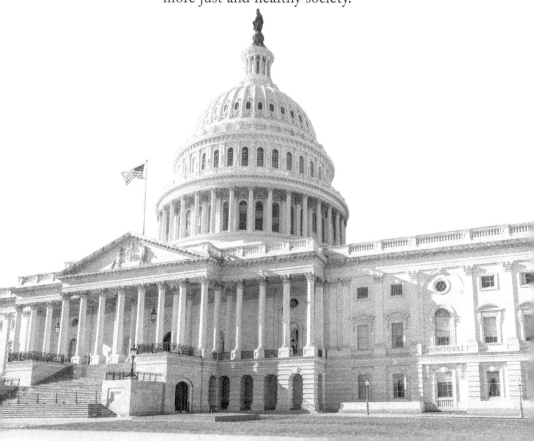

TABLE OF CONTENTS

PREFACE

These are perilous times for the people in the United States. The danger we face as a nation involves various threats to the sustainability of our democracy and the mental health crisis our country currently faces. This book provides a detailed and multidimensional analysis of numerous factors underlying these perilous times. My professional training in the Human Development Counseling doctoral program at Vanderbilt University, my 40+ years of clinical experience as a social justice advocate in different work settings, and my research and professional publications are all invaluable in helping me acquire the knowledge and skills necessary to undertake the challenge of writing this book.

With this background in mind, I conducted a comprehensive, multi-year analysis of numerous factors fueling the serious threats to our nation's democracy and our collective mental health. Among the factors I found to have a particularly adverse effect on our nation's democracy as well as a negative impact on the mental health of millions of people in our nation are the lies and false conspiracies articulated by former President Donald Trump and his supporters.

The results of numerous surveys in early and mid-2023 indicated more than 70 percent of Republican Party members continued to believe Trump's lies about the ways the 2020 presidential election was alleged to have been stolen from him. That's 70 percent of Republican Party members who continue to believe this lie despite the total lack of evidence supporting this serious psycho-political falsehood. From a psycho-political perspective, this staggering statistic sadly persists to the present time. The reasons for making the previous statement are detailed throughout this book.

The unquestionable loyalty of millions of Trump supporters, who believe his lies without providing valid evidence, is similar to the psychological reactions millions of German citizens manifested in the early 1930s as they became increasingly mesmerized by another popular, authoritarian fascist: Adolf Hitler. History repeats itself in this and other important ways and are discussed in the new integral theory of mental health and human development presented in this book.

One of the interesting and challenging aspects of writing this book is the importance of keeping abreast of significant psycho-political events that have occurred over the past several years. During this time, I have been involved in synthesizing my research and theoretical findings related to these complex issues into this publication. Numerous important events related to my research findings explain how more current political events continue to fuel the political divisiveness that was more fully activated during Trump's four years as president. These events and the increasing support from Trump supporters and members of the Trump cult represent genuine threats to our nation's democracy are also addressed throughout this book.

Among the most significant events that provide insights into the strength and viability of Trumpism in the United States occurred during the Spring/Summer/Fall of 2022 with the nationally televised House of Representatives report on the January 6, 2021 insurrection in Washington DC. This report and the results of the midterm elections, which took place on Tuesday, November 8, 2022, are highlighted in the following pages because many political pundits believed these events to be indicative of Donald Trump's waning political power and popularity.

However, in 2023, Donald Trump was indicted on ninety-one counts in four federal courts. Most pundits thought these legal problems would negatively impact Trump's political power and popularity. Instead, Trump's popularity consistently increased among his MAGA supporters as reflected in numerous polls related to his possible candidacy for the Republican Party's nomination for the 2024 presidential election. Given the relevance of these historic events for the perilous times in which we are all situated, I felt compelled to describe factors that contributed to these contradictory reactions throughout this book.

This book is divided into two parts. Part 1 is comprised of Chapters 1–6 which discuss a broad range of issues of relevance to the title of this book. Chapter 1 puts a spotlight on three words that are key to the essence of our nation's democracy: *We the People.* This chapter also explores the meaning of various foundational terms and concepts addressed in the following chapters, including the definitional meaning of the term, *a psycho-political perspective;* a concept that is the centerpiece of this book.

Chapter 2 outlines a new, expansive, and multidimensional definition of White racism and White supremacy as these psycho-social pathologies continue to be manifested in our country. It also provides a detailed description of a new theory of a multiracial/multicultural democracy entitled the RESPECTFUL theory (RT). RT is anchored in the new psycho-political perspective detailed later in this chapter.

Chapter 3 discusses the potential promise of the ongoing evolution of our multiracial/multicultural democracy when and if it is supported and sustained by a majority of people in the United States. Chapter 4 proceeds to describe some of the important pitfalls that may undermine the full realization of the fragile multiracial/multicultural democracy in our nation.

Chapter 5 explores Trump's psychology and describes the meaning of *Trumpism* from a psycho-political perspective. Chapter 6 discusses some of the similarities and differences that characterize the different Trump supporters that have emerged during his 2015–2016 campaign and his 2017–2020 presidential term. Specific attention is directed to the meaning of the *Trump cult* and the impact of this cult on the psycho-political consciousness and mental health of the United States.

Part 2 is comprised of Chapters 7–15. Chapter 7 discusses the crisis of the mental health system in the United States. This chapter also describes the impact of Trump's presidency and the Trump cult on our nation's increasing mental health problems manifested among millions of people.

Chapter 8 provides a detailed description of a new theoretical model referred to as the *integral theory of mental health and human development from a psycho-political perspective.* Numerous new terms and concepts are introduced and defined in this chapter. Among these new terms and concepts include the definition of the four quadrants that comprise the new integral theory.

Chapter 9 is entitled *Awakening*. This title was chosen to highlight the ways increasing numbers of persons in the United States are *awakening* to a new consciousness described in this chapter. Particular attention is directed to the meaning and relevance of such concepts as *collective consciousness, collective unconsciousness, a sane society, mass psychology in the Age of Trump, malignant normalcy,* and their relevance for the new integral theory.

In Chapters 10–15, I draw from the knowledge of six major theoretical forces that have been and continue to be utilized in mental health professional training programs and clinical practices across our country. This includes research-based information drawn from the psychodynamic force, the cognitive behavioral force, the existential/humanistic force, the multicultural/social justice force, the neuroscience force, and the community counseling force.

The latter force provides readers with a detailed description of many practical mental health and human development intervention strategies that are designed to stimulate the revitalization of the mental health professions. The goal of this final chapter is to assist readers in expanding their understanding of some of the psychological, emotional, behavioral, racial/cultural, community, and neurological factors that are important to address to effectively ameliorate our country's mental health crisis.

As the title of this book suggests, it is intentionally aimed at stimulating new thinking and imagination about what can happen *Beyond the Lies* that currently mark the serious psycho-political divisiveness in our nation. Among the questions addressed in this book include the following: What will happen in our country's future? What will our nation's democracy look like in the future? How can interested persons support the evolving multiracial/multicultural democracy in the United States? What can be done to address the adverse impact of Trumpism on healthy human development? Why is it important to support efforts that assist large numbers of persons in diverse populations to realize optimal mental health from a psycho-political perspective?

As an anti-racist, engaged intellectual, and social scientist, I address all of the above questions in the following pages of this book. It is my hope that describing the perilous psycho-political dangers currently threatening our nation will generate the establishment of new actions among *we the people* to support the ongoing evolution of a multiracial/multicultural democracy in our nation.

In the continuing struggle for social justice and peace,

Dr. Michael D'Andrea

The Fall of 2023

Springfield, Massachusetts

PART 1

Part 1 of this book is comprised of Chapters 1–6. Chapter 1 provides an overview of key issues and concepts that are foundational throughout this book. The issues and concepts detailed in these chapters are intentionally aimed at identifying, defining, and analyzing multiple factors that help to explain the complexity of the current threats to our nation's democracy, the rapid rise of authoritarianism and fascism, and the mental health crisis in the United States.

CHAPTER 1

WE THE PEOPLE

One of the biggest lies out there is that no matter what race or religion you are, it doesn't matter. Now that's a lie and we all know it. If we don't talk about these problems and take them on, they're going to get much, much worse.

Spike Lee, movie producer and director

True democracy in America is a young, fragile experiment that must be defended if it is to endure.

Adam Serwer, Atlantic Magazine

Introduction

The first three words in the United States Constitution are the most powerful: *We the People*. These words declare that the Constitution derives its power not from a king or a congress, but from the people themselves. This concept of popular sovereignty is the foundation upon which our democratic republic is supposed to operate. The popular sovereignty and overall mental health of our nation largely depend on the accurate information *We the People* receive from our elected officials and other government persons.

The history of our country has been marked by numerous historic crossroads that have shaped the evolution of our democracy. These crossroads have also impacted *We the People* in various ways. This includes the effects of these crossroads on the overall mental health of our nation.

Unfortunately, lies and misinformation embedded in many of these crossroads by political leaders have had and continue to have a negative impact on the psychological well-being of millions of people in the United States. These untruths undermine the responsibility *we the people* have in being accurately aware and knowledgeable of whatever challenges, policies, and actions our democratic government implements as engaged citizens strive to sustain and strengthen our democracy.

Crossroads in Our Nation's History

As I wrote this book, I was reminiscent of some of the key historic crossroads that impacted the United States for better or worse. I was reminded that there was no guarantee that positive outcomes would inevitably emerge from the many crossroads we have and continue to face as a nation. As I pondered these issues, I imagined what things might look like today if the colonialists were defeated in the Revolutionary War against England during our first national crossroad.

I wondered what our society would look like now if the South had won the civil war. While I may not know the specific differences that might have followed the South's hypothetical Civil War victory, I am certain there would have been numerous changes in the persona of our country if the confederacy had been victorious.

I also wondered how our nation would be different if Germany and/or Japan were victorious in World War II.

I reflected on the changes that might have occurred if the United States never got involved in a failed military presence in Vietnam.

Additional crossroads in our nation's history occurred during the first two Reconstruction eras. These psycho-political eras clearly had and continue to have substantial effects on *we the people*. This includes the initial short-term Reconstruction policies implemented with the support of Northern soldiers occupying the Southern states after the Civil War. This military occupation was done to ensure that the new amendments to the Constitution supporting the rights of African Americans were followed in the southern states.

The second Reconstruction era was marked by the Civil Rights Movement of the 1960s and 1970s. I wondered what our nation would be like today if these two historic democracy-promoting processes never occurred.

Once again, our nation faces an important crossroad. That crossroad involves three interconnected factors, which include the rise of Trumpism, the large number of people in our society who support Trump's authoritarian leadership style, and the current mental health crisis in the United States.

As discussed in more detail later in this book, numerous social scientists have reported the ways that our nation's mental health crisis is exacerbated by the rise of Trump, Trumpism, and the millions of people who support Trump; especially those persons comprising the Trump cult (See Chapter 6).

The Current Crossroads Facing Our Nation

The current crossroads we face as a nation involves unique challenges that elected officials and we the people face in making decisions that will have short- and long-term implications for our nation's democracy and mental health. Given the acceleration of the emotional and psychological energy millions of people generate in their unquestionable support of Donald Trump and *Trumpism*, it is possible that the former president may again run for the presidency in the 2024 election. It is also possible that Trump could be re-elected president in that election.

In writing this book, the research findings escalated my concern about the real possibility that supporters of *Trumpism* could indeed succeed in replacing our vulnerable democracy with authoritarian and fascist principles. With this backdrop in mind, I repeatedly emphasize that it would be a serious mistake to underestimate the seriousness of our current psycho-political situation. I stress this point in light of the outcomes of the November 8, 2022 midterm elections in which the Democratic Party did better than most journalists predicted and 2023 polls that describe Trump's increasing popularity despite his legal problems.

History teaches us that the ongoing rise of authoritarianism and fascism, fueled by the tenets of White racism and White supremacy, will continue with or without the possible candidacy and electability of Donald Trump in the 2024 presidential election. This can occur especially as a small and growing number of Republican politicians are signaling their interest in challenging Trump in the 2023 – 2024 Republican primary season.

Unhelpful Comments About Trump and His Supporters/Cult

During the multiple years I have been involved in researching the current crossroads in our nation, I noticed that many people had similar comments when describing their reactions to Trump's leadership style, his political philosophy (often referred to as *Trumpism*), and reactions to the millions of Trump supporters in the United States. The following quotations are among some of the common reactions people had in discussions of Trump, Trumpism, and his many supporters:

"Trump is crazy," "The people that follow everything Trump says are jerks," "The people that support Trump without asking any questions are like a cult," and "Trump is so narcissistic, he only cares about himself and his power to do whatever he wants," "The people that continue to support Trump have lost their minds," and "I just don't understand why Trump and his supporters are so hostile and self-centered. They seem to have trouble just getting along with people who do not think like they do."

Such comments are often driven by emotional reactivity. But they do little to help people understand the multidimensional nature of Donald Trump, Trumpism, and the persons who comprise the Trump cult. As a social scientist, one of my hopes is that readers will experience new thinking about Trump and his supporters (and especially his cult members) as a result of reading this book (see Chapter 6). The information presented in the following pages is aimed at answering several important questions including the following:

- Why does Trump think and act the way he does? (See Chapter 5)
- Why do Trump supporters (especially persons who comprise the Trump cult) think, feel, and act in the way they do during these perilous times? (See Chapter 6)

- Why is the mental health of so many people in the United States adversely impacted by Trump, Trumpism, and Trump's supporters (especially those persons comprising the Trump cult)? (See Chapter 7)

To address these questions, I draw from research findings in multiple disciplines to describe the serious crossroads we presently face as a nation. In doing so, I explore historical, psychological, emotional, racial, cultural, neuroscientific, social, economic, and political theories and research findings, all of which will expand readers' understanding of these perilous times. In the spirit of full disclosure, it is also hoped that the information presented in this book will encourage many readers to strengthen the evolving multiracial/multicultural democracy in our nation in whatever way they believe they can be helpful.

A Nation in Peril: Moving Beyond the Lies

The word *peril* is defined as "serious and immediate danger." With that definition in mind, it is clear that the United States is in psycho-political peril. Numerous facts (not personal opinions) provide clear evidence of the specific ways our democracy is teetering on the edge of being transformed into a government characterized by authoritarian and fascist political principles.

Some people reading this book will disagree with the above statement. However, one of the many lessons I learned in conducting my research for this book included the different ways people construct the meaning of democracy, authoritarianism, and fascism. These different concepts frequently result in confusion that adversely impact healthy, vibrant, and important psycho-political discussions. Confusion, frustration, and anger frequently occur when people operate from different definitions of such concepts as *authoritarianism* and *fascism* in particular.

When people's negative emotional reactions are heightened in discussions related to Trump's leadership style and his many lies, this commonly results in premature termination of such discussions by one or both of the discussants. Relational cultural theory (RCT) explains how and why such frustrating interactions frequently result in seriously *ruptured relationships*.

Former President George W. Bush offered helpful suggestions for ways to avoid ruptured interpersonal interactions during psycho-political discussions. He did so in a speech in September 2021 at a memorial service in Shanksville, Pennsylvania; the site where Flight 93 was brought down thanks to the heroics of the passengers who revolted against the 9/11 hijackers. As former President Bush stated:

> In the weeks and months following the 9/11 attacks, I was proud to lead an amazing, resilient, united people. When it comes to the unity of America, those days seem distant from our own.
>
> A *malign force* seems at work in our common life that turns every disagreement into an argument, and every argument into a clash of cultures. So much of our politics has become a naked appeal to anger, fear, and resentment that leaves many of us worried about our nation and our future together.
>
> On America's day of trial and grief, I saw millions of people instinctively grab their neighbors and rally for the cause of one another. That is the America I know.
>
> At a time when religious bigotry might have flowed freely, I saw Americans reject prejudice and embrace people of the Muslim faith. That is the nation I know.
>
> This is not mere nostalgia; it is the truest version of ourselves. It is what we have been—and what we can be again.

The Optimal Mental Health Theory From a Psycho-Political Perspective

Later in this book, I describe ways to move beyond the mental health crisis in our country by becoming more aware, knowledgeable, and committed to fostering *optimal mental health from a psycho-political perspective (OMH)*. Former President George W. Bush's above comments explain some of the characteristics of what OMH is (See Chapter 7 & Chapter 8).

For now, I want to emphasize that the comments made by former President Bush invite us to be more effective, respectful, and healthier in our interpersonal interactions, especially with persons operating from different constructions of the meaning of justice, mental health, and human development. This is not to suggest that everyone will or should be endlessly patient by trying to hang in there during political discussions with people having different views and values.

Individuals would do well to withdraw from toxic psycho-political interactions when they begin to experience the negative impact of such interactions on his or her mental health. This book acknowledges the importance of finding ways to engage in difficult psycho-political discussions even if they result in incremental new insights and the genesis of mutually empathic connections with others. It also affirms the importance of withdrawing from harmful and toxic interactions when they occur in such situations as noted above.

In my research endeavors, I have found it useful to check in with other discussants to make sure respondents are on the same page regarding the meaning of controversial psycho-political words/concepts utilized in such discussions. One of the basic points made in interpersonal psychology is the usefulness of making such check-ins to increase mutual understanding of key terms/concepts in difficult interactions.

I include definitions of terms used throughout this book to ensure there is clarity between the meaning of the words as used by myself, the author of this book, and the reader's understanding of the meaning of these concepts. Because the terms *authoritarianism, fascism,* and *psycho-political* are used throughout this book, they are defined below. Definitions of other terms and concepts frequently used in the following pages are also defined to foster greater clarity and mutual understanding of the author's intentionality and prevent readers from misinterpreting the author's intent in using these words and concepts.

Definition of Words/Concepts

Authoritarianism is defined as individuals and governments who are anchored in the importance of gaining blind submission to authority by large numbers of people, as opposed to supporting individual freedom of thought and action. Authoritarian governments result in political systems that concentrate power in the hands of a charismatic individual or a small elite who do not feel responsible to *we the people.*

An authoritarian government holds power and makes policies without the consent of the majority of people comprising a nation. Authoritarian governments make an effort to use their power to suppress dissent and exert control over the dissemination of information among the general public.

Fascism is defined as a far-right political ideology characterized by dictatorial power, forcible suppression of opposition, and strong regimentation of society. Fascism rose to prominence in early 20th-century Europe. The first fascist movements emerged in Italy during World War I before spreading to other European countries. As a political ideology, fascism is opposed to liberalism and democracy.

Fascists believe that liberal democracy is obsolete. They value and strive to stimulate the mobilization of society under a totalitarian one-party state.

A rising fascist state is led by leaders like Donald Trump. Fascism rejects the belief that violence is automatically negative and views political violence as a means to achieve the implementation of an authoritarian state. An example of this fascist violence was exhibited in the failed January 6, 2021 insurrection in the United States capital; an effort to violently overthrow our government.

Extreme forms of authoritarianism and fascism often become manifested in a generalized belief in racial purity, usually complemented with some variant of racism and/or bigotry against demonized "Others."

Hopefully, the above definitions help to clarify the meaning of authoritarianism and fascism as used throughout this book. Some, perhaps many people might still question the validity of the assertion that Trump and *Trumpism* underlie increasing support for the rise of authoritarianism and fascism as outlined in the above definitions. Concrete evidence (not personal opinions) is presented below to further support this psycho-political perspective.

Psycho-political: The term *psycho-political* refers to the interaction between people's mental health, human development, and politics. It denotes the psychological, emotional, and behavioral impact of politics and political structures, policies, expectations, and governance on healthy human development for better or worse.

The January 6, 2021 Insurrection: The Power of Lies

Detailed evidence presented by the January 6 House Committee in nationally televised hearings during the spring, summer, and fall of 2022 was clarifying and compelling. The evidence presented by this committee and the many witnesses' testimony unequivocally point to the historic fact that thousands of Trump supporters followed orders given by former President Donald Trump resulting in an attack on our nation's capital in an unlawful act of violent insurrection.

What made this attack particularly unique was that it was not initiated by foreign adversaries. The January 2021 insurrectionists were loyal Trump supporters willing to obey his orders to "fight and fight like hell or you will lose your country forever," without any questions asked. Many were members of White supremacist groups and extreme alt-right-wing White nationalist organizations. These are the same groups and organizations the FBI previously announced were the greatest threat to our national democracy, peace, and security.

These threats were reflected in behaviors exhibited by former President Trump as he poured fuel on the fire of hatred and violence when he repeatedly articulated the *Big Lie* in his 10:00 a.m. speech at the *Stop the Steal Rally* on January 6, 2021, in Washington DC. This *Big Lie* was based on the inaccurate assertion that the 2020 Presidential election was stolen by the Democratic Party leaders and their supporters.

Reports about the violence, assaults, deaths, and psychological injuries many persons experienced during the insurrection were heartbreaking and unlawful. These injuries and deaths targeted law enforcement professionals whose courage and commitment were vital in re-taking the Capitol Building from Trump's insurgents on January 6, 2021. These false assertions consistently lacked any concrete evidence.

As the reader continues to absorb the information presented in this book, it will become clear that the comprehensive analysis I have undertaken in my research focuses on the rise of White racism and White supremacy and their correlation with increased racial/cultural hatred in our society in general and the January 6, 2021 insurrection in particular. Using a psycho-political approach in reporting conclusions drawn from my comprehensive multi-year study points to a greater understanding as to how and why the malignant psycho-political cancers of White racism and White supremacy are foundational factors underlying the current perilous threats to our nation's democracy.

The reader will repeatedly be presented with research findings shared throughout this book to clarify how and why the historically metastasized impact of White racism and White supremacy are central factors driving the negative emotions, hostility, and hatred that fueled the January 6, 2021 insurrection. These same psycho-political factors are embedded throughout the history of the United States and were strongly activated throughout former President Trump's presidency. It is further noted that the perpetuation of these malignant psycho-political factors continues to exclude millions of people of color from exercising their full constitutional rights; rights that have been ensured to White persons throughout the founding and evolution of our country.

Given the long and continuing racial history of state-sanctioned violence against people of color in general and African Americans in particular, it is not hard to find persons who would agree that the outcome of the January 6, 2021 insurrection would have been different if the majority of persons involved in efforts to violently overthrow the United States government were Black and Brown people. In light of the history of state-sanctioned racial violence that continues to occur in our country, it is not hyperbolic to suggest that, if the January 6, 2021 insurrection was mainly comprised of Black and Brown people, there could have been a repeat of the 1989 Tiananmen Square protests and massacre this time in Washington, DC.

Again, the Call for Racial Justice

During these perilous times, the people of the United States are once again pressed to address the complex problems of White racism and White supremacy in our nation. The murders of George Floyd, Breonna Taylor, and many other unarmed Black and Brown men and women by law enforcement officials promote renewed concern about the persistence of White racism and White supremacy in our nation and their threat to our country's democracy and mental health.

Enduring demands for corrective action to address this country's long and continuing legacy of White racism and White supremacy is part of the ongoing pursuit of racial justice in the United States. A couple of unique factors are particularly instrumental in distinguishing the current call to eradicate the complex forms of White racism and White supremacy in the United States than has been achieved in the past.

First, social media provides unequivocal evidence of the indisputable murders of unarmed Black and Brown men and women by law enforcement persons. Such was the case when Darnella Frazier video-recorded the murder of George Floyd by police officer, Derek Clauvin, on June 1, 2020. The impact of this video recording penetrated some of the apathy and indifference that have marked many White persons' inactions to previous displays of racially violent injustices.

Second, the rising number of White persons, who willingly and publicly displayed their abhorrence to these murders, demonstrated their support for racial justice. This support was manifested in increased White participation in rallies and protests in response to the murders of Black and Brown men and women then has been manifested in the recent past. While this level of multiracial unity has too often been absent in the past, recent White support for racial justice and the eradication of state-sanctioned racial violence marks a new willingness among rising numbers of White persons to engage in public demands for social justice and the implementation of a genuine and comprehensive multiracial/multicultural democracy in the United States.

Despite this meaningful progress, a major barrier impeding our country from more effectively purging White racism and White supremacy from our country is the narrow and provincial ways many people–especially White persons–construct meaning of the intimately interconnected concepts of White racism and White supremacy. This chapter and others that follow encourage readers to expand their collective understanding of the multidimensional nature of White racism and White supremacy. Throughout this book, readers are encouraged to support the ongoing evolution of our multiracial/multicultural democracy by taking a stronger anti-racist stand for corrective action in whatever ways they are willing and able to implement in the future.

As a White anti-racist social scientist, I have spent the past 40+ years exploring the many idiosyncrasies of White racism and White supremacy through my personal and professional experiences. These experiences are complemented by the numerous years I have worked as a faculty member and researcher in several universities and colleges across the United States.

The insights I gained from these experiences increased my understanding of the need to expand our collective understanding of the definition and meaning of White racism. The following information is intentionally designed to assist readers in thinking in more comprehensive, expanded, and accurate ways about the manner in which racial injustices and various forms of racial violence continue to be perpetuated in our country.

Definition of Terms/Concepts

White supremacy is defined as racial beliefs and ideas purporting a natural superiority of the White human race over other racial groups. In contemporary usage, the term *White supremacist* has been used to describe societal groups espousing nationalist, racist, and/or fascist doctrines. These White supremacist groups have often relied on violence to achieve their goals.

From the 19th to the mid-20th century the doctrine of White supremacy, was largely taken for granted by political leaders and social scientists in Europe and the United States. The 19th-century French writer and diplomatist Arthur de Gobineau wrote about the superiority of the White race, maintaining that Aryans (Germanic peoples) represented the highest level of human development. According to 19th-century British writers such as Rudyard Kipling, Charles Kingsley, Thomas Carlyle, and others, it was the duty of White Europeans to bring civilization to nonwhite people through beneficent imperialism. This was referred to as the *White man's burden.*

Several attempts were made to give White supremacy a scientific footing early in the 20th century. This was done as various institutes and renowned scientists published research findings asserting the biological superiority of White people. Those ideas were bolstered by a new intelligence testing science. This new science asserted major innate differences in the intellectual ability among people in diverse racial groups. Such tests alleged that northern Europeans always scored higher than Africans on intelligence tests.

In the United States—especially in the South—in the era of slavery and the subsequent Jim Crow period of legal racial segregation, White supremacy enjoyed broad popular and political support. An emerging White supremacy doctrine was especially associated with violent groups such as the Ku Klux Klan (KKK), which enjoyed success in the United States (particularly in the 1920s).

It is also important to note that many nonviolent individuals and groups also believed fervently in White supremacist ideas throughout our country's history. By the mid-1950s and early 1960s, however, overtly racist doctrines and behaviors fell into deep disfavor across much of the Western world, a development that was hastened by both desegregation and decolonization.

During the late 1950s and 1960s, hostility again increased among many White persons. Much of this hostility was in reaction to the Americans civil rights movement and political efforts to pass new anti-racist federal legislation. Among the most notable political accomplishments occurring in this regard included the passage of the 1964 Civil Rights Act and the 1965 Voting Rights Act. White hostilities were further activated in reaction to Supreme Court decisions invalidating many racially discriminatory laws.

White supremacists as well as many social conservatives resented what was perceived to be the U.S. government's adoption of and acquiescence to psycho-political measures such as affirmative action, school busing, and rules against racial discrimination in the housing market. This resentment contributed to the growth of various groups and movements that actively preached White supremacy, including traditional KKK organizations, neo-Nazi organizations, and many evangelical groups.

These collective hostilities ultimately manifested themselves in the development of a reactionary *White Power* movement. This movement was intentionally aimed at counteracting *Black Power* doctrines gaining widespread popularity and support in Black communities across the United States during the 1960s and 1970s.

In early 2016, the presidential campaign of real-estate developer Donald J. Trump, the eventual Republican nominee, attracted significant support from White supremacists and White nationalists. Persons who self-identify as supporters of these groups celebrated a growing pride in *White identity* development while lamenting the alleged erosion of White political and economic power. These psycho-political reactions were also energized by what was perceived to be a decline of *White culture* in the face of increased non-white immigration and the rise of multiculturalism in the United States.

During this time, Trump admirers included members of the *alt-right* (alternative right) political movement, a loose association of relatively young White supremacists, White nationalists, extreme libertarians, and neo-Nazis. These supporters resonated with Trump's repeated questions about the validity of former President Barack Obama's American birth certificate prior to and during the 2016 campaign.

This White enthusiasm was further stimulated by Trump's vows to build a wall along the U.S.–Mexico border, deport some 11 million persons living in the United States illegally, and banning immigration of Muslims, all of which further unleashed many of his supporters' proclivity for White racism and White superiority. Research findings generated by the Southern Poverty Law Center (SPLC) confirmed that the manifestation of these intentional and explicit forms of White racism and White supremacy by the president of the United States contributed to substantial increases in hate crimes directed at minorities, most notably towards African Americans, Muslims, Latinx persons, and Jews.

White racism: As used throughout this book, the meaning of *White racism* is drawn from the 1981 work of Dr. James Jones in his important book entitled, *Prejudice and Racism*. According to Jones, *White racism* occurs as a result of the transformation of race prejudice and/or ethnocentrism through the exercise of power against a racial group defined as inferior by individuals and institutions with the intentional or unintentional support of the entire culture. My research endeavors add to Jones's work by creating a comprehensive, multi-factor definition of White racism that is detailed in Chapter 2.

How to Classify This Book: A Consciousness Raising Endeavor

Readers may have different perspectives when it comes to classifying this book. It would be accurate to classify it as a non-fiction, research-based book that discusses numerous factors contributing to the perilous times in which we live.

It would also be accurate to think of this book as a new mental health theory that is relevant for our perilous times. This theoretical perspective is referred to as the Integral Theory of Mental Health and Human Development from a Psycho-Political Perspective that includes the concept of optimal mental health (See Chapter 8). It is important to add that this book can also be classified as a *consciousness raising* endeavor.

Definition of Term/Concept

The term *consciousness raising* is defined in a couple of ways. First, consciousness raising is fundamentally defined as providing people with information that expands their awareness of, interest in, and support for individual, group, societal, and global changes.

From a psycho-political perspective, this book is designed to be a resource aimed at assisting people to become more aware of personal, social, and/or political issues; particularly those issues that adversely impact the mental health of millions of people in our society.

Historically, the concept of *consciousness raising* is a key factor related to various forms of feminist activism popularized in the United States in the 1960s. It has also been and continues to be an essential component in the fields of multicultural counseling and psychology. Among many mental health professionals, the consciousness raising process is viewed as a precursor for the implementation of social justice advocacy to stimulate mental health and human development in the 1990s through the present time.

Common issues related to *consciousness raising* thoughts and ensuing actions include a greater understanding and awareness of the adverse impact of breast cancer and AIDS as well as the traumatic conflicts emerging from the history of the genocide of Native American people and the perpetuation of various forms of White racism. All of these issues have an impact on the mental health of millions of people in our nation. Promoting such awareness is often regarded as the first step to changing the way societal, governmental, and cultural institutions deal with the above issues.

The concept of *consciousness raising* has also been addressed in a variety of other disciplines. This includes and is not limited to the mental health professions, liberation psychology, philosophy, and spiritual studies to name a few. The following pages build on the use of the *consciousness raising* concept by incorporating it into theories of counseling, psycho-therapy, and human development that are hallmarks of the mental health professions and used to address the perilous times our nation currently faces (See Chapters 7–15).

Summary

This chapter opens with two quotations, one by Spike Lee and the other by Adam Serwer. The points made in these quotations are foundational for much of the information presented throughout this book.

Chapter 1 emphasizes the importance of three keywords repeated throughout this book. In highlighting the importance of understanding the complex meaning of *We the People* in a democratic society, I alert the reader that this concept will be central in all the ensuing chapters.

Readers are encouraged to be cognizant of the many crossroads that have impacted our nation in positive and/or negative ways. The hazardous psycho-political crossroads we are currently experiencing are marked by a rise of authoritarianism and fascist principles at the expense of our democracy.

The next section in Chapter 1 discusses why it is important to pause to discuss the meaning of specific words and concepts that might serve as negative triggers in psycho-political discussions. It is pointed out that negative triggers frequently result in the premature termination of interpersonal interactions among persons with different psycho-political perspectives. This includes differences commonly evident among Trump supporters and people not supportive of Trump's Make America Great Again (MAGA) movement.

Attention then shifts to uncovering the numerous lies made by Trump and his supporters related to the 2020 presidential election in general and the tens of thousands of persons comprising the Trump cult who participated in the failed January 6, 2021 insurrection. These lies were largely unveiled as a result of a year-long investigation culminating in a series of nationally televised reports by the House January 6 Congressional Committee.

As highlighted in Chapter 1, it is important to recognize that the vast majority of persons testifying in these televised reports were members of the Republican Party and individuals who voted for Trump in the 2016 and 2020 presidential elections. These persons described the various legal indiscretions the former president exhibited throughout his presidency; especially as they related to Trump's encouragement for his supporters to "fight and fight like hell" in the January 6, 2021 violent insurrection.

Many members of the Republican Party and other persons supportive of Donald Trump's authoritarian leadership style echoed Trump's false allegations that the 2020 presidential election resulted in a *Big Lie*. The perpetuation of this false accusation, claiming that major voter fraud occurred during the 2020 presidential election has and continues to result in unsubstantiated doubts about the integrity of our nation's elections.

Trump and his supporters' failure to provide any evidence that would validate these false assertions resulted in 60 of the 61 lawsuits filed by Trump and his supporters being dismissed in numerous court hearings as frivolous and without merit. Chapter 1 sheds light on the different factors that contribute to these perilous times. These issues are repeatedly addressed in various ways throughout this book.

The next section in Chapter 1 is entitled: *Again, A Call for Racial Justice*. Included in this section are detailed definitions of terms and concepts frequently used in this book. These terms include *White Supremacy* and *White Racism*. Earlier in this chapter, the terms *authoritarianism* and *fascism* are defined. It is hoped that defining key words and concepts in this and other chapters will be helpful in adding to readers' awareness and understanding of the meaning of these essential terms and concepts from a psycho-political perspective.

I build on the above points and issues throughout this book by discussing the relevance of these terms and concepts to describe the current mental health crisis in our country (See Chapter 7). I also present numerous action strategies that can assist readers in considering ways that *we the people* can implement practical actions to prevent the hostility, hatred, and divisiveness that continue to be manifested during these perilous times.

The term *multiracial/multicultural democracy* has been incorporated in this chapter and will continue to be used throughout this book. Chapter 2 provides readers with detailed definitions of these important terms and concepts. Thus, the primary purpose of the next chapter is to unpack the meaning and definition of our multiracial/multicultural democracy.

Lastly, my overall goal is to have this book classified as a *consciousness raising* endeavor. In doing so, I hope readers will find the information in Chapter 1 and the ensuing chapters interesting and helpful to the point of taking action to support, strengthen, and sustain the ongoing evolution of our nation's multiracial/multicultural democracy.

CHAPTER 2

OUR MULTIRACIAL/ MULTICULTURAL DEMOCRACY

I'm not concerned with your liking or disliking me. All I ask is that you respect me as a human being.

Jackie Robinson, Major League Baseball player, 1954

We are living in a multicultural society. Our role as leaders is to enable grappling with this situation, even when multiculturalism is difficult.

Reuven Rivlin, Israeli politician and lawyer who served as the tenth president of Israel between 2014 and 2021

Introduction

Chapter 2 builds on the first chapter in a number of important ways. First, this chapter describes the multidimensional manifestation of White racism and White supremacy in the United States. Throughout this chapter the reader's attention is directed to how these different manifestations of White racism play a significant role in undermining our nation's democracy and mental health.

Chapter 2 is also aimed at stimulating the reader's thinking about an extended definition of a multiracial/multicultural democracy. To achieve this goal, I outline a new theory entitled: *A RESPECTFUL theory of a multiracial/multicultural democracy (RT)*.

As promised in Chapter 1, I will continue to provide definitions of key terms used throughout this book. This is done to model ways to increase more respectful interpersonal discussions with persons that have different psycho-political perspectives/values during these perilous times. I continue to provide definitions in this chapter and all ensuing chapters so readers will have greater clarity about the meaning of key terms as they are used throughout this book.

Definition of Terms/Concepts

The term *culture* is a key concept used throughout this book. For that reason, the meaning of this term is defined here to clarify how it is used in this and other chapters. *Culture* has been defined by Dr. Thomas Parham, a pioneer in the multicultural counseling and psychology movement, as a complex constellation of shared experiences, morals, values, customs, traditions, and histories distinguishing different cultural groups from one another.

Dr. Parham expands this definition by adding that *culture* provides people with a general design for living and a pattern for interpreting reality. This definition extends beyond people who self-identify with a specific racial or ethnic group and includes persons in other marginalized and devalued groups.

The term *multicultural* refers to a broad range of identities that impact people's psychological, cognitive, emotional, and behavioral development as well as their individual and collective sense of well-being. Early in the multicultural movement, particular attention was directed to the negative ways a *socialization process*, impacted by White racism and White supremacy, adversely affect the personal development of persons of color in the United States with a particular focus on African Americans. A number of these groups are listed later in this chapter. The term *multiracial* describes people who are composed of, involving, or representing various races.

Particular attention is now directed to the negative impact of the ongoing problem of White racism and White supremacy as overarching factors effecting the socialization of large numbers of people in our nation. The following section directs the reader's attention to a theoretical framework that is helpful in expanding our individual and collective understanding of these toxic societal aspects of these racial human power dynamics.

Expanding Our Thinking About White Racism in the 21st Century

Historically, many White persons have learned to think of White racism in very constricted ways. In doing so, they associate images of White racism as primarily being intentional and overt behaviors that are obscene, hateful, and harmful.

Over the past several decades, social scientists have expanded the definition of White racism. For full disclosure, I want to acknowledge that I greatly appreciated working with the late Dr. Donald C. Locke, a former professor at North Carolina State University and a pioneer in the multicultural/social justice counseling movements. Over several years, Dr. Locke and I engaged in discussions and informal research endeavors aimed at expanding the narrow definition of White racism.

In the following section of this chapter, I detail the creation of a multidimensional model of White racism that resulted from the scholarly discussions Dr. Locke and I had on these issues over several years. The following discussion of this expanded model of White racism is dedicated to Dr. Locke's legacy via his many important contributions resulting in a more comprehensive (and consequently a more accurate) definition of the different types of White racism perpetuated in the United States today.

Overt Intentional White Racism

Overt intentional White racism is reflected among White persons commonly associated with the Ku Klux Klan and other domestic terrorist groups. What distinguishes this type of racism from others is the way White people openly, intentionally, and without any remorse express hatred and engage in violent actions towards persons of color.

Stereotypic and generalized comments made by Donald Trump when describing Mexicans coming to this country as drug dealers and rapists are examples of overt intentional White racism. Trump continued to exhibit this type of racism in his infamous comments about what he referred to as "shit hole countries" when commenting on Haiti and other African nations.

Additional ways Trump's presidency contributed to the increased activation of overt forms of intentional White racism include his assertion of the moral equivalence of the motivations of the White supremacists and White anti-racists during the August 11–12, 2017 protests in Charlottesville, Virginia. As Trump stated, "There are good people on both sides of the protests in Charlottesville."

Overt Unintentional White Racism

Overt Unintentional White Racism is similar to overt intentional racism as both reflect open and public displays of racist behaviors. One main difference is that overt unintentional racism, while open and public, is not done consciously with racist intent.

One of my colleagues told me of a situation he experienced when he was working as an athletic counselor in a large public university. The situation my colleague described below is an example of overt unintentional White racism.

During one of the men's basketball team's practices at the University where my colleague was employed, a frustrated White player said to another player, "Get your cotton-picking hands off me," when this Black teammate was playing tight defense to stop him from making a shot near the basket. This incident caused an uproar among Black players who demanded an apology from their White teammate.

As my colleague worked with the team to address this racially charged situation, the African American players acknowledged that they did not believe their White teammate's comment was an intentional racist act. Furthermore, the African American players expressed the belief that their White teammate unconsciously manifested this racist comment out of ignorance of its negative impact on African Americans.

Ultimately, this event turned into an important learning experience as the White player expressed remorse and embarrassment. He also expressed interest in learning more about the ways White people exhibit overt unintentional racism without understanding its negative impact on persons of color.

Covert Unintentional White Racism

Covert Unintentional White racism refers to behaviors that are not overt or intentional, but nevertheless allow racial injustices to go unchallenged in harmful ways. An example of this type of White racism occurs when good-hearted, well-meaning White teachers, counselors, and other school/university officials participate in the administration of racially biased tests and other culturally biased education assessments.

Education researchers point out that numerous educational tests and assessment processes used in public schools are often not validated nor found to be reliable when utilized among racially/culturally diverse students. These researchers explain how such racially flawed tests and assessment processes often have an adverse impact on many non-White students' educational opportunities and outcomes.

As controversial as it may be, it is important to recognize that persons participating in covert unintentional White racism typically acknowledge that they are simply following school/university mandated policies. In using this excuse to legitimize the work they do in the field, good-hearted and well-meaning White school personnel are nevertheless complicit in perpetuating this form of racism in our nation.

Stating that they are simply following school/university policies result in the perpetuation of structural racism in our society and high-light one way that covert unintentional White racism is maintained by many people in such situations. This includes law enforcement professionals involved in shooting unarmed Black and Brown men and women in our society. In many of these situations, law enforcement persons assert that their actions were legitimized by institutional policies related to protective engagement in such racist atrocities.

One of the ways some White people think about these reactions can be explained, in part, by Sigmond Freud's psychodynamic theory (See Chapter 10). For now, it may be useful to point out that Freud's psychodynamic theory suggests that, when people experience anxiety in their interpersonal interactions with others, they commonly unconsciously employ defense mechanisms to alleviate their anxiety. Among the more common defense mechanisms that are particularly relevant for the present discussion include what are referred to as *projection* and *rationalization.*

Social scientists like Stanley Milgram in his 1965 Obedience Research and Philip Zimbardo's Stanford Prison Study provide evidence relevant for this discussion. The results of these investigations led researchers to conclude that many people in our society readily conform to the demands of persons in authority positions often without question. This includes following immoral institutional/structural policies and practices when abiding to the demands of persons in authority positions.

The above comments represent one of the many ways this book strives to give psychology, counseling, and human development theories away to *we the people* (as noted in the Preface). Readers will hopefully become more aware of the psychological complexity manifested in toxic ways by Trump, Trump supporters, and the Trump cult; and perhaps experience even an incremental increase in their understanding, empathy, and compassion for Trump's supporters and persons in the Trump cult.

Some, perhaps many, readers will conclude that the above recommendation is not something they are able to do at the present time. Too idealistic! Despite these reactions, I am committed to describe what is referred to as *optimal mental health* in Chapters 7 and 8. In doing so, I explain why this level of mental health is necessary if our nation is to effectively address the unprecedented psycho-political challenges we face during these perilous times.

Covert Intentional White Racism

Covert intentional White racism is arguably the most pervasive and harmful racial injustice in our nation. This type of White racism has a serious negative impact among large groups of persons of color when compared to the more limited adverse effect of overt intentional and overt unintentional White racism.

One does not have to openly express racial hatred or articulate obscene racial comments publicly to be guilty of covert intentional racism. Instead, this form of racism occurs when White persons create policies and/or support another person's or organization's policies intentionally designed to dominate racial minority persons.

A pattern of actions implemented by former President Donald Trump over an extended period of time are examples of how covert intentional White racism continues in our society. Examples of this pattern of White racism include the following:

- A court decision in the 1970s found Donald Trump guilty of implementing racially discriminating housing policies while building his real estate empire in New York City;

- Trump supported the "Stop and Frisk" strategy in New York City as this institutional racist policy was implemented daily from 2004–2012;

- President Trump worked to dismantle the Fair Housing Act–a federal legislative policy that supports African Americans' chances to secure fair housing opportunities in our nation;

- Trump's false accusations that cities with large populations of Black voters, including Detroit and Philadelphia, have a history of major voter fraud that contributed to his loss in the 2020 election;

- Trump's order to then Attorney General Jeff Sessions to have immigrant children stripped from their parents at the Mexican–U.S. border in an effort to migrate to the United States; and

- Attacks against Black professional football players, who supported Colin Kaepernick's protest of police brutality toward Black persons in the United States by kneeling during the national anthem at the beginning of professional games.

The purpose of describing the four types of White racism outlined above is to help White persons develop a more comprehensive, expansive, and accurate understanding of the ways White racism continues to be a broad-based toxic force in our society. It is hoped that the information presented in this chapter will motivate more White readers to work with other anti-racist allies to promote a greater level of racial justice by finding ways to diminish the perpetuation of all four of these forms of White racism in their communities.

Unprecedented Demographic Changes

Mental health professionals and related social scientists have developed an expansive knowledgebase over an extended period of time that describes the range of reactions White people have to the substantial demographic changes occurring in all aspects of our society. This includes demographic changes in our schools, universities, workplaces, social, and athletic organizations as well as religious, ethnic, racial, and cultural communities to name a few.

As stated in Chapter 1, it is not possible to overstate the substantial psychological, emotional, and behavioral implications emerging from the unprecedented demographic transformation of the United States. With this in mind, it is disappointing to see the dearth of information available that would help persons in the general public to more accurately understand the relationship between the unprecedented demographic changes occurring in the United States and the positive as well as the negative responses many White persons have in response to this psycho-political phenomena.

Among the central purposes of this book is to assist readers in expanding their understanding of the psychological, emotional, and behavioral reactions many people have to the unprecedented demographic transformation of the United States. It also describes positive ways interested readers can address the unprecedented demographic transformation rapidly unfolding in our nation.

These issues are highlighted throughout this book as my research findings indicate that eradicating the various forms of White racism and White supremacy is essential in strengthening the ongoing evolution of our nation's multiracial/multicultural democracy. It is also acknowledged that strengthening our country's multiracial/multicultural democracy by eradicating White racism and White supremacy has the potential to address the mental health crisis in our country; a crisis that has been exacerbated by former President Trump, the increasing popularity of Trumpism, and the mental health problems manifested by persons experiencing heightened stress as a result of Trump's leadership style (See Chapters 6 and 7).

The Primary Factor in White People's Resistance to a Multiracial/Multicultural Democracy

My research findings indicate that the increasing activation of the four types of White racism described above over the past seven years correlate with a large number of people who express strong emotional and behavioral support for former President Donald Trump. As a psycho-political phenomena, this support is grounded in a variety of psychological, emotional, behavioral and political factors that activate a growing awareness, anxiety, frustration, anger, and hostility as result of the unprecedented racial-cultural transformation of our nation's demography.

The United States of America has historically been a country comprised of a majority of persons who come from White, western European, English-speaking, and Christian backgrounds. From the beginning of our nation, this demographic profile elevated the status of White persons in general and White men in particular. This elevation resulted in the development of a racial psychology that falsely affirms the specialness and supremacy of White persons above persons of color.

Over the past several decades, researchers have reported the unfolding of unprecedented changes in the demography of the United States. These research findings further indicated that this demographic transformation will culminate in a majority of persons living and working in our nation who come from non-White, non-western European, non-English speaking, and increasingly non-Christian backgrounds by 2042. These changes will ultimately result in the United States becoming what is referred to as a *minority majority nation*.

Racially different students already constitute the majority of public-school students in most urban schools in the U.S. The unprecedented nature of these transformative demographic changes has a tremendous impact on the psychology of many White persons in the United States. Safe it is to say here that many, perhaps most, White persons will experience a broad range of reactions as our nation continues on the path to becoming a minority majority country.

Among the reactions large numbers of Trump supporters articulate at Trump's political rallies include the following: "We will take our country back," "All of these immigrants are taking over our country and we are going to take it back," and "This is our country and we are not going to let you people take it away from us." Researchers with the Southern Poverty Law Center (SPLC) conducted important studies describing the various negative psychological, emotional, and behavioral reactions that continue to be manifested among Trump's supporters and especially those persons who comprise the Trump cult in response to the rapidly increasing and unprecedented transformation of our country's demography (See Chapters 5 and 6).

Responding to My Critics

I have been criticized by some colleagues in the mental health professions for asserting that eradicating the various forms of White racism and White supremacy perpetuated in the United States are central in addressing these perilous times. Some colleagues have argued that issues related to economic injustice, increasing political divisiveness, the environmental crisis, differential health-care services (especially as manifested during the Covid pandemic), challenges facing our national education system, and injustices manifested in our country's judicial/prison system are equally important when addressing our nation's current perilous times.

I strongly agree with the important impact these additional factors have on the mental health crisis we currently face in these perilous times. However, my research endeavors led me to examine how various forms of White racism and White supremacy correlate with all of the factors listed above. When I examined research findings that include data related to the relationship between persons in marginalized racial and cultural groups and the national and global environmental crisis we are all facing, I found a direct correlation between the environmental crises and the manifestation of what is referred to as *environmental racism*.

When I examined research findings that focused on the potential relationship between economic injustices and people in marginalized racial and cultural groups, I found a direct correlation between these injustices and the negative impact of White racism and White supremacy.

When I reviewed research studies that examined the potential relationship between the increasing political divisiveness in the U.S., I found a direct correlation between our current political divisiveness and persons in different racial groups.

When I examined the results of studies that focused on the potential relationship between healthcare and people in different racial and cultural groups, I found a direct correlation between these outcomes and the negative impact of White racism and White supremacy.

When I examined the potential relationship between differential education outcomes and people in different racial and cultural groups, I found a direct correlation between negative educational outcomes and the impact of White racism and White supremacy among African Americans and Latinx students in particular.

These collective research findings led me to several conclusions. First, the results drawn from the above listed multidisciplinary research findings indicate that the primary factors driving these perilous times is the perpetuation of various forms of White racism and White supremacy described earlier in this chapter.

Second, Trump and Trump's supporters continue to assert that the 2020 presidential election was stolen from the former president. Such allegations are partially based on the assertion that substantial voter fraud occurred in urban areas where large numbers of Black and Brown registered voters commonly support Democratic Party candidates. Numerous researchers, social scientists, and journalists have pointed out that these false accusations continue to be made without any concrete evidence supporting such lies.

Third, my research efforts resulted in the conclusion that Trump and many of his supporters exhibit a pattern of emotional reactivity, cognitive rigidity, and agitated/hostile behavioral patterns which are not consistent with the optimal mental health theory detailed in Chapter 8.

The above-stated factors represent what can be referred to as a negative psychological-emotional-behavioral-developmental syndrome that directly conflicts with the optimal mental health theory discussed later in this book.

It needs to be further asserted that these harmful psycho-political outcomes represent barriers to the on-going evolution and sustaining of a multiracial/multicultural democracy in our nation. The following section is aimed at clarifying and expanding the reader's thinking about the meaning of *multiculturalism* in the 21st century.

The RESPECTFUL Theory of a Multiracial/ Multicultural Democracy (RT)

Expanding the Definition of Multiculturalism and Our Nation's Socialization Process

In 1997, my colleague Dr. Judy Daniels and I developed the RE-SPECTFUL theory of multicultural counseling and psychotherapy as faculty members at the University of Hawaii. In doing so, we helped to expand the definition of multiculturalism as it previously existed. I have adapted this theoretical framework in my continuing research endeavors to support the on-going evolution of our nation's multiracial/multicultural democracy. In adapting this original theory to the current perilous times, it has been renamed as the RESPECTFUL Theory for a Multiracial/Multicultural Democracy (RT).

It is important that people in a multiracial/multicultural democracy understand the ways individuals are positively and/or negatively impacted by our society's socialization process. In a society that continues to be impacted by a *socialization process* anchored in various forms of White racism and White supremacy (See Chapter 1), it is important for *we the people* to understand ways these social injustices and toxic mental health dynamics adversely impact healthy human development. This includes being aware of the ways that the socialization process effects both the beneficiaries (White people) and victims (i.e., persons of color) of a nation still perpetuating various forms of White racism and White supremacy.

The RT identifies how social injustices contribute to negative psychological, cognitive, emotional, and behavioral outcomes among White persons as well as people in marginalized racial/*cultural groups*. While an individual's personal identity may be dominated by one cultural variable (i.e., an individual's racial/ethnic identity), most people consciously and unconsciously operate from the interface of multiple cultural identities.

The 10 factors comprising the RT are listed below. A brief description of each factor is presented to assist readers in developing an expanded understanding of the meaning of *multiculturalism* as used throughout this book.

Religious/spiritual identity: Most persons in the United States acknowledge the importance of their religious/spiritual identity. However, religious/spiritual injustices, the perpetuation of inaccurate stereotypes and overt bigotry (especially as manifested towards Jewish and Muslim persons) continue to underlie rising levels of religious/spiritual violence in the United States.

Economic class identity: Researchers have reported the significant impact economic class factors have on human development. The socialization impact of economic class identity development occurs among all people regardless of their location in poor, working class, middle class, and economically elite cultural groups.

Sexual/Gender identity: Researchers have reported that persons in sexual minority groups (i.e., lesbian, gay, bisexual, transgender groups) are routinely subjected to injustices, stereotyping, discrimination, and overt violence. These injustices adversely impact the mental health, physical safety, and overall well-being of persons in sexual minority groups. The ongoing evolution of the multiracial/multicultural democracy holds the potential to address these injustices in ways that foster the realization of new forms of mental health as discussed in Chapter 9.

Political identity: The heightened divisiveness manifested in our nation today is largely due to the differences in people's political identities. Clear differences are commonly exhibited by persons who self-identify as right-wing/Republican, liberal/Democratic, or Independent Party loyalists to name a few. People who support these political parties/organizations typically share experiences, morals, values, customs, traditions, and histories that are different for each group. These latter points are consistent with the definition of culture as described above and, thus, are included in the new RT.

Ethnic/racial identity: This component of the RT is addressed in various ways throughout this book. RT emphasizes the importance of becoming aware and knowledgeable of the stages of ethnic/racial identity development theories. This is important as research shows how people operating at different ethnic/racial identity stages manifest different ways of thinking and feeling about the ongoing perpetuation of White racism and White supremacy in the United States.

Given the nature of the rapidly changing demography of our country, the on-going evolution of our multiracial/multicultural democracy movement depends, in part, on increasing people's understanding of ethnic/racial identity development theories. As noted in the Preface, one of the purposes of writing this book is to give psychology, counseling, and human development theories away to readers to increase their understanding of the multidimensional nature of our perilous times. In doing so, I hope to increase readers' understanding of the relevance of ethnic/racial identity development theories for the work mental health professionals do in the field.

Mental health professionals are often hesitant to address political dynamics in their professional lives. This hesitancy continues to exist despite a substantial rise in research publications describing how the stages of White, African American/Black, Latinx, Asian, and indigenous persons ethnic/racial identity development represent diverse political perspectives and responses to White racism and White supremacy. Chapter 13 provides more detailed information describing the characteristics of racial/ethnic identity development stages and their relevance for the new integral theory of mental health and human development presented in this book.

Chronological challenges: Researchers have described the various ways persons in different chronological groups experience developmentally unique and stressful challenges across the lifespan. This has resulted in an increased understanding of the ways that interpersonal encounters have a positive and/or negative impact on people's development during the infancy, childhood, adolescence, early adulthood, middle adulthood, and late adulthood stages.

Suggesting that people operating from different chronological stages constitute unique cultural groups may be hard for some readers to contemplate. If you find it hard to consider how persons at different chronological stages can be viewed as unique *cultural groups,* it is important to recall the definition of the term *culture* as used in this book.

Human development researchers explicitly and implicitly describe how people moving through chronological stages across the lifespan commonly realize new and untapped dimensions of their design for living and a pattern for interpreting reality. With this in mind, persons in different chronological stages meet the definition of *culture* as used throughout this book and, thus, are included in an expanded definition of *multiculturalism.*

Traumatic experiences: Dr. Gabor Maté is an internationally respected physician and author with expertise in addiction, stress, and trauma. In his most recently published book entitled, *The Myth of Normal: Trauma, Illness and Healing in a Toxic Culture*, Dr. Maté defines trauma as, "… an inner injury, a lasting rupture or split within the self, due to difficult or harmful environmental events." He further explains that "trauma is a psychic injury, lodged in the nervous system, mind, and body, lasting long past the originating incident." I have adopted the definition of *trauma* presented by Dr. Maté later in this book.

Research findings uncover the degree to which social injustices manifested in micro- and macroaggressions contribute to the heightened stress levels reported by people in marginalized, traumatized, and oppressed groups in the United States. Among the marginalized groups I have directed attention in my research endeavors include observations of the differential stress levels African Americans, Latinx persons, Native Americans, and Native Hawaiians experience in their daily lives.

Particular insights were gained from my clinical experiences and research endeavors with persons in the above listed groups. This includes learning about the different reactions persons manifest as a result of traumatic experiences they encounter in their own lifetimes as well as being impacted by horrific historical events resulting in ongoing intergenerational trauma.

Drs. Eduardo and Bonnie Duran (2019) referred to the transmission of these intergenerational forms of trauma as the *soul wound* from a Native American perspective. Dr. Joy Angela DeGruy is an author, academic, and researcher previously employed at Portland State University's School of Social Work. As a result of her twelve years of quantitative and qualitative research endeavors, Dr. DeGruy developed her theory of post traumatic slave syndrome (PTSS). Her findings are published in the book entitled, *Post Traumatic Slave Syndrome – America's Legacy of Enduring Injury and Healing*.

The concepts of the soul wound and PTSS are two ways of constructing new meaning of the ongoing impact of intergenerational trauma. The perpetuation of these forms of trauma adversely impacts the healthy development of large numbers of persons from indigenous groups and African Americans in our nation.

Supporting the ongoing evolution of a multiracial/multicultural democracy in the United States provides a greater probability of effectively addressing these intergenerational forms of trauma from a psycho-political perspective. Readers interested in gaining a greater awareness and knowledge of intergenerational trauma and its relevance for the work mental health professionals do in an increasingly multiracial/multicultural 21st-century society would do well to secure the books written by Drs. Maté, the Durans, and DeGruy.

Family identity: Researchers describe the different types of families in the United States. This includes intact traditional, divorced, blended, multi-racial, and lesbian/gay/transgender parent-headed families to name a few. These diverse families commonly manifest characteristics consistent with the definition of *culture* presented above.

This includes diverse families who share life experiences, morals, values customs, and histories. Such families commonly impact familial members by transmitting a general design for living and a pattern for interpreting reality. Given the important ways diverse families impact familial members' mental health for better or worse, they are included in the RESPECTFUL theory of a Multiracial/Multicultural Democracy (RT).

People with unique physical, cognitive, developmental, and/or psychosocial human characteristics: This component of the RT includes persons who experience negative stereotyping, prejudices, and biases as a result of manifesting what has traditionally been referred to as a disability in their lives. The term, disability, has traditionally been defined as physical, cognitive, psycho-social, or developmental conditions that impair, interfere with, or limit a person's ability to engage in routine activities and interactions.

Persons, who support the new integral theory discussed in this book, recognize that this definition of disability can be viewed in a number of ways. First, the new integral theory acknowledges that people in our nation are often socialized to consciously and/or unconsciously adopt negative views and feelings about people with disabilities. Such thoughts and feelings can and often do result in a generalized non-empathic view among many people not labeled with a disability.

Second, the meaning of the term *socialization process* is a central concept in the new integral theory of mental health and human development from a psycho-political perspective. This powerful and lasting psycho-social-neurological-cultural process is described throughout this book and detailed in Chapter 8.

Third, mental health professionals sometimes fail to assess and address the relevance of our nation's multidimensional socialization process when working with clients in general and individuals labeled with a disability in particular. This can result in unintentional adverse mental health outcomes with people labeled with a disability. Such an adverse impact may result from being victimized by inaccurate, disempowering, and culturally-biased words, beliefs, and values, about persons labeled as disabled.

Fourth, becoming aware of the power and impact of our socialization process to consciously and unconsciously perpetuate various psycho-political-social injustices is another key feature of the new integral theory. It is important to realize that the concepts generated in the socialization process can result in damaging the mental health of persons labeled as having a disability. As a result, the RT discussed in this chapter uses the term, *People with Unique Physical, Cognitive, Developmental, and Psychosocial Human Characteristics* to address this aspect of human diversity.

Location of residence and language style: The United States is comprised of diverse residential areas including rural, suburban, and urban settings. Each of these residential areas are comprised of persons who typically communicate with different accents, dialects, and, in many cases, different languages. Incarcerated persons often adopt prison language as a way of coping with the stresses of incarceration. People who are hearing impaired commonly use sign language to communicate with other persons.

While the above listed residential locations and language nuances are often marked by positive environmental conditions, they are also characterized by negative and toxic dynamics sustained by what Dr. Martin Luther King Jr. called "the strangulation of poverty and economic inequities."

People living in diverse residential settings are often distinguished by their shared experiences, morals, values, customs, traditions, and histories. These factors are also complemented by the different ways people in diverse residential settings develop a general design for living and a pattern for interpreting reality. The points highlighted in the above two sentences are the basis for including persons living in rural, suburban, and urban areas as culturally different from each other.

The RT model stresses the importance of incorporating a comprehensive view of human development into the work mental health practitioners do. The 10 factors that comprise the RT do not represent an exhaustive listing of all the variables affecting healthy human development. Rather, these factors have been selected because research findings in each of the above 10 categories highlight the positive and negative effects that predictably occur when people are impacted by the interface of multiple RT factors on one's optimal mental health and their sense of well-being.

Summary

This chapter opens with quotations by Jackie Robinson and Reuven Rivlin. These quotations were selected because the ideas presented in them are relevant for much of the information discussed in this chapter.

Chapter 2 builds on a number of concepts presented in the first chapter in a variety of ways. Given the ways that White racism and White supremacy continue to have a negative impact on the ongoing evolution of the current multiracial/multicultural democracy, Chapter 2 details a comprehensive model of these societal cancers. The aim of this new theoretical framework is to extend readers' thinking about the meaning of White racism and White supremacy in our 21st century society. To achieve this goal, I discuss four quadrants of White racism including: overt intentional, overt unintentional, covert unintentional, and covert intentional forms of White racism.

I proceeded to identify White racism and White supremacy as primary factors fueling the increasing political divisiveness and hatred in our nation. These malignant societal problems are enhanced as a result of the unprecedented demographic transformation occurring in the United States.

Essentially, I join with other social scientists, journalists, and social justice/antiracist advocates who point to the relationship between the unprecedented demographic transformation of our nation and the increasing levels of political divisiveness fueled by the ongoing perpetuation of different forms of White racism and White supremacy; all of which are major threats to our country's democracy. I incorporate research results from different disciplines to make the assertion that the key factors in the current threats to democracy in the United States are both historic and current manifestations of White racism and White supremacy. As a result of drawing these conclusions, I have received numerous criticisms from colleagues in the mental health professions.

These critics point out that other issues besides White racism and White supremacy are equally, if not more, important factors in my psycho-political analysis. Among the factors critics commonly raise in this regard include such important psycho-political factors like differential educational outcomes, differences in annual family income, and the global climate crisis, to name a few of these serious challenges.

As a social scientist, my response to these critics is to point out that racial factors are indeed consistently correlated in investigative findings that study the above-stated challenges. Consequently, I am committed to continue to operate from the ethical standards that require researchers to accurately report findings in their investigative efforts. I believe it is also important to highlight the data generated in research findings when drawing the above stated research findings. This is a process I refer to as *listening carefully to research data*.

I also acknowledge the important role mental health professionals can play in helping to educate *we the people* from a scientific perspective using data to enhance critical thinking among the masses of people in our nation and not by formulating conclusions largely based on unsubstantiated opinions or *gut feelings* as Donald Trump proudly explains. Such unsubstantiated opinions and gut feelings are the hallmarks of the lies and misinformation presented by Trump, his supporters in general, and persons comprising the Trump cult in particular.

As stated earlier, this book is a clarion call to mental health professionals. In making this call, I outline specific strategies that can be implemented in a more comprehensive manner that include the application of the new integral theory of mental health and human development highlighted throughout this book.

Moving forward in Chapter 2, I present another new theory. This new theoretical model expands previous definitions of multiculturalism. The RESPECTFUL theory of a multiracial/multicultural democracy (RT) provides mental health professionals and persons in the general public with a new way of thinking about multiculturalism that is particularly relevant for the ongoing evolution of our nation's democracy.

Chapters 3 and 4 build on the concepts and new theories presented in this chapter. In doing so, the following chapter illuminates the potential promise of the ongoing evolution of the multiracial/multicultural democracy movement in the United States. Chapter 4 details important pitfalls that have and continue to undermine the realization of the untapped potential of a multiracial/multicultural democracy in our nation.

CHAPTER 3

THE PROMISE

Philosophers, historians, and politicians have been asking a profound question of late. Are we living at a hinge of history, a moment of tremendous change that will influence the future of democracy in the United States as well as the fate of our species?

Jacqueline Adams, correspondent

I think a lot of this is about race and entitlement ... and now, we're at a stage where you basically have to use violence to overthrow the results of a democratic election to protect White minority power. In any society where you have such a divide over how you see reality, that's an unstable country.

Dr. Renee Romano, Oberlin College professor

Introduction

This chapter builds on numerous issues presented in Chapters 1 and 2. It highlights the potential promise beholden to the ongoing evolution of a multiracial/multicultural democracy in the United States. The discussion of the potential promise of our multiracial/multicultural democracy is tempered by doubts many people have about our government ever realizing a vibrant, genuine, comprehensive, and inclusive democracy; a democracy where all people are entitled to and protected by the rights and responsibilities outlined in our nation's constitution.

These doubts are exacerbated by a legacy of historic injustices and state-sanctioned racial violence that our nation owns. These injustices are detailed later in Chapter 4 and referred to as *pitfalls*. There are two main reasons why it is important to balance the inevitable pain people experience in the face of continuing injustices, state-sanctioned violence, and White supremacy with a renewed commitment to strengthen our fragile multiracial/multicultural democracy.

First, renewing our collective commitment to strengthen our nation's multiracial/multicultural democracy necessitates readers to increase their awareness and understanding of both the promise and potential fulfillment of the principles upon which our country is grounded. It is hoped that the information presented in this chapter and other chapters in this book will stimulate increased awareness and understanding of these issues.

Second, as described in Chapter 2, the unprecedented demographic transformation of our country is rapidly unfolding; ushering in the United States becoming an increasingly multiracial/multicultural democracy. Given the unprecedented nature of this psycho-political phenomenon and the perpetuation of White supremacy and White racism in our nation, it is important that all people in our society have opportunities to acquire new racial and cultural competencies. As discussed later in this chapter and other chapters in this book, acquiring such competencies underlies our individual and collective success, empowerment, and happiness.

As discussed in Chapter 1, it is important for people functioning from different political values and beliefs to be aware of some of the concrete ways to navigate difficult political discussions during these perilous times. As noted earlier, there is an increased possibility for more positive political discussions to occur by taking time to clearly define key words and concepts that may otherwise trigger negative interpersonal interactions among persons with different psycho-political perspectives. The concept of *socialization* is a key term described in this chapter and included in a discussion of the new integral theory of mental health and human development (See Chapter 8). For these reasons, the term *socialization* is defined below.

Definition of a Term/Concept

Socialization is defined as an ongoing process whereby an individual acquires a multidimensional personal identity by consciously and unconsciously learning about the norms, values, behavior, and social skills appropriate to his or her cultural position in society. This definition complements the earlier discussion of the meaning of *culture* which states that culture consciously and unconsciously provides people with a general design for living and a pattern for interpreting reality.

Three important concepts underlie the concept of socialization. First, the socialization process is integral to the ways people in all societies construct meaning of their life experiences.

Second, the socialization process in the United States continues to be impacted by racial concepts fueled by White supremacy. This aspect of the socialization process validates and negates the legitimacy, dignity, and value of people's personal, cultural, and racial identities.

Third, the ongoing evolution of the multicultural and social justice counseling and psychology movements continue to be impacted by persons in a broad range of societal groups who have and continue to advocate for their validation as part of an expanded multicultural family. These advocacy efforts resulted in a more inclusive definition of multiculturalism including millions of persons in marginalized groups who continue to be subjected to various social injustices that adversely impact their mental health, human development, and sense of well-being.

The Potential Promise of a Multiracial/ Multicultural Democracy

1. Realizing an authentic, inclusive, and comprehensive democracy.

The United States has never realized its full potential to live up to the principles upon which our nation was founded. When referring to *We the people* in early political documents, the founding fathers exposed the myopic nature of their personal and political socialization.

From the beginning of the United States, the phrase "We the people" referred only to White males, most of whom had to possess property to validate their right to life, liberty and the pursuit of happiness. This narrow view of political liberties and freedom discounted any sense of equality or protection of the lives, liberties, and happiness of women, indigenous people, and persons of African descent.

Another way of stating this is that the personal and political socialization of the founding fathers of the United States resulted in a very limited psycho-political consciousness. The limitations of this narrow psycho-political consciousness resulted in generations of unfathomable pain, misery, psychological oppression, economic injustices, and inconceivable forms of state-sanctioned violence and death.

Despite the psycho-political limitations and flaws in our founding fathers' personal and political socialization as well as the horrors ensuing from their limited racial justice consciousness, the seeds of a fuller, more inclusive, and comprehensive democracy were planted in the consciousness, unconsciousness, collective consciousness, hearts, and souls of other people across the history of our nation. These new, powerful, and revolutionary forms of consciousness resulted in an increased understanding that our founding fathers' flaws and limitations as well as the important commitment for *we the people* to make an expanded commitment to support the untapped potential and ongoing evolution of our nation's multiracial/multicultural democracy.

One of the major principles embedded in the new integral theory of mental health and human development described in Chapter 8 is the way our national socialization impacts our individual and collective racial consciousness for better or worse. As stated in Chapter 2, millions of people in culturally diverse groups continue to experience physical and psychological harm, in part, due to the flaws and limitations resulting from the founding fathers' political psychology and personal socialization.

During these perilous times, *we the people* are called upon to ensure that the lies proliferating by Donald Trump, his supporters, and his cult followers are overcome by expanding and sustaining our multiracial/multicultural democracy. These perilous times invoke the hope, faith, and love demonstrated by Dr. Martin Luther King Jr. and the countless number of people whose unearned suffering, physical injuries and, in many cases, their deaths, resulted from a commitment to exhibit non-violent resistance to social injustices in the United States.

With this backdrop in mind, the first potential promise described here is the assertion that *we the people* can and must be successful in expanding our democracy by overcoming the lies and violence perpetuated by Donald Trump and his supporters. From a practical psycho-political perspective, this involves supporting and sustaining the fragile multiracial/multicultural democracy now under serious and violent attacks by treasonous elements determined to support the rising forces of authoritarianism and fascism in our nation (See Chapter 1).

I outline specific action strategies that are recommended for interested readers' consideration throughout this book. Here it is suggested that persons interested in supporting the ongoing evolution of our nation's multiracial/multicultural democracy, at a minimum, would do well to exercise their individual and collective right and responsibility to vote in all future local, state, and federal elections. As former President Barack Obama and others have stated, "Elections have consequences."

2. The promise of developing more complex critical thinking skills from a psycho-political perspective.

The psycho-political analysis presented in this book emphasizes the importance of becoming knowledgeable of our nation's racial/cultural history. This book stresses the need to more accurately understand the present threats to our democracy and not repeat the same mistakes our country has made in the past when stumbling in efforts to develop a truly inclusive and comprehensive democracy. Educators in our nation's schools are particularly well-positioned to play a central role in realizing this promise.

This requires preparing lessons that help students learn how to determine whether information they have accessed on social media is valid or not; in other words, it necessitates greater institutional efforts to stimulate critical thinking from a psycho-political perspective than has been done in the past.

A multiracial/multicultural democracy flourishes in a society that effectively nurtures the critical thinking skills of all the people. It also requires educators and mental health professionals to work together to agree to the types of political activism that is not only aimed at promoting healthy human development, but to create connections with other allies at the local and state levels. These alliances are aimed at ensuring local, state, and national political policies are discussed and implemented to support the ongoing evolution of our multiracial/multicultural society.

3. Developing multiracial/multicultural competencies during the unprecedented demographic transformation of the United States.

Another potential promise, which is important to realize in a nation rapidly becoming a minority majority society, is the need for all persons to become more culturally competent than they have been in the past. This book directs attention to the impact of White supremacy on the history of the United States and the need to address the hegemonic implications of this psycho-political phenomenon during a time of unprecedented demographic transformation.

Definition of a Term/Concept: The term *hegemonic* is a derivative of the word *hegemony*. As used in this book, *hegemony* is defined as the dominance of one racial/cultural group's worldview, language, and social beliefs as well as its economic, educational, familial, and workplace values and traditions over other cultural/racial groups.

Chapter 1 begins a discussion of the ways that White supremacy and White racism represent toxic hegemonic conditions that adversely impact the healthy development of the victims of such hegemony. This includes people in groups comprising an expanded definition of multiculturalism presented in the new RESPECTFUL theory (RT) discussed in Chapter 2. It is important to continue to point out that research findings clearly describe how the unprecedented demographic transformation of the United States continues to negatively affect the healthy psychological, cognitive, emotional, and behavioral development of many perpetrators of such hegemony. This point underscores the need for *we the people* to acquire multicultural competencies in our 21st century culturally and racially diverse society.

The fields of counseling and psychology have made substantial progress in describing specific multicultural competencies mental health professionals need to develop to work effectively and ethically with racially and culturally diverse persons. In keeping with my promise to give away counseling and psychology concepts and theories to the readers of this book, I have adapted one of the most widely utilized set of multicultural counseling and psychology competencies in the psycho-political perspective presented in this book.

Appendix A, included at the end of this book, lists 25 multicultural competencies tailored for mental health professionals as well as interested persons in the general public. It is hoped that persons committed to developing any and/or all of the competencies listed on Appendix A will find greater satisfaction and effectiveness when dealing with the unprecedented demographic transformation of our nation.

One of the important goals for writing this book is to outline ways that mental health professionals, who have intentionally developed many of the multicultural counseling competencies formally endorsed by the American Counseling Association (ACA) in 2003, to move our national attention to the importance of mainstreaming the above stated competencies.

It is emphasized that there is a moral imperative for mental health professionals to increase their multicultural competence, especially when working with people whose health has been compromised by White supremacy and different forms of White racism. The new integral theory extends this moral imperative to include the need for support from national mental health associations and organizations to develop and implement strategies that result in large numbers of people in the mainstream of our society acquiring a broad range of multicultural competences. Key in realizing this potential promise is an increased awareness and understanding of the ways that the unprecedented demographic changes discussed in Chapter 2 are central in eradicating White supremacy and White racism while simultaneously fostering new forms of optimal mental health (See Chapters 8 and 9).

4. Fulfilling the promise of eradicating White supremacy and White racism in the United States.

In February 2003, I published an article describing the meaning and manifestation of White supremacy and White racism in our society. That article also described the relevance of these malignant societal dynamics for the mental health professions. One of the purposes in highlighting these points was to describe the multiple factors that beg for the emergence of a new era in mental healthcare in the United States.

The new integral theory illuminates specific ways the mental health professions can address the challenges of this new era by supporting the incorporation of psycho-political factors in professional training programs, revised ethical standards, individual and community-based mental health assessments, and in the clinical practices and related mental health and human development services routinely employed by mental health practitioners.

The eradication of these social cancers will not occur automatically. Given the extensive history and complexity of White racism and White supremacy in our country, it is imperative to understand that their eradication will necessitate a long-term process and a moral-psycho-political cleansing among the dominate racial group in our society. The success of this cleansing largely depends on the willingness of White people in the United States to increasingly support and sustain the ongoing evolution of our nation's multiracial/multicultural democracy.

To successfully realize this potential psycho-political cleansing, it is important to look beyond the demographic changes occurring in our nation and understand the relevance of such concepts as postmodernism, moral equivalence, and false equivalence. These terms are critical to understand given their relevance for the new integral theory of mental health and human development.

Understanding the basic meaning of postmodernism, moral equivalence, and false equivalence is useful in promoting a truly multiracial/multicultural democracy that fosters new forms of optimal mental health in our society. These concepts are defined below.

Definition of terms/concepts

Postmodernism represents a 20th-century movement characterized by broad skepticism of what is often thought of as universal truths fostered by dominant social-cultural-political groups in society. This includes asserted truths that are not necessarily valid among diverse cultural-racial groups. Many postmodernists hold one or more of the following views: (1) there is no objective reality; (2) there is no scientific or historical truth (objective truth); (3) science and technology (and even reason and logic) are not vehicles of human progress but suspected instruments of established power. Many postmodernists deny that there are any beliefs about reality that are objective or universally accurate statements about reality (D'Andrea, 2000).

Moral Equivalence: The term *moral equivalence* is typically used in political arguments and debates. It draws comparisons between opposing concepts to make a point that one psycho-political perspective is just as bad as another or just as good as a different perspective. Moral equivalence theory allows someone to appear both objective and detached from such arguments or debates.

The general form of this concept is described in the following postmodern ways:

- The actions of A are morally equivalent to the actions of B, therefore A is just as good or bad as B, regardless of what the actual actions are.

- Doing X is morally equivalent to doing Y, therefore someone doing X is just as good or bad as someone doing Y, regardless of what X and Y actually are.

False equivalence: As used in this book, the term *false equivalence* is defined as the belief that two opposing concepts thought to be morally equivalent are based on flawed or false reasoning. Colloquially, a false equivalence is often called *comparing apples and oranges.*

This book reflects an understanding of postmodernism and the importance of its foundational principles as well as its weaknesses when discussing issues related to multiculturalism in general and the ongoing evolution of our nation's multiracial/multicultural democracy in particular. The concept of *moral equivalence,* particularly as it applies to *Trumpism,* unfounded conspiracy theories, and lies that continue to be used to damage the ongoing and fragile evolution of the multiracial/multicultural democracy in our nation is rejected throughout this book. This controversial perspective is addressed in greater detail in Chapters 5 and 6.

5. The strengths and potential promise in supporting the ongoing evolution of our fragile multiracial/multicultural democracy.

The issue cutting across every aspect of American politics today is whether— and how—our nation can survive as a multiracial/multicultural democracy. A key question related to this issue is stated as follows: Have decades of struggle to more fully integrate racially and culturally diverse persons into the ongoing evolution of the fragile multiracial/multicultural democracy in the United States resulted in positive outcomes?

Thomas Edsall, a long-time journalist with the New York Times, published a synthesis of data generated from numerous quantitative and qualitative research endeavors in September 2021. This synthesis of important research findings provides answers to the above question. Edsall's article is entitled, "How Strong is America's Multiracial Democracy?" The following section summarizes a broad range of research findings included in Edsall's synthesis of multiple investigations.

A study published in 2020 entitled, "The Long-Run Effects of School Racial Diversity on Political Identity," examined how the end of race-based busing in Charlotte-Mecklenburg schools, an event that led to large changes in school racial composition, affected the partisanship of students as adults. The authors of this study, Stephen Billings, of the University of Colorado, Erich Chyn, of Dartmouth University, and Kareem Haggag, of U.C.L.A.'s Anderson School of Management, found that "a 10-percentage point increase in the share of minorities in a student's assigned public school decreased their likelihood of registering as a Republican by 8.8% as adults." The drop was "entirely driven by White students (a 12% decrease)."

The researchers suggested that the results of this study can, in part, be explained by recognizing that intergroup contact (resulting from school integration) is an important factor in empowering White students to formally register with a political party that more closely matched their political identity in adulthood. Several theoretical frameworks provide predictions for how exposure to more minority peers may shape party affiliation.

According to the researchers, one of the chief factors that help to explain the above stated investigative findings is referred to as the *contact hypothesis*. The contact hypothesis was initially posited by Gordon Allport, a professor of psychology at Harvard University, in his classic 1954 book, *The Nature of Prejudice*. Allport wrote that prejudice may be reduced by equal status contact between majority and minority groups in the pursuit of common goals. This effect is greatly enhanced if this contact is sanctioned by institutional supports (i.e., by law, custom, or local atmosphere), and provided it leads to the perception of common interests and a common humanity between members of diverse racial groups.

Two additional publications by independent investigators provide further support for the positive impact and relevance of the contact hypothesis. The first study was published by Scott Carrell, Mark Hoekstra and James West, economists at the University of California-Davis, Texas A&M and Baylor University entitled, "The Impact of College Diversity on Behavior toward Minorities." The results of this study indicated that White students, who were randomly assigned a Black roommate in their freshman year, were more likely to choose a Black roommate in subsequent years.

Another publication resulted in research findings reported by Salma Mousa, a political scientist at Yale University entitled, "Building Social Cohesion Between Christians and Muslims through Soccer in Post-ISIS Iraq." The results of this investigation indicated the positive impact of religious-based and caste-based intergroup contact among culturally and religious-diverse members of their soccer team. In essence, team members with different cultural and religious identities reported increasingly positive interpersonal relationships as a result of their unique team membership based on shared athletic goals.

In an August 2021 paper entitled, "Race and Income in U.S. Suburbs: Are Diverse Suburbs Disadvantaged?" Ankit Rastogi, a postdoctoral fellow at the University of Pennsylvania's Center for the Study of Ethnicity, Race and Immigration, challenges two common assumptions many White persons make related to their beliefs about residential locations largely comprised of people of color. Rastogi points out that many (perhaps most) White people believe that Black and Brown people are largely concentrated in large, economically disadvantaged, urban areas.

However, as a result of using data from the 2019 American Community Survey, Rastogi reports the following findings:

1. By and large, racially diverse suburbs are middle class when comparing their median household income with the national value ($63,000). The most multiracial suburbs host populations with the highest annual median incomes of $85,000 or more.

2. Black and Latinx median household incomes surpass the national value in racially diverse suburbs.

By 2010, Rastogi points out that majorities of every major demographic group lived in suburbs including 51% of Black Americans, 62%

of persons of Asian descent, 59% of Latinx ancestry, and 78% White persons. Rastogi's research findings acknowledged that many people of color stated they chose to live in suburbs because they see them as desirable, resource-rich communities with good schools and other public services.

In addition, Rastogi's research findings indicated that:

3. Roughly 45 million people of color and 42 million White people lived in suburbs in 2019 with persons of color, on average, living in middle-class contexts. These research findings may lead many White persons to question stereotypes of race, residential populations, and over generalizations about economic disadvantage of persons of color residing in suburbs.

4. Rastogi correctly points to some optimistic trends related to residential and economic characteristics of people of color. These findings are complemented by other investigative findings relevant to positive educational outcomes that are, in part, fostered by important diversity and affirmative action policies.

Among numerous research publications relevant to the above statements include the following investigative findings in a March 2021 report sponsored by the Pew Research Center entitled, "The Growing Diversity of Black Americans." Among some of the striking educational-social changes that have occurred in recent decades include the following:

5. From 2000 to 2019, the percentage of African Americans with at least a bachelor's degree rose from 15 to 23 percent, as the share with a master's degree or higher nearly doubled from 5 to 9 percent.

6. At the same time, the share of African Americans without a high school degree was cut by more than half over the same period, from 28 to 13 percent.

The evidence of Black educational and economic progress noted in the above research findings lends support for the belief that such progress has been underreported—indeed minimized—in recent years. Refuting some of the common negative stereotyping many (perhaps most) White persons have about the above stated accomplishments of persons of color in general and African Americans in particular is relevant for the psycho-political perspective presented in this book.

In part, this progress has and continues to occur because of the increasing representation of racially diverse persons as elected officials at the local, state, and federal levels of our government. There is a correlation between the increasing number of racially diverse elected officials' efforts to address covert intentional and unintentional White racism by successfully promoting new education, housing, and economic statutes and policies that contribute to the positive outcomes and accomplishments described above. Space limitations do not enable a more comprehensive summary of other research documented accomplishments directly tied to the increasing representation of elected persons of color at all levels of our government.

The collective publication of the above-stated research findings is a testament to the importance of supporting and sustaining the ongoing evolution of our nation's multiracial/multicultural democracy. This is particularly important during the current perilous times when Donald Trump, his supporters, and cult followers are committed to do what is ever necessary to advance their racist, authoritarian, fascist, and obscene plans to "Make America Great Again!"

6. The potential promise of a new model for healthy human development

One of the most important potential promises underlying the psycho-political analysis described in this book is the hope and belief that our nation will not only survive these perilous times but thrive in substance and content in the future. The basis for this hope and belief is anchored in the ongoing energy, commitment, courage, and risk-taking manifested by a majority of people in the United States supportive of the ongoing evolution of our multiracial/multicultural democracy. This perspective is based on the title of this book –*Beyond the Lies*– especially as it relates to the ways that supporters of our nation's democracy address the lies perpetuated by Donald Trump and his supporters.

Having worked for more than 40 years as a mental health professional, community organizer, social justice advocate and anti-racist, I have learned from experience that the realization of this potential promise will not come easily, nor is it automatically guaranteed. It will require much time, energy, courage, commitment, unity, and risk-taking to overcome the perilous times we currently face as a nation.

The test of these efforts will be reflected in the degree to which a majority of people, particularly mental health professionals, implement concrete actions aimed at promoting the sort of consciousness that is accompanied by actions which increase the psycho-political impotence of Donald Trump and his supporters. I am aware that some readers will predictably disagree with the above-stated analysis and suggestions.

Nevertheless, numerous actions will need to be taken to combat the rising authoritarianism and fascism in our country. The key to achieving this important challenge is to keep our collective eyes on the prize. That prize being our collective commitment to implement concrete action strategies to counter what Dr. Robert Lifton (2017) refers to as the *malignant normalcy* in our society. The following comments made by Dr. Lifton offer a taste of the complex and important meaning of a *malignant normalcy*:

> The concept of the malignant normalcy in our nation requires us to recognize the urgency of the situation in which the former president is the bearer of profound instability and untruths. As mental health professionals, we need to act with ethical passion in our efforts to reveal what is most dangerous and what, in contrast, might be life-affirming in the face of the malignant normality that surrounds us.

Another guiding principle outlined throughout this book is an acknowledgement that *we the people* have no guarantee that our current form of government will continue. This is a reality we would do well to face given the unprecedented efforts by Donald Trump and his supporters/cult followers to dismantle the fragile experiment we call *democracy*.

A third guiding principle is the importance of becoming more knowledgeable of how and why these perilous times represent toxic psycho-political conditions that are fertile terrain for disordered ways of being. Such disordered ways of being may succeed in giving birth to a level of authoritarianism and fascism in the United States few readers believe could occur in our nation. I have previously asserted that these toxic conditions are particularly important for mental health professionals to address if counselors, psychiatrists, psychologists, social workers and other allied professionals are to remain relevant and viable in a culturally and racially diverse 21st century.

It has been discouraging to experience the level of resistance, hostility, and apathy many mental health professionals exhibit when discussing the need to affirm and publicly support the ongoing evolution of our nation's multiracial/multicultural democracy. The primary goal in supporting the incorporation of a psycho-political perspective into our national mental health system is to foster and sustain the healthy development of larger numbers of persons in diverse groups than we have done in the past.

As noted in Chapter 1 and repeated throughout this book, mental health professionals are called upon to openly acknowledge the growing psychological threats to the lives of millions of people in our society. Increasing numbers of researchers continue to document how and why many people are at-risk for mental health problems when subjected to and accepting the lies and injustices perpetuated by Donald Trump, his supporters, and members of the Trump cult (See Chapters 5, 6 & 7). It is necessary but not sufficient to acknowledge how the driving force of Trumpism builds on a historic legacy of racial injustices, including ongoing forms of state-sanctioned violence among persons in multiracial/multicultural groups.

It is simultaneously important to acknowledge that survey results indicate millions of people in the United States continue to articulate support for the former president and Trumpism. These issues are detailed in Chapter 6 entitled, Trump Supporters and the Trump Cult.

Additional potential promises underlying the realization of a stronger and sustained multiracial/multicultural democracy are discussed in the following chapters. Chapter 4 also directs readers' attention to a number of serious pitfalls that represent real and ongoing threats to our current imperfect democracy.

The Primary Factor in White People's Resistance to a Multiracial/Multicultural Democracy

As noted at different points throughout this book, many, perhaps most, White persons will experience a broad range of reactions as our nation becomes a minority majority country. Among the reactions large numbers of Trump supporters articulate at political rallies include the following: "We will take our country back," "All of these immigrants are taking over our country and we are going to take it back," and "This is our country, and we are not going to let you people take it away from us." Researchers with the Southern Poverty Law Center (SPLC) conducted important studies describing the negative psychological, emotional, and behavioral reactions that continue to be manifested among Trump's supporters, especially among those persons comprising the Trump cult (See Chapter 6).

Mental health professionals have developed a growing knowledge-base that describes reactions White people have to the substantial demographic changes occurring in all aspects of our society. This includes demographic changes in our schools, universities, workplaces, social and athletic organizations as well as religious, ethnic, racial, and cultural communities to name a few. Given this knowledge-base, it is not possible to overstate the substantial psychological, emotional, neurological, and behavioral impact of the unprecedented demographic transformation of the United States.

Hopefully, the information presented in this book will stimulate a new consciousness among readers–the sort of new consciousness that is anchored in an expansive awareness and understanding of the need to support our nation's evolving multiracial/multicultural democracy from a psycho-political and mental health perspective. It also describes positive ways interested readers can address the unprecedented demographic transformation rapidly unfolding in our nation by developing new multicultural competencies (See Appendix A at the end of this book).

Summary

This chapter focuses on the potential promise of the multiracial/multicultural democracy movement in the United States. It also describes doubts many people have about our nation ever being able to realize a genuine, comprehensive, and inclusive democracy.

Keeping with the commitment I made in Chapter 1, numerous terms relevant to the information presented in this and other chapters are defined for the reader's clarity. Among the key terms defined in this chapter include *socialization* and *hegemony*. The following section of Chapter 3 summarizes research findings describing the positive impact of integrated schools, universities, athletic teams, and communities. These empirical findings further highlight why it is important to support the ongoing evolution of the multiracial/multicultural democracy in the United States.

Another potential promise of the multiracial/multicultural democracy movement relates to its possibility to replace our country's *malignant normalcy* with *optimal mental health*. This discussion begins by defining what is meant by *malignant normalcy* as outlined by Dr. Robert Lifton. It continues in Chapter 8 where the concept of *optimal mental health* is described in greater detail.

Once again, this chapter ends with a renewed call for mental health professionals to effectively ameliorate the complex crisis in our nation's mental health system. It is suggested that it would be useful to incorporate a psycho-political perspective in our professional training programs, clinical practices, and research endeavors in the future.

This chapter is followed by Chapter 4, which is designed to bring balance to the discussion of the potential promise of the ongoing evolution of our nation's fragile multiracial/multicultural democracy. It does so by detailing some of the key pitfalls that are a part of our past as well as those that lay ahead in strengthening our democracy for all the people in our country.

CHAPTER 4

THE PITFALLS

This is not the end…

This is not even the beginning of the end…

But this is the end of the beginning…

Winston Churchill, 1942

Come gather 'round people wherever you roam

And admit that the waters around you have grown

And accept it that soon you'll be drenched to the bone.

If your time to you is worth savin,' then you better start swimmin'

Or you'll sink like a stone

For the times they are a-changin'.

Come writers and critics who prophesize with your pen

And keep your eyes wide the chance won't come again

And don't speak too soon for the wheel's still in spin

And there's no tellin' who that it's namin'.

For the loser now will be later to win for the times they are a-changin'.

Come senators, congressmen please heed the call

Don't stand in the doorway don't block up the hall

For he that gets hurt will be he who has stalled

There's a battle outside and it's ragin'.

It'll soon shake your windows and rattle your walls.

For the times they are a-changin'.

–Bob Dylan, The Times They Are a Changin'

Introduction

This chapter adds to important points made in Chapter 3. Among the points included in Chapter 3 are descriptions of the potential promise that is linked to the ongoing evolution of the multiracial/multicultural democracy in our society. This includes discussions of the potential promise to (a) realize a more inclusive and comprehensive democracy in our nation, (b) ways to stimulate an increase in people's critical thinking skills, (c) the need to fuel a greater level of multiracial/multicultural competence among mental health professionals and persons in the general public, and (d) ongoing efforts to eradicate White supremacy and White racism in our society.

This chapter balances several points made in Chapter 3 by juxtaposition pitfalls that represent impairments to the continuing evolution of our multiracial/multicultural democracy. This includes discussions that describe the pitfall of disinformation and lies, the pitfall of the historic and ongoing problem of anti-intellectualism in our society, the pitfall of subverting voting rights, the pitfall of state-sanctioned racial violence, and multiple factors contributing to our present perilous times. The following sections of this chapter provide more detailed discussions of these influential pitfalls.

1. Multiple factors contributing to our perilous times.

According to the Human Rights Foundation, today more than half of the people on earth are governed by anti-democratic rulers. From Milan, Italy, to Manila, Philippines, from Walsall, Poland to Washington, DC, authoritarian leaders are on the rise. Thus, as Tarso Luis Ramos acknowledged, "*We the people* should not make the mistake of thinking that what's happening in the United States is unconnected to these global trends."

Tarso Luis Ramos is a social scientist with Political Research Associates. He drew the following conclusions from his study of the current perilous times that have national and global implications:

> Different from the past, in recent decades the descent from democracy into authoritarianism is more likely to occur through this slow corruption and erosion of democratic institutions than from a sudden event such as a military coup. Authoritarians are often elected, before dismantling democracy from within.

> Ramos's analysis includes the following observations of the common elements that drive liberal democracies towards authoritarianism, including:

> Severe economic inequality;

> The rise of theocratic religious movements; and

> The rise of racial/ethnic nationalist movements and political parties that define the perilous situation we are currently experiencing in racist and other exclusionary ways.

The economic, religious, and racial/ethnic dynamics listed above are present in Trump's coalition and that is not by accident. While these points are discussed in more detail later in this book, it is important to highlight the point that in the United States, where racial hierarchy has always been a central organizing principle for society and politics, demographic change is an especially powerful lever for would-be authoritarians. Consider that in the short history of the modern nation-state; it's hard to find an example of a democracy that has survived a transition in which the dominant racial/ethnic/religious group became a numerical minority.

As numerous historians and social scientists have reported, democracy can be, and often is, sacrificed in order to maintain the cultural, economic, military and political power of the dominant group. A thoughtful reflection of the United States' post-Civil War history reveals that, rather than accept the multiracial democracy of Reconstruction in the southern states, Southerners increasingly implemented racial terrorism and the creation of a one-party racial organization across the South. That's not to single-out the southern states as forms of structural racism permeate every corner of this country.

2. The pitfall of disinformation and lies.

The idea of operating from a political platform of deliberate lies and advancing mistruths to cover up for one's own failures and missteps is nothing new. Hitler was one of the first in modern times to intentionally mislead the public for his own political advantage. At the current time it appears that millions of people in the United States continue to believe in and support the disinformation and lies propagated by Donald Trump, his supporters, and members of the Trump cult.

Dr. David Childs, a faculty member at Northern Kentucky University, has written about these issues in an article entitled, "The Danger of Disinformation and Anti-Intellectualism in Today's Society." Among the points included in this article that are relevant for a discussion of our perilous times are stated below:

> One of the troubling aspects of the times that we live in is that many people do not trust long established institutions because of the proliferation of disinformation. Indeed, reputable organizations and institutions such as the *New York Times, The Washington Post,* well established universities and the Americans Academy of Arts and Science are challenged by the general public and written off as biased and dangerous institutions.
>
> As a result, many people struggle with differentiating between valid and invalid sources of information. When people do not have the ability to differentiate between valid and invalid information sources, they become susceptible to disinformation and misinformation.

This susceptibility contributes to people's vulnerability to many false conspiracy theories based on unsubstantiated claims. Many of these unsubstantiated conspiracy theories are primarily aimed at maintaining and expanding the authoritarian political power that Donald Trump and his supporters in the Republican Party are so desperately working to sustain. The essence of these conspiracy theories is driven by fantastic disinformation that can more accurately be described as bizarre and preposterous lies.

Perhaps the most egregious of these lies is what Trump, his supporters, and members of the Trump cult refer to as "The Big Lie." As Misinformation Reporter, Anya Wagtendonk, writes in her article entitled, "The Big Lie's Lasting Damage to Americans Democracy":

> Almost half of all the Americans polled indicate that they don't believe President Joe Biden legitimately won the 2020 election. This is the 'Big Lie' that inspired the insurrectionists to attempt to block the certification of the presidential election on January 6, 2021, and remains at the center of the democratic emergency in the United States.

> Behind this false belief is a concerted disinformation campaign funded by allies of the former president. The campaign and high-profile supporters orchestrated rallies around the country that popped up days after the 2020 election took place. But even two years after Biden took office, the Big Lie continues to have a strong pull on the Republican Party.

> The unsubstantiated belief that U. S. elections are vulnerable to corruption threatens to undermine voters' faith in democracy itself as that faith is an essential part of what energizes our democracy.

3. The pitfall of anti-intellectualism.

The United States was founded by some of the most influential intellectuals in history. Thomas Jefferson, Benjamin Franklin, Alexander Hamilton; they were all children of the Enlightenment, and the constitution reflects this fact. But after the first few decades of governing and as the country expanded westward, hostility towards intellectuals increased.

In his book entitled, *America's Longstanding History of Anti-Intellectualism and the Current War on Reason,* Conor Lynch pointed out that as "America became increasingly industrialized ... uneducated businessmen rose to be the tycoons of industry, which further increased the Americans belief that education is impractical, elitist, and morally decedent." Lynch further contends that corruption in American politics is at its peak when anti-intellectualism is at its highest.

While the rise of anti-intellectualism was notable during the 19th century, it was only when the progressive movement emerged in the early twentieth century, led by the rough-riding Harvard educated Theodore Roosevelt, was the importance of intellectualism reinstated in order to strengthen and sustain our democracy. At that time, intellectuals once again became prominent in Americans life. President Franklin Roosevelt's political philosophy and implementation of his New Deal policies accelerated the role intellectuals played in running the government during the 1930s.

However, distrust and belittling of intellectuals increased during the mid-20th century and continues to be increasingly evident during the early 21st century. Today, anti-intellectualism can be seen in schools around the country, where administrators choose to teach children *alternatives* to evolution, like the pseudo-scientific creationism, which asserts fictitiously that a divine entity created life on earth and claims this to be *scientific*. It can also be seen in Washington DC, where politicians like Donald Trump and his supporters in the Republican Party assert that the environmental crisis is a hoax fabricated by the Democratic Party as well as respected scientists in our nation.

In the 1980's, Jerry Falwell and the *moral majority* began their counter-revolution against the political system that had become increasingly secular. Falwell and his followers, like Pat Robertson, wanted Christianity to once again play an important role in America's political structure. This role increased the influence of the religious right among many politicians, especially those politicians who expressed anti-intellectual sentiments. Ronald Reagan brought back the strong distrust of the intellectual world. Since then, many other politicians have become increasingly hostile towards any evidence that might be contrary to their anti-intellectual ideological beliefs.

According to Lynch, heightened anti-intellectualism in the United States is grounded in a general skepticism and hostility towards highly educated experts. According to Lynch, President Obama was continuously labeled *professorial* when he ran for president, as if this was a bad thing. Expanding on this point, Lynch's observations led him to acknowledge that Obama was too intelligent and academic for many

Americans who would have preferred an emotional and populist politician, or to be accurate, a demagogue.

In making this observation, Lynch suggests that many Americans crave personality, not intellect or expertise. Consequently, many politicians continue to demonstrate that anti-intellectualism is not a thing of the past as it is deeply rooted in American society today.

What ultimately fuels distrust of intellectuals and education is insecurity. Researchers have noted that many people view intellectualism as something that is foreign, elitist, and aristocratic. In high schools around the country, athletes are glorified, while intellectual students are called *nerds* or *geeks*. While our international academic standing continues to sink, spending on athletics increases, while academics and instruction get snubbed.

Anti-intellectualism was recently heightened in many states and manifested in ugly confrontations with public school officials, including threats and physical violence inflicted on school board members often perpetuated by persons who self-identify as MAGA supporters. Another form of anti-intellectualization is manifested in low academic scores in classes like social studies that focus on students' knowledge of citizenship. A recent poll in Oklahoma (a strong Republican State) revealed that a measly 2.8% of public-school students in that state passed a standard test on students' knowledge about citizenship.

Scientific issues, like climate change are denied by significant percentages of the Americans population. Unsubstantiated conspiracy theories continue to be embraced by large numbers of people in our nation as does the unquestionable belief in Trump's Big Lie; a lie that undermines the foundational cornerstone of our democracy.

In contemporary America, it is more important than ever to examine our anti-intellectualist history and the loss of interest among many people in staying informed about what is happening in the nation and the world which is increasingly becoming a thing of the past. With this backdrop in mind, it is important to resist longstanding stereotypes that our culture has placed on rational thinking, highly educated individuals. In a globalized world, hostility towards issues related to intellectualization can only make America unexceptional, and we all know how very important exceptionalism is to Americans today.

4. The pitfall of subverting voting rights.

In 2020, the world witnessed the United States navigate a presidential election amid growing White supremacy, structural racism, misinformation, and elected officials deliberately exacerbating ugly economic, social, cultural, and racial divisions. At the same time, the raging Covid-19 virus revealed gross government negligence, shaped in part by institutional racism that disproportionately impaired Black and Brown communities from the pandemic's physical, psychological, economic, and political impact.

The presidential elections of 2020 saw the highest voter turnout since 1900. The results of this election underscored this country's deep-seated social, cultural/racial, and political divides. There was strong support for Joe Biden (81 million total votes casted for Biden in 2020) and 74 million total votes for former President Donald Trump as most Americans voted strictly along party lines.

Shortly after the 2020 presidential election, Trump and his allies organized a series of Stop the Steal rallies across the nation. Trump supporters attended these rallies and many turned up at voter recount sites to directly observe the alleged fraud they were convinced had hijacked Trump's victory. Anya Wagtendonk, the Misinformation Reporter referenced above, emphasized the outcomes of these events in the following ways:

> Many Trump supporters, who attended the Stop the Steal rallies, continued to communicate with other like-minded allies online where their rage fomented. All of this culminated in a violent breach of the Capital. But the dramatic events of January 6, 2021 were not the end of the Big Lie's influence. It is reshaping how future elections are administered nationwide. According to the Brennan Center for Justice, 19 states have enacted at least 33 new laws since January 2021 that restricts voting access.
>
> The Big Lie continues to loom large over the political system in other ways. According to *The Washington Post*, at least 163 Republicans who have embraced Trump's false claims are

running for statewide positions that would give them authority over the administration and certification of future elections. Few Republicans have gone out of their way to disavow these actions.

Today, an important question to be addressed is: How can we build a democracy that truly reflects and serves all Americans in an equitable manner? First, we must not be afraid to name the failed systems of power that lead to social division and inequity in the first place. Then we must begin to replace those systems with new ones that support a truly inclusive, multiracial democracy.

5. The pitfall of state-sanctioned racial violence. Implications for White racism, White supremacy, intergenerational trauma, and the mental health of the United States.

This section of Chapter 4 provides readers with research-based knowledge related to the ways that our nation's long history of state-sanctioned violence against persons of color in general and African Americans in particular has and continues to be manifested in our nation. My research in writing this book led me to explore state-sanctioned racial violence that permeates the history of the United States.

As for myself, I would rate my own experiences in elementary, secondary and post-secondary schools as being above average from an educational perspective. Despite these positive educational experiences, I was surprised, disappointed, and concerned that I had not been taught about the degree to which state-sanctioned racial violence was as American as apple pie.

As I continued my research for this book, I decided to talk with colleagues and friends about their own educational experiences as they related to the degree to which they learned about the persistence of state-sanctioned racial violence throughout our nation's history. Although a non-scientific approach to exploring these issues, it was disturbing to find that the responses my colleagues and friends expressed matched my own educational experiences. This included a lack of teaching and learning about the history of state-supported racial violence in our nation.

Recognizing that the information I secured in my research on state-sanctioned racial violence was important to disseminate with other White persons who may have never learned about these horrific social injustices in school, I decided to present these findings in this book. What follows is information related to factual documentation (not my opinion) of the frequent implementation of state-supported racial violence fueled by White supremacy and White racism during the history of our nation. A side reason for including a description of these violent injustices here is to assist the reader in becoming more culturally competent in the United States (See Chapter 3, Appendix A).

One of my research findings resulted in becoming more aware of the number of African Americans who were murdered by state-sanctioned lynchings throughout the history of the United States. Researchers calculated that more than 6,500 African Americans were victims of racial lynching in the United States between 1865 and 1950. When I read this research finding, I had to reread it to make sure this was the actual number of African Americans lynched between 1865 and 1950. At the risk of repeating myself, I want to again point out that more than 6,500 African Americans were victims of state-sanctioned racial lynchings between 1865 and 1950.

I paused to think about the large number of African Americans who were subjected to death by lynching without having their rights for court hearings with legal representation or having their due process rights respectfully guaranteed.

What a powerfully negative political part of our country's history.

I also thought about the genocidal practices imposed on the Native people of this land resulting in countless deaths, physical and psychological injuries, and intergenerational trauma as a result of such state-sanctioned violence.

I was deeply distressed by all of this information! How could my educational experiences, along with those of many other White people in our society fail to educate us about this profoundly brutal, violent, and unjust part of our country's history! My conclusion was that the failure of our nation's school system to teach about the brutality and injustice of these horrific murders were important and awful examples of the ways that White supremacy was, and in many instances, continue to be perpetuated in our schools.

Such White supremacy continues to enable our educational institutions to simply omit this part of our country's history from the curriculum. Currently, the governor of the State of Florida, is advocating for public schools in that state to not use any learning strategies that create discomfort among white students. This includes prohibiting learning strategies that explore the depth of White supremacy, White racism, and White privilege as manifested throughout our country's history.

As I proceeded with my research for this book, I learned a great deal about state-sanctioned massacres that were brutal and unjust parts of our nation's history. As a result of this learning, I made a commitment to do what I can to provide information about these injustices and mass homicides in whatever way I could in my personal and professional life.

Also, as stated in the Preface and ensuing chapters, I have reiterated that one of the main goals of this book is to increase readers' awareness and knowledge of a broad range of issues related to the ways that White supremacy and White racism continue to be manifested in our society. As a result of this learning, I decided to include the following description of the numerous state-sanctioned racial and cultural massacres that have occurred throughout history for a couple of reasons.

First, I hope the following descriptions of the state-sanctioned violence directed to African Americans and Native Americans Indians help to increase the reader's awareness of these horrific injustices, especially for those persons whose education experiences failed to promote such learning in these areas.

Second, I have faith that reading the ensuing information about state-sanctioned racial massacres (perhaps for the first time among many readers) will stimulate a greater level of understanding, and perhaps compassion, for the ways these violent actions resulted in persistent intergenerational trauma among many African American and Native American people in the United States today.

State-Sanctioned Racial Massacres of African Americans in the United States

The 1875 Massacre in Clinton, Mississippi

The Clinton Massacre began on Sept. 4, 1875, in the small town of Clinton, Mississippi. It occurred at a Republican rally to introduce the party's candidates who were running for political office in the upcoming November 1875 state elections.

Over 1,500 Black Republicans and their families gathered on the grounds of the former Moss Hill plantation for a barbecue and political rally. Approximately 100 Whites also attended, including a few Democrats from the nearby town of Raymond.

While a Republican was giving a speech, shots were fired. When the gunfire ended, a total of five African Americans, including two children, and three white people were dead, and nearly thirty others were wounded.

The following days were marked by violence and bloodshed as the White mob indiscriminately shot and killed nearly fifty African Americans in Clinton and the surrounding area. In addition, the White mob murdered a White school teacher working in the African Americans community.

Although Governor Ames requested federal troops to assist in restoring order, President Ulysses Grant denied the request on September 14, 1875, and adopted a policy of non-intervention, leaving Ames and the local Black and White Republicans without protection.

The Wilmington Massacre of 1898

The Wilmington insurrection of 1898, also known as the Wilmington Massacre of 1898 or the Wilmington coup of 1898, was a riot and insurrection carried out by White supremacists in Wilmington, North Carolina on Thursday, November 10, 1898. The White press in Wilmington originally described this event as a race riot caused by Black people. However, since the late 20th century, the insurrection has been characterized as a *coup d'état*, the violent overthrow of a duly elected government by a group of White supremacists.

Multiple causes brought this violent overthrow about. In part, the Wilmington massacre was the result of a group of North Carolina's White Southern Democrats conspiring and leading a mob of 2,000 white men to overthrow the legitimately elected local biracial government in Wilmington. These White Southern Democrats expelled Black and White political leaders from the city, destroyed the property and businesses of Black citizens built up since the American Civil War including the only Black newspaper in the city, and killed an estimated 60 to more than 300 people. It has been described as the only incident of its kind in American history because other violent racial incidents did not result in the direct removal and replacement of elected officials by unelected individuals.

The Wilmington coup is considered a turning point in post-reconstruction North Carolina politics. It was part of an era of more severe racial segregation and the effective disenfranchisement of African Americans throughout the South, which had been underway since the end of the southern reconstruction era.

Other states soon passed similar laws. Laura Edwards wrote in *Democracy Betrayed* (2000): "What happened in Wilmington became an affirmation of White supremacy not just in that one city, but in the South and in the nation as a whole." This historic event affirmed that invoking Whiteness eclipsed the legal citizenship, individual rights, and equal protection under the law that Black Americans were guaranteed in the Fourteenth Amendment of the U.S. Constitution.

Tulsa's Black Wall Street Massacre, May 30, 1921

My ongoing research efforts resulted in increased knowledge about the years following World War I. After that war, there was a substantial spike in racial tensions, including the resurgence of the Ku Klux Klan, numerous racial lynchings, and other acts of racially motivated violence as well as efforts by African Americans to prevent such attacks from occurring in their communities. Tulsa was a highly segregated city with most of the city's 10,000 Black residents living and working in an area called Greenwood. This was an economically thriving area that included

Black run businesses that resulted in what was referred to as the Black Wall Street of the south.

By 1921, fueled by oil money, Tulsa was a growing, prosperous city with a population of more than 100,000 people. But crime rates were high and vigilante justice of all kinds were not uncommon.

On May 30, 1921, a young Black teenager named Dick Rowland entered an elevator at the Drexel Building, an office building on South Main Street in Tulsa. At some point after that encounter, the young White elevator operator, Sarah Page, screamed. Rowland fled the scene. The police were called and the next morning they arrested Rowland.

By that time, rumors of what supposedly happened on that elevator had circulated through the city's White community. A front-page story in the *Tulsa Tribune* published on May 30th reported that the police arrested Rowland for sexually assaulting Page.

As evening fell, an angry White mob gathered outside the courthouse, demanding the sheriff to hand over Rowland. Sheriff Willard McCullough refused and his men barricaded the top floor of the courthouse to protect the Black teenager.

Around 9 p.m. on May 30, 1921, a group of about 25 armed Black men—including many World War I veterans—went to the courthouse to offer help guarding Rowland. After the sheriff turned them away, some of the White mob tried unsuccessfully to break into the National Guard armory nearby.

With rumors still flying of a possible lynching, a group of around 75 armed Black men returned to the courthouse shortly after 10 p.m., where they were met by some 1,500 White men, many of whom carried weapons. After shots were fired and chaos broke out, the outnumbered group of Black men retreated to Greenwood.

Over the next several hours, groups of White Tulsans—some of whom were deputized and given weapons by city officials—committed numerous acts of violence against Black people, including shooting an unarmed Black man in a movie theater.

The false belief that a large-scale insurrection among Black Tulsans was underway, including reinforcements from nearby towns and cities with large African American populations fueled a growing hysteria. As dawn broke on June 1, 1921, thousands of White citizens poured into the Greenwood District, looting and burning homes and businesses over an area of 35 city blocks. Firefighters who arrived to help put out fires later testified that White rioters had threatened them with guns and forced them to leave.

According to a later Red Cross estimate, some 1,256 houses were burned; 215 others were looted but not torched. Two newspapers, a school, a library, a hospital, churches, hotels, stores, and many other Black-owned businesses were among the buildings destroyed or damaged by fire. Fatalities of the Tulsa Massacre vary greatly. Estimates range between 30 and 300 men, women, and children reportedly died during this massacre.

The Rosewood, Florida Massacre of January 1923

The Rosewood massacre was a racially motivated carnage of Black people and the destruction of a Black town that took place during the first week of January 1923 in rural Levy County, Florida. At least six Black people and two White people were killed during this massacre, though eyewitness accounts suggested a higher death toll of 27 to 150 persons. The town of Rosewood was destroyed in what contemporary news reports characterized as a race riot. Florida had an especially high number of lynchings of Black men in the years before the massacre, including a well-publicized incident in December 1922.

Though it was originally settled in 1845 by both Black and White people, black codes and Jim Crow laws in the years after the Civil War fostered segregation in Rosewood (and much of the South). Employment in Rosewood was provided by pencil factories, but the cedar tree population soon became decimated and White families moved away in the 1890s settling in the nearby town of Sumner, Florida. By the 1920s, Rosewood's population of about 200 was entirely made up of Black citizens, except for one White family that ran the general store there.

On January 1, 1923, in Sumner, Florida, 22-year-old Fannie Taylor was heard screaming by a neighbor. The neighbor found Taylor covered in bruises claiming a Black man had entered the house and assaulted her.

The incident was reported to Sheriff Robert Elias Walker with Taylor specifying that she had not been raped.

Fannie Taylor's husband, James Taylor, a foreman at the local mill, escalated the situation by gathering an angry mob of White citizens to hunt down the culprit. James also called for help from White residents in neighboring counties, among them a group of about 500 Ku Klux Klan members who were in Gainesville for a rally. The White mob prowled the area searching for any Black man they might find.

Law enforcement persons found out that a Black prisoner named Jesse Hunter had escaped earlier from a chain gang and immediately designated him as a suspect. The White mob focused their searches on Hunter, convinced that he was being hidden by Black residents. The searchers were led by dogs to the home of Aaron Carrier in Rosewood. Aaron Carrier was the nephew of Sarah Carrier, who did the laundry for Taylor. White men in the mob dragged Aaron Carrier out of his house, tied him to a car and dragged him to Sumner where he was cut loose and beaten.

Sheriff Walker intervened, putting Aaron Carrier in his car and driving him to Gainesville, where he was placed in the protective custody of the sheriff there. Another White mob showed up at the home of a blacksmith named Sam Carter. The White mob proceeded in torturing Aaron Carrier until he admitted that he was hiding Jesse Hunter and agreed to take them to the hiding spot. Carter led them into the woods, but when Hunter failed to appear, someone in the mob shot Sam Carter. His body was hung on a tree before the mob moved on.

The sheriff's office attempted and failed to break up the White mob and advised Black workers to stay in their places of employment for safety. As many as 25 people, mostly children, took refuge in the home of Sarah Carrier when, on the night of January 4, 1923, armed White men surrounded the house in the belief that Jesse Hunter was hiding there.

Shots were fired in the ensuing confrontation. Sarah Carrier was shot in the head and died, and her son, Sylvester, was also killed by a gunshot wound. Two White attackers were also killed. The gun battle and standoff lasted overnight. It ended when the door to Sarah Carrier's home was broken down by White attackers. The children inside the house escaped through the back entrance and made their way to safety through the woods where they hid.

News of the standoff at the Carrier house spread with newspapers inflating the number dead and falsely reporting bands of armed Black citizens going on a rampage. Even more White men poured into the area believing that a race war had broken out. Some of the first targets of this influx were the churches in Rosewood which were burned down. Houses were then attacked, first by setting fire to them and then shooting people as they tried to escape from the burning buildings.

Lexie Gordon was one of those murdered, taking a gunshot to her face as she hid under her burning house. Gordon had sent her children fleeing when White attackers approached but, suffering from typhoid fever, she stayed behind. Many Rosewood citizens fled to the nearby swamps for safety, spending days hiding in them. Some attempted to leave the swamps but were turned back by men working for the sheriff.

James Carrier, brother of Sylvester and son of Sarah, did manage to get out of the swamp and take refuge with the help of a local turpentine factory manager. A White mob found him anyhow and forced him to dig a grave for himself before murdering him.

Florida Governor Cary Hardee offered to send the National Guard to help, but Sheriff Walker declined the help, believing he had the situation under control. Mobs began to disperse after several days, but on January 7, 1923, many returned to finish off the town, burning what little remained of it to the ground, except for the home of John Wright.

A special grand jury and prosecutor were appointed by the governor to investigate the violence. The grand jury heard the testimonies of nearly 30 witnesses, mostly White men, over several days, but claimed to not find enough evidence for prosecution. The surviving citizens of Rosewood did not return, fearful that the horrific bloodshed would reoccur.

The story of Rosewood faded away quickly. Most newspapers stopped reporting on it soon after the violence had ceased, and many survivors kept quiet about their experience, even to subsequent family members. It was not until 1982 when Gary Moore, a journalist for the *St. Petersburg Times*, resurrected the history of Rosewood through a series of articles that gained national attention.

The living survivors of this massacre, at that point all in their 80s and 90s, came forward, led by Rosewood descendant Arnett Doctor and demanded restitution from Florida. This action led to the passing of a bill awarding the victims of the Rosewood Massacre a total of 2 million dollars and creating an educational fund for descendants.

State-Sanctioned Massacres of Native Americans Indians

The first 100 years of the United States existence was filled with travesties like the Civil War and the enormous slave trade that flourished in the South. In addition, Manifest Destiny and the inherent racism involved with the *White man's burden* led to a number of horrible massacres of the Native American Indian population. Some are well-known, like the Wounded Knee Massacre.

But there are other terrible examples that people in a growing multiracial/multicultural democracy movement need to be aware from a psycho-political perspective. The following information draws from the work of Michael Van Duisen.

The Sand Creek Massacre in 1864

At Sand Creek in the Colorado territory in 1864, the Cheyenne village of around 800 Native Americans was supposed to be protected territory. Chief Black Kettle had brokered a deal with a nearby U.S. Army fort for his people's safety, but this proved to be an outright lie.

Colonel John Chivington had decided that winning battles against local Native American tribes was the best way to become a territorial delegate to Congress. When the spring of 1864 proved fruitless for battle, he used a 700-volunteer militia to burn Native American villages.

On November 29, 1864, just one day after Black Kettle's deal, the Colorado Volunteers attacked Sand Creek. Nearly all the Cheyenne men were out hunting, leaving the women, children, and elders with no one to protect them. Between 100 and 400 Native Americans were reportedly slaughtered. Although Chivington was denounced by much of the country, he was never formally charged with anything.

The Camp Grant Massacre of 1871

Shortly after the start of President Ulysses S. Grant's "Peace Policy" toward Native Americans, the Camp Grant Massacre occurred in southern Arizona on April 30, 1871. The local Apache tribe had recently agreed to live at Camp Grant via an order by Lieutenant Royal E. Whitman, who also pledged to provide the Native Americans with food.

Public opinion turned against the military in Arizona, declaring them unable to protect the territory's citizens. A handful of Americans, some Mexicans, and some rival Native American tribesmen sneaked up on the peaceful village in the middle of the night.

Most of those killed were women and children because the men were out hunting for food. The perpetrators of the massacre had used unfounded claims of Apache depredations to justify their murder. Although 104 men were charged with murder, all were acquitted at trial.

The 1860 Wiyot Massacre

In an act of genocide on a small tribe, the Wiyot Massacre took place on February 26, 1860. Smaller attacks on the Wiyot tribe occurred later that week. For at least 1,000 years, the tribe had lived off the northern coast of California on what is now called Indian Island. The peaceful Wiyot had just completed their annual world renewal ceremony, marking the start of their new year.

The men were out gathering supplies when a small group of White men crossed Humboldt Bay and slaughtered women, children, and the elderly. Sixty to two hundred Native Americans were estimated to have died in this massacre. The local sheriff lied, citing revenge for cattle rustling as the reason for this massacre. In reality, a local militia wished to be federally recognized as a state militia to receive money from the government. The militia leader believed that massacring local tribes would accomplish that goal, but it didn't work.

The 1852 Bridge Gulch Massacre

The Bridge Gulch Massacre against the Wintu tribe of northern California took place on April 23, 1852. Shortly before the attack, a man named John Anderson was killed, with his riderless mule returning to a nearby corral. Nearly 70 men set out after the perpetrators, who were reportedly members of the Wintu tribe.

Surrounding a part of the small valley known as Bridge Gulch, the men attacked early in the morning, shooting nearly every man, woman, and child they saw. Over 150 Native Americans were killed, and only two small girls survived. They were taken back to the town and adopted by White parents.

The Three Knolls Massacre in 1865

By 1865, the Yana tribe's population had dwindled to fewer than 100 in northern California around Lassen Peak. After the murders of several nearby White people during a raid, hunters tracked the culprits to Three Knolls, where the Native Americans slept.

Determined to rid the area of any remaining natives, the settlers attacked, killing dozens of Native Americans. Only a handful escaped.

A Yana tribesman named Ishi was present at the massacre as a small child and he and his family eventually hid in some nearby mountains for almost 40 years. 1n 1911, he emerged as a frail, elderly man—the last of his people—to tell his fantastical story.

The Marias Massacre of 1870

The deadliest massacre of Native Americans in Montana's history was a mistake. Colonel Eugene Baker had been sent by the government to *pacify* a rebellious band of the Blackfeet tribe.

Eventually, Baker's men tracked the tribe to a village along the Marias River. On January 23, 1870, the men surrounded the village and prepared to attack. But a scout recognized some of the painted designs on the lodges and reported to Baker that this was the wrong band. Baker replied, "That makes no difference, one band or another of them; they are all [Blackfeet] and we will attack them."

Most of the Native Americans men were out hunting, so the majority of the 173 massacred were women, children, and the elderly. When Baker discovered that the survivors had smallpox, he abandoned them in the wilderness without food or shelter, increasing the death toll by 140.

The Yontocket Massacre of 1853

The Tolowa people laid claim to territories in northwestern California and southern Oregon that were continuously encroached upon by White settlers. By 1853, a "war of extermination" had been going on for a while, with settlers forming makeshift militias and slaughtering any Native American Indian they encountered.

In the fall of that year, the Tolowa and other tribes came together to pray at Yontocket, the spiritual center of their universe, and to perform the world renewal dance. Unknown to them, a group of White people, led by J.M. Peters, was slowly creeping upon the camp.

Surrounding the Tolowa, the men began firing, indiscriminately slaughtering everyone in sight. Peters, who lost no men during the massacre, reportedly said that "scarcely an Indian was left alive." By the end of the violence, hundreds of people had been killed.

The Clear Lake Massacre in 1850

An island in Clear Lake, California, was renamed Bloody Island after the massacre of the indigenous Pomo tribe there in 1850. As a result of severe mistreatment, including rape and murder at the hands of White men who had taken various members of the tribe as slaves, the Pomo people attacked, killing two men and escaping to a nearby lake.

Captain Nathaniel Lyon, a soldier in the U.S. Cavalry and other men set off into the woods to find the offending tribe. The men discovered the hidden camp a short time later.

After failing to successfully reach the tribe, which had taken refuge on an island in the lake, the soldiers built a handful of boats, loaded them with cannons, and attacked. From 100 to 400 Native Americans were killed. A local newspaper originally declared the massacre to be tantamount to state-sponsored genocide but reversed course four days later, calling it a "greatly exaggerated" story.

The Bear River Massacre in 1863

Perhaps the deadliest massacre of Native Americans in U.S. history, the Bear River Massacre, has remained in obscurity largely because it occurred during the Civil War. The Northern Shoshone called present-day southeastern Idaho home and it was there that they were attacked.

Mormon settlers had been progressively taken more land from the Native Americans, appropriating nearly all of the arable territory. Striking back at those stealing their land, the Shoshone soon saw themselves in the crosshairs of Colonel Patrick Connor and 200 California volunteers, who vowed to take no prisoners.

At daybreak on January 29, 1863, the soldiers attacked, brutally killing nearly 250 Native Americans. They raped any women who hadn't been killed, used axes to crush the skulls of the wounded, and set fire to all the lodges.

Using a Psycho-Political Perspective to Analyze Such Race-Based Violence and Death

Three important questions are the outgrowths of the above information about state-sanctioned racial violence that beg to be addressed. The first question is stated as follows: How does one explain the horrific, traumatic, and irrational historic massacres listed above?

The second question seeks to understand: What were the neurological and psychological outcomes manifested by victims of such state-sanctioned and race-based traumatic violence?

Third, the psycho-political perspective discussed throughout this book emphasizes the importance of understanding how the mental health of the United States is affected by the above listed massacres and other state-sanctioned acts of violence and death?

A preface in addressing the above three questions is to remind readers of the definition of *trauma* as used in the psycho-political perspective presented in this book. In Chapter 2, the definition of *trauma* is presented by Dr. Gabor Maté in his most recently published book entitled, *The Myth of Normal: Trauma, Illness and Healing in a Toxic Culture*. Dr. Maté defines trauma as "an inner injury, a lasting rupture or split within the self, due to difficult or harmful environmental events." He further explains that "trauma is a psychic injury, lodged in the nervous system, mind, and body, lasting long past the originating incident."

In responding to the first question, I refer to my research endeavors that point to the various forms of White racism and White supremacy as being central to our nation's history and current perilous times all of which have implications for our country's present mental health crisis. This assessment extends the psycho-political perspective presented in this book by pointing to the worst, most inhumane forms of White supremacy that were manifested in the racial massacres discussed above.

When addressing the second question, I point to advances in neuroscience and epigenetics which provide helpful information to more fully understand how the above stated massacres not only cause serious and lasting trauma for the victims of such state-sanctioned racial violence, but also have a lasting impact on the collective consciousness of the perpetrators of such violence (See Chapters 9 and 10 for more detailed discussion of these issues).

It is hoped that readers will become more aware of the symptoms of both direct and intergenerational trauma as a result of learning about the massacres outlined above and other forms of state-sanctioned racial violence which continue to occur in our society. This awareness can be fostered by acquiring new knowledge about the on-going direct and intergenerational trauma emerging from historic racial/cultural massacres as well as the disproportional shooting and killing of unarmed Black and Brown men and women by law enforcement personnel across our country in the 21st century. The acquisition of such knowledge can contribute to a consciousness raising experience that is one of the goals of this book as stated in Chapter 1.

It is further predicted that an increased multiracial/multicultural democracy in the United States will be augmented by increased calls for reparations. Such reparations will, in part, need to be aimed at securing some semblance of justice due to the injuries of large numbers of persons of color who continue to experience direct and intergenerational trauma due to many acts of state-sanctioned racial violence.

Advances in neuroscience and our knowledge of epigenetics will also be helpful in future reparation discussions to ensure justice is realized for persons of color suffering injury from the various forms of trauma Dr. Maté details in his most recent book on these topics. These issues are discussed in greater detail later in this book.

Summary

The issues discussed in this chapter are in juxtaposition to those presented in the preceding chapter. Chapter 3 discusses the multidimensional potential promise of a multiracial/multicultural democracy to promote mental health, healthy human development, peace, and justice in our society. In contrast, this chapter describes important pitfalls that must be confronted to maintain and expand democracy in the United States.

The first section of Chapter 4 provides an overview of multiple pitfalls that can impair support for the ongoing evolution of a multiracial/multicultural democracy in our nation. This section is followed by a discussion of the *pitfall of disinformation and lies* used to undermine our democratic institutions and promote authoritarianism and fascism in the United States.

A closely related pitfall is discussed in the next section of this chapter. This involves exploring the historic and current pitfall of anti-intellectualism that persists in our country and the relevance of this pitfall for the rising support of authoritarianism and fascism as defined in this book.

A more immediate pitfall is a strategy repeatedly employed throughout the history of our nation to undermine the ongoing evolution of a multiracial/multicultural democracy. This involves continuing efforts to subvert voting rights in our nation. Researchers have reported that, from 2021 through 2022, Republican Party leaders in several states introduced over 200 legislative proposals restricting various voting rights; especially the voting rights of persons of color. This includes passing repressive legislative policies related to early voting, mail-in voting, and increased gerrymandering to name a few.

Republican Party members are leading a charge since the 2020 presidential election to change voting right policies at the state level. These efforts are in response to the unsubstantiated allegations about massive voting fraud that falsely resulted in stealing the election from Trump. This is a well-constructed strategy that can result in victories for Trump supporters in the future.

Given the potential impact of these systemic changes on future election outcomes, members of the Democratic Party and other allies would do well to implement state-wide voting proposals that promote more progressive and liberal voting policies. Mental health professionals would do well to demonstrate support for these endeavors by supporting voting registration and voting education initiatives in the communities where they live and work.

The final section of this chapter discusses the historic and current pitfalls of state-sanctioned racial violence. In addition to describing the manifestation of various forms of historic state-sanctioned racial violence in our country, the final section of this chapter highlights the implications of this violence for White supremacy, White racism, intergenerational trauma, and their adverse impact on the mental health of the United States today.

The following chapter adds to many of the ideas and concepts discussed in Chapters 1–4. It does so by exploring the similarities and differences between Donald Trump as a human being and the activation of Trumpism from 2015 to the present time.

CHAPTER 5

TRUMP AND TRUMPISM

Trump is a human being who has been shaped by the people that raised him and the mental/emotional deficiencies that came from those life experiences. He created a universe focused on his beliefs and what's required for survival.

Bill Newgent, published in Politically Speaking

While it is unethical to speak about matters that one has insufficient information about, it is also unethical to withhold an assessment on which one has more than enough information–especially when societal safety is at stake. Failure to disclose serious mental problems, especially in a democracy, where the electorate must be informed to make the right choices, could have catastrophic consequences.

Dr. Bandy X. Lee

Introduction

This chapter is designed to accomplish a threefold purpose. First, it discusses who Donald Trump is as a human being. The research methods employed to explore these issues began by utilizing what psychologists and other allied mental health professionals refer to as the *alpha personality*. The definition of this term is provided below as it is relevant in understanding Trump as a human being. This concept was used in gathering data that describe how Donald Trump's supporters, as well as his detractors, come to think about him as a human being with a focus on Trump's psychology in general and his cognitive, emotional, and behavioral characteristics in particular.

Second, this chapter describes why mental health professionals have published serious concerns about the danger Donald Trump presented during his presidency and continuing now as a potential candidate for the 2024 presidential election. This chapter and other chapters in this book highlight those concerns as they represent the ethical responsibility mental health professionals have to warn communities and the nation at-large of real dangers that any individual and certainly the president of the United States might present as a human being and a person in a powerful position in our nation.

Third, this chapter concludes with a discussion of the similarities and differences between Donald Trump, the rising popularity of Trumpism, and a discussion of the emotional basis for the large number of people who support the authoritarian leadership of former President Trump.

Donald Trump is a Human Being with Attributes and Deficiencies

As the title of this section of Chapter 5 suggests, the reader's attention is directed to increasing one's understanding of Donald Trump as a human being. Before addressing these issues, it is readily acknowledged that every person has attributes and deficiencies as they relate to their *human beingness*.

Trump's supporters continue to acknowledge their perceptions of his positive attributes. This is in sharp contrast to the list of Trump's deficiencies as perceived by his detractors. These deficiencies have resulted in numerous mental health professionals expressing serious concern about the potential danger Trump has and continues to pose for our nation's democracy and mental health. These issues are discussed in greater detail later in this book. It is also important to acknowledge that these important points are detailed in another book entitled, *The Dangerous*

Case of Donald Trump: 27 Psychiatrists and Mental Health Experts Assess a President with Dr. Bandy Lee as the primary editor (Lee, 2017).

What does it mean to say Donald Trump is a human being from a psycho-political perspective? In answering this question, this book highlights the ways that a complex *socialization process* impacts human development for better or worse. Chapter 3 defines the *socialization* process as an ongoing dynamic whereby all human beings consciously and unconsciously learn to respond to the norms, values, behavioral expectations, and social skills viewed as being appropriate and normal in our society.

This book illuminates the negative effect White racism, White supremacy, and other social injustices have on our collective and individual development via our socialization. In responding to the first question listed above, it is important to be cognizant of the ways Donald Trump's racial and gender socialization contributes to his overall personality development. While these issues are addressed later in this chapter, I use the term *alpha personality* when reporting the different reactions Trump's supporters and detractors have about his human beingness.

In discussing these issues, Mary Wright, a writer with *Curious Mind* magazine states:

> There is a set of cultural values, biases and stressors commonly viewed as being necessary in achieving happiness and success in one's life in general and in a person's career in particular. These cultural values, biases, and stressors, while not universal, contribute to the development of an *alpha personality*.

> The alpha personality is comprised of human characteristics that include: a strong sense of self-determination, conviction in beliefs, ambition and the desire to work hard, resilience, a desire to be in control, confident, seeking new challenges, goal-driven and a strong drive to ensure a career that results in large financial income and security.

Many Trump supporters point to these human characteristics as evidence of one's personal development and success in life. From a psycho-political perspective, it is important to be cognizant of the views articulated by multicultural researchers who point out that the above stated characteristics are anchored in cultural/racial/gender specific values, biases and stressors sustained by the dominant racial-gendered-economic group in our society.

The information presented in the following section of this chapter comes from a synthesis of multiple sources. This includes recorded comments made by a broad range of Trump supporters and detractors during news broadcasts produced by FOX News, CNN, and MSNBC.

My research efforts in writing this book also resulted in securing over 100 publications from a variety of professional and news media outlets. Using qualitative and historic research methods, I relied on comments made in televised interviews as well as in many publications related to Trump and his leadership style during his 2015–2016 presidential campaign and throughout his 2016–2020 presidency.

Based on the results of these research methods, I summarize comments made by both Trump's supporters and his detractors in response to questions designed to draw out their thoughts, feelings, and perceptions of Trump as a human being.

Question #1: What does the term *a strong sense of self-determination* mean and what is its relevance for the perceptions of Trump as a human being by both his supporters and his detractors?

Definition of Terms/Concepts

Self-determination is a combination of attitudes and abilities that lead people to set goals for themselves and to take the initiative to reach these goals. It means making one's own choices, learning to effectively solve problems, and taking responsibility for one's life choices.

Trump Supporters: A summary of comments made by Trump supporters indicate very positive reactions to his persistent self-determination as evidenced by his creation of a billion-dollar real estate empire. In numerous FOX News broadcasts, Trump supporters emphasize that his self-determination is exactly what needs to be done to Make America Great Again (MAGA).

Trump Detractors: Trump's detractors point to Trump's major economic losses during the 1980s and 1990s to highlight how his self-centered determination contributed to unprecedented losses in his real estate endeavors.

According to many detractors, Trump's self-determination is marked by a heightened self-centeredness, which is a factor that contributes to an insatiable ego and need for unquestionable loyalty from persons involved in his business and political endeavors. According to journalists at CNN and MSNBC, this ego-heightened demand for unquestionable loyalty was intensified during his presidency with what Dr. Bandy Lee referred to as an equally powerful sense of personal insecurity. More information related to this powerful insecurity is presented later in this chapter.

Question #2: What does the term *conviction in beliefs* mean and what is its relevance for the perceptions of Trump as a human being by both his supporters and his detractors?

Definition: A *conviction* is a firm belief that an individual has regarding particular life experiences and subjects.

Trump Supporters: Interviews with several FOX News hosts during Trump's 2015–2016 campaign and 2016–2020 presidency resulted in a pattern of Trump's supporters pointing to his exceptionally strong conviction in following his gut feelings as they relate to his decision-making skills.

Trump Detractors: One of Trump's detractors is Dr. Bandy Lee, a forensic psychiatrist and an expert on violence and violence prevention. Dr. Lee is also the author of the book entitled, *Profile of a Nation: Trump's Mind, America's Soul* and is the editor of another New York Times bestselling book entitled, *The Dangerous Case of Donald Trump*. These publications highlight the frequent ways Trump's convictions and firm beliefs were driven by what he believes to be his exceptional gut feelings. As Dr. Bandy reported:

> There can be little room for doubt over Donald Trump's belief in his greatness. What are the sources of this belief? Some have attributed his confidence and convictions to the fact that he believes in his superior 'gut' to guide him through any course of action he faced in life. He said there was no need to prepare for trade negotiations with the Chinese president because 'I know it better than anyone knows it, and my gut has always been right.' He said on one occasion that his decisions about which candidates to endorse were based on 'very much my gut instinct.'

Question #3: What does the term *a desire to be in control* mean and what is its relevance for the perceptions of Trump as a human being by both his supporters and his detractors?

Definition: The *goal to be in control* is one of the alpha personality characteristics that people often direct their attention. While the goal of being in control is often about controlling oneself in stressful times, it often leaks into the desire to control others.

Trump's Supporters: Comments in televised news broadcasts and in news publications by Trump supporters reflected approval and appreciation for Trump's desire to be in control of the challenges he faced as president and the leader of the MAGA movement. Trump recognized the importance of reinforcing the positive impact of his desire to be in control during a press briefing on April 15, 2020. President Trump then stated that he has "absolute powers" that include "total control over the coronavirus, the nation's governors, the efficacy of coronavirus cures, and everything else in America."

Trump's Detractors: A summary of comments made by numerous Trump detractors illuminated their rejection of the idea that the powers of any U.S. president are absolute. One of Trump's detractors talked about the negative reactions many people in our nation had when former president Richard Nixon famously said "if the president does it, it's not illegal."

This detractor added that Trump goes much further as he literally states that there is absolutely nothing the president cannot do, that the Office of the President of the United States has control over everything like the Pope's claim to infallibility. A number of mental health professionals have expressed concern over what appears to be an increasing frequency that Trump discusses the importance of his control and power in many of his press conferences and off-the-cuff comments with journalists. Such behaviors could be viewed as being consistent with obsessive-compulsive thinking and behaviors (Gilligan, 2017; Jhueck, 2017).

Dr. Bandy Lee (2017) joins the voices of others who express concern about the combination of a person's feelings of insecurity as a catalyst for the repeated pattern of obsessive-compulsive behaviors rooted in a lack of an individual's confidence. These concerns become exacerbated when they are combined with alarm over the impact of psycho-political stressors that represent exaggerated beliefs about the total control

Trump expounds in press conferences where he repeatedly emphasized these points.

Question #4: What does the term *confidence* mean and what is its relevance for the perceptions of Trump as a human being by both his supporters and his detractors?

Definition: *Confidence* is a feeling of self-assurance arising from one's appreciation of his or her abilities and personal qualities.

Trump Supporters: Many Trump supporters positively responded to what they perceived as his *confidence* being a key factor underlying his success as a business leader, president of the United States, the leader of the MAGA Movement, and as a human being.

Trump Detractors: In John Bolton's book entitled, *The Room Where It Happened* (2022), he stated that he viewed Trump to be lacking in confidence and clarity of thought. He describes Trump's thought process when it comes to matters of governance and policy as being "like an archipelago of dots, leaving the rest of us to discern or create policy." By Bolton's account, "Former President Trump's overall insecurity held the possibility of a grand spectacle that allures the president without consideration of other factors."

Additional Assessment of Problematic Behaviors Repeatedly Manifested by Donald Trump

Numerous researchers have expanded our understanding of the problematic behaviors repeatedly manifested by Donald Trump. Malcolm Nance, a global expert on terrorism, extremism, and insurgency elaborates on these issues in his recently published book entitled, *They Want to Kill Americans: The Militias, Terrorists, and Deranged Ideology of the Trump Insurgency.* In doing so, Nance documents how and why Trump, his supporters, and Trump cult members represent ongoing dangers to our nation's democracy including future acts of seditious violence to achieve their goals.

This section of Chapter 5 focuses on some of the problematic behaviors that continue to be manifested by Donald Trump. These behaviors represent on-going dangers to our nation's democracy; many of which go unaddressed by many Trump supporters and especially among members of the Trump cult (See Chapter 6).

Trump's Pattern of Racist Behaviors

Researchers (including the author of this book) provide evidence describing specific ways the former president has and continues to manifest racist comments, policy decisions, and actions over an extended period of time. This includes racist reactions throughout his 4-year presidential term. Some of the specific racist behaviors repeatedly exhibited by Trump are those described in Chapter 2. As other researchers have noted, such behaviors increase the potential to activate additional forms of racism among persons in the general public who self-identify as White nationalists and/or White supremacists.

Pathological Liar

A pathological liar is an individual who chronically tells grandiose lies that may stretch or exceed the limits of believability. While most people lie or at least bend the truth occasionally, pathological liars do so habitually. Whether or not pathological lying should be considered a distinct psychological disorder is still debated within the medical, mental health, and academic communities.

However, when the Washington Post Fact-Checker Team members first started recording then President Donald Trump's false or misleading claims, they recorded 492 suspect claims in the first 100 days of his presidency. On November 2, 2020 alone, the day before the 2020 presidential election, Trump made 503 false or misleading claims as he barnstormed across the country in a desperate effort to win reelection.

This astonishing jump in falsehoods is the story of Trump's tumultuous reign. By the end of his term, Trump had accumulated 30,573 untruths (what I refer to as lies) during his presidency averaging about 21 erroneous claims a day. What is especially striking is how the tsunami of untruths kept rising the longer he served as president and became increasingly unmoored from the truth.

Trump averaged about six claims a day in his first year as president, 16 false claims a day in his second year, 22 misinformation points a day in this third year and 39 claims a day in his final year. Put another way, it took him 27 months to reach 10,000 false claims and an additional 14 months to reach 20,000. He then exceeded 30,000 lies and pieces of misinformation less than five months later.

The above description of patterns of behavior manifested by former President Donald Trump caused much concern among many people in the general public. These toxic behaviors contributed to the rise of a psycho-political phenomenon referred to as *Trumpism*.

Trumpism

The following section of this chapter is designed to achieve two goals. First, it provides an overview of four factors that have contributed to the rapid rise of Trumpism in the United States. The work of Dr. David Tabachnick, a professor in political science at Nipissing University, is particularly clear in describing these four factors.

Second, following Tabachnick's well-written overview of the four factors that contribute to the popularity of Trumpism in our nation, I draw from a broad range of research findings published by individuals in diverse disciplines to outline a more detailed description of the factors that have and continue to perpetuate Trumpism in our society. Although the information in this section is likely to appeal to readers who are interested in developing a more comprehensive and detailed understanding of Trumpism, I try to translate such research findings in ways that will appeal to anyone in the general public interested in gaining a better understanding of this concept without having been trained as a professional researcher.

Four Factors Stimulating Increased Support for Trumpism in the United States

Dr. David Tabachnick's publication entitled, *The Four Characteristics of Trumpism*, is important reading to understand some of the factors thought to contribute to the rapid popularity of Trumpism in the United States. Tabachnick begins his analysis by first describing the genesis of Trumpism in the following manner:

> The Republican Party's nomination of Donald Trump in the 2016 presidential election year gave the world a new term: *Trumpism*. Obviously, Trumpism is linked to the person, Donald Trump, but its roots run much deeper, intertwining contemporary and traditional political trends in such a way that makes it both

uniquely American and distinct from European fascism of the last century.

The four characteristics that define Trumpism are distillations of a much more complicated phenomena. These four characteristics provide a brief explanation of the surprising appeal of Trumpism in the United States... The ongoing success of Trumpism demands more serious thinking about its origins and future.

Celebrity

Whether movie stars running for office appear on late-night talk shows, *celebrity* has long played a role in Americans presidential politics. Celebrity has empowered Trumpism in two unique ways. First, unlike other politicians that seek to frame or reframe their image through positive media coverage during their campaigns, Trump's celebrity persona as a CEO and tough decision-maker was already cemented and well-suited to his desired political image. With this tremendous advantage over his rivals and despite his many blunders on the campaign trail, this image has endured even under withering criticism that would destroy any other candidate.

Second, the celebrity character of Trumpism appeals to citizens that would otherwise be disengaged from politics. He serves as a placeholder for many White persons' unsatisfied wants and dreams. The ability to translate the cultural capital of celebrity into political capital has motivated many voters for Trump.

Nativism

The second factor in Tabachnick's analysis is listed as *Nativism*. In discussing this factor, he emphasizes the following:

Nativism reaches back to the mid-19th century and the short-lived American Party that combined anti-immigrant sentiment with conspiracy theories about foreigners. Following in the same tradition as Nativism, Trumpism first emerged as part of the birther movement. While already debunked in the mainstream,

Trump's 2011 public and calculated demand that then President Barak Obama release his full birth certificate kept him in the media spotlight for well over a year. This year-long spotlight greatly helped Trump develop an initial phase of political support. In the late summer of 2015, Public Policy Polling released a national survey that showed 61 percent of Trump supporters still self-identified as birthers.

Under the triumphalist banner "Make America Great Again," Trump's articulated fear of foreigners explains the broad approval for his impractical pledges to build a wall along the Mexican border and deport all illegal Immigrants as well as his unworkable plan to ban all Muslim immigration.

The Outsider

The third factor Tabachnick presents emphasizes the important impact that Trump's status as "The Outsider" generated among millions of persons in our nation who have come to support Trumpism. In emphasizing these points, Tabachnick states the following:

> Normally, anti–establishment politicians must convince political supporters that they stand in opposition to the entrenched power structure. Ronald Reagan did this very well during his first campaign for governor of California in 1967. 'I am not a politician,' Reagan was fond of saying. 'I am an ordinary citizen with a deep-seated belief that much of what troubles us has been brought about by politicians; and it is high time that more ordinary citizens brought the fresh air of common-sense thinking to bear on these problems.'

> Trumpism finds strength from the unusual position of the insider-outsider. Trump, the archetypal billionaire insider, often brags that his opponents are "puppets" of big donors like the Koch Brothers.

> Even though he has never run for office, he is too rich and knows the establishment too well to have to curry favor from elites, including leaders in the Republican Party.

Populism

Lastly, Tabachnick provides a compelling perspective as to the impact of populism on the development of Trumpism. As Tabachnick noted:

Trumpism appeals to a large group of anti-intellectuals, conspiracy-minded, and alienated malcontents, the same type of voter that backed third party Presidential candidates Ross Perrault in the 1990s and George Wallace (in the 1960s and early 1970s). In these ways, Trumpism embodies a particular kind of American populism composed of a mishmash of overt patriotism and economic nationalism, along with a vague commitment to the middle class and an aggressive but indefinite foreign policy.

Like all populism, Trumpism relies on the rhetoric of resentment, but is thin on specifics. To the thorny issue of race and police brutality, Trump responds to the chant "Black Lives Matter" by saying "All Lives Matter"; an easy applause line on the campaign trail. Unrestrained by any ideological limitations, Trump is also able to defend some form of universal healthcare "Because the insurance companies are making a fortune as they have control over the politicians."

Attacks by mainstream media, his political opponents, and even bona-fide conservatives, only serve the narrative that Trumpism threatens the established power structure, further framing Trump as the Savior of the disenfranchised.

These four characteristics of Trumpism make it a unique phenomenon that has surprising appeal across the political spectrum which also extends beyond Trump himself. Much to the consternation of Republican elites, it also stands well outside of conservative political ideology. The remaining question of whether it has enough appeal to win the GOP nomination for the 2024 presidential election and go on to the White House for a second time will be answered soon.

While Donald Trump is a conduit that helped promote the rise of Trumpism in the United States, this toxic psycho-political phenomenon has its roots in past White nationalist and White supremist groups including the Tea Party Movement of the 1990s. The following sections of this chapter provide detailed information that defines the meaning of Trumpism and several other variables related to the rise of Trumpism in our nation.

Trumpism as a Movement

Trumpism is a term for the political ideologies, social emotions, style of governance, political movement, and set of mechanisms for acquiring and keeping control of power associated with Donald Trump and his political base. The Trumpism movement started its development during Trump's 2016 presidential campaign. For many scholars, it denotes a populist political method that suggests nationalistic answers to political, economic, and social problems. As such, Trumpism became manifested into such policy preferences as immigration restrictionism, trade pro-tectionism, isolationism, and opposition to entitlement reform during Trump's presidency, all of which represented the emergence of a new political movement.

Gavriel Rosenfeld, a professor of history at Fairfield University, details key points related to Trumpism. These points are presented below to add to the reader's thinking about the meaning of Trumpism.

> As a movement, Trumpism is still in flux, but its extremist drift – as shed disturbingly by the widely aired footage of mob violence at the January 6, 2021 insurrection in our nation's capital, the outlandish behavior of Marjorie Taylor Greene, and the ongoing possibility of domestic terror attacks lends credence to new claims that Trumpism should be seen as a form of *American fascism*.

> While this charge is an important one that deserves serious scrutiny, it is premature to fully endorse it. While Trumpism is undeniably defined by fascist traits, a personality cult, hostility to liberal democracy, and violent action, certain questions linger.

> First, can Trumpism be seen as a fascist movement if its composition is still undeveloped and its goals are still unclear? Many different groups were present at the sacking of the U.S. Capitol. A partial list of these groups includes the White supremacist Proud Boys, Three Percenters, NSC-131ers, Christian Nationalists preaching the message of Jesus, libertarian gun fanatics such as the Boogaloo

Boys, and QAnon true believers fighting the "deep state." These groups have little in common aside from their anger against the liberal "establishment." While some of them, it now appears, coordinated their actions at the Capitol on January 6, 2021, the majority were unconnected by any central command structure.

In contrast, traditional fascist parties were steered in a clear direction by dominant leaders pursuing clear goals. To be sure, fascist parties did not appear fully formed on the political stage and took time to develop... It took years before the Nazis rose above their competitors and gained anything resembling political traction. Trumpism is arguably at a similar moment, with the potential to develop in multiple directions; which one it will head in, however, remains unknown.

This fact raises a second question: Can Trumpism acquire a clear identity (fascist or otherwise) with its leader out of power? Trump may linger as a political force, but since he is no longer the sitting president—and especially since he has been banned from Facebook— his wings have been clipped. It remains unclear, therefore, how his movement will evolve going forward. Trumpism without Trump as president may simply end up adrift.

Third, even if Trump remains an inspirational figure for Trumpism, can the movement be seen as fascist if the leader himself is not? Scholars remain divided about whether Trump's political beliefs can be linked to fascism in any real sense. I have written elsewhere that, at best, he can be seen as a "situational fascist," as someone who stumbled into fascistic modes of behavior at the very end of his presidency, when, in the face of electoral defeat and possible criminal indictments, he incited violence to hold on to power. To this day, it remains unclear what beliefs, if any, Trump subscribes to beyond personal self-interest. Trumpism thus remains something of a political cipher.

For all of these reasons, it is difficult to compare Trumpism to other political movements whose names derive from their leaders. There is a long list of such movements—Bonapartism, Leninism, Stalinism, Maoism —but they were all defined by an ideologically rigid, top-down relationship between strong leaders and willing followers. There is no real precedent in American history for a political movement being closely tied to a single figure for any significant period of time before the emergence of Trump.

With these points in mind, it may be best to view Trumpism through a new political prism. Because fascism has unavoidable connotations related to Europe and World War II, we may do well to view Trumpism as something uniquely new and American. Trumpism can be seen as the product of the United States's early 21st century political crisis. It is a crisis with deep-seated origins and Trump is its symptom, not its cause. Like other rightwing populist movements around the world today, its immediate origins are rooted in the nation's turbulent history.

Rather than describing Trumpism as a version of classical fascism, we may want to see the movement in terms of its most notorious slogan, "Make America Great Again," and conceptualize it as "MAGA-ism." Although the term is unwieldy and has only been embraced by scattered commentators, it has the benefit of reminding us that right wing nationalism in the United States is likely to persist long after Donald Trump leaves the political scene for good.

The Emotional Underpinnings of Trumpism

As a political method, Trumpism is not driven by any particular ideology. Sociologist Michael Kimmel states this point in the following way: "Trumpism is not a theory [or] an ideology, it's an emotion. And that emotion is righteous indignation that the government is screwing 'us.'"

Kimmel (2018) further notes that "Trump is an interesting character because he channels all that sense of what Kimmel calls an 'aggrieved entitlement.'" This term is defined as "the sense that those benefits to which people believed they are entitled have been snatched away by unseen larger and more powerful forces. These persons feel themselves to be the heir to a great promise, the American Dream, which has turned into an impossible fantasy for the very people who were supposed to inherit it."

Researchers give differing emphasis to which emotions are important to Trumpism followers. Michael Richardson argues in the *Journal of Media and Cultural Studies* that "disgust of traditional politicians is among the primary affective drivers of the political success of Trumpism." A core strategy of Donald Trump, both as candidate and president, has been to use Trumpism to manufacture fear and contempt towards undocumented migrants (among other groups).

In accounting for Trump's 2016 election and his ability to sustain high approval ratings among a significant segment of voters, Erika Tucker argues in her book, *Trump and Political Philosophy,* that though all presidential campaigns have strong emotions associated with them, Trump was able to recognize and then gain the trust and loyalty of those who like him. These emotional reactions underlie the energy that activates Trumpism. Tucker also asserts that "Political psychologist Drew Westen was right in arguing that Democrats are less successful at responding to affective politics–issues that arouse strong emotional states in citizens."

Like many academics examining the populist appeal of Trump's messaging, Hidalgo-Tenorio and Benítez-Castro point out that, "The emotional appeal of Trumpism is key to its polarizing effects, this being so much so that Trumpism would be unintelligible without the affective component."

The Convergence of the Social Media, Familial Bonding, Emotionality and Entertainment

Communications scholar Michael Carpini states that, "Trumpism is a culmination of trends that have been occurring for several decades. What we are witnessing is nothing short of a fundamental shift in the relationships between journalism, politics, and democracy." Among these shifts, Carpini identifies "the collapsing of the prior media regime's presumed and enforced distinctions between news and entertainment."

Journalist Olivier Jutel notes that "Donald Trump's celebrity status and reality-TV rhetoric of 'winning' and 'losing' corresponds perfectly to the values underlying Trumpism." Jutel also acknowledges that it is important to recognize that "Fox News and conservative personalities from Rush Limbaugh, Glenn Beck and Alex Jones do not simply represent a new political and media voice. Rather, they embody the convergence of politics and media in which affect and entertainment are the central values of Trumpism."

Studying Trump's use of social media, anthropologist Jessica Johnson finds that social emotional pleasure plays a central role in the sustaining of Trumpism. As Johnson states: "Rather than finding accurate news meaningful, Facebook users find the affective pleasure of connectivity addictive, whether or not the information that comprises Trumpism is factual, and that is how Trumpism captivates subjects as it holds them captive."

The American way of affirming upward mobility for the deserving is, according to academics such as Michael Kimmel and Arlie Hochschild, a promise that many Americans feel has been denied them due to forces described within Trumpism. Social media scholar Daniel Kreiss summarizes that, "Trumpism gives Trump supporters hope that they would be restored to their rightful place at the center of the nation and provided a very real emotional release from what is perceived to be an oppressive chain of political correctness."

Kreiss's 2018 account of conservative media personalities found that information underling Trumpism became less important than providing a sense of familial bonding with other Trump supporters. Hochschild further explains that the familial bond of trust is manifested with FOX News star personalities. As Hochschid (2016) suggests, "Bill O'Reilly is like a steady, reliable dad. Sean Hannity is like a difficult uncle who rises to anger too quickly. Megyn Kelly is like a smart sister. Then there's Greta Van Susterena and Juan Williams, who came over from NPR. They're all different, just like a family."

Conservative columnist George Will considers Trumpism similar to fascism, stating that Trumpism is "a mood masquerading as a doctrine." National unity is based "on shared domestic fears – for fascists, the "Jews," for Trump, the media ("enemies of the people"). Solutions to these fears come not from tedious "incrementalism and conciliation," but from the leader (who claims "only I can fix it").

Trump's political base is kept entertained with mass rallies, but inevitably the strongman develops a contempt for those he leads. This contempt is based on machismo, and in the case of Trumpism, "appeals to those in thralled to country-music manliness: 'We're truck-driving, beer-drinking, big-chested Americans too freedom-loving to let any itsy-bitsy virus make us wear masks.'"

In his published reports of the results of his survey research that describes how Trumpism is well suited to social media, Brian Ott writes that, "Commentators who have studied Trump's public discourse have observed speech patterns that correspond closely to what I identified as Twitter's three defining features [simplicity, impulsivity, and incivility]."

Media critic Neal Gabler has a similar viewpoint, writing that, "What FDR was to radio and JFK to television, Trump is to Twitter." All of these points help to fuel the sort of *outrage discourse* that characterizes much of Trump and Trumpism.

Outrage discourse expert Patrick O'Callaghan argues that social media is most effective when it utilizes the type of communication which Trump relies on. As early as 2011, sociologist Sarah Sobieraj and political scientist Jeffrey M. Berry describe the social media communication style commonly used by Trump long before his presidential campaign and presidency.

These social scientists explained that *outrage discourse* involves efforts to provoke visceral responses (e.g., anger, righteousness, fear, and moral indignation). Trumpism supporters frequently manifest outrage discourse at Trump's cantankerous political rallies, in videotaped media interviews, and in interactions they have with Trump's detractors.

Among the characteristics that mark this form of outrage discourse include the use of overgeneralizations, sensationalism, misleading or patently inaccurate information, and partial truths about opponents, who may be individuals, organizations, or entire communities of interest (e.g., progressives or conservatives) or circumstance (e.g., immigrants).

In their critical analysis of the above stated issues, Sobieraj and Berry discuss how using Trumpism to stimulate outrage via social media sidesteps the messy nuances of complex political issues in favor of melodrama, misrepresentative exaggeration, mockery, and improbable forecasts of impending doom. These researchers point out that this sort of "outrage discourse is not so much discussion as it is verbal competition, political theater with a scorecard."

Within such communication settings as Twitter and Facebook, it matters little to social media companies whether much of the information spread is false. As digital culture critic Olivia Solon points out, "The truth of a piece of content is less important than whether it is shared, liked, and monetized."

The results of a 2022 Pew Research Survey study found 62% of U.S. adults polled indicated they get their news from social media. Solon expressed alarm with these research findings by pointing out that "the news content on social media regularly features fake and misleading stories from sources devoid of editorial standards." Despite this warning, many Trumpism supporters receive and share political information via social media without verifying the accuracy of this information.

Democracy Won in the 2020 and 2022 Elections! (Well, at least for the time being!)

Donald Trump received more than 74 million votes compared to Joe Biden's more than 81 million votes in the 2020 presidential election. It is reasonable to suggest that the huge number of people who voted for Donald Trump in the 2020 election represent evidence of the continuing popularity of Trump and Trumpism. In spite of this popularity, the more than 81 million votes for the Democratic Party candidate resulted in a victory for both Joe Biden and American democracy; at least for the time being.

Members of the Republican Party predicted that a tsunami was going to occur from the 2022 midterm elections. More specifically, it was asserted that a large number of Republican candidates – many who were endorsed by Trump – would be elected to the House of Representatives. This prediction would have resulted in the largest majority of Republican House representatives than has occurred in the recent past.

However, rather than a tsunami, the 2022 midterm elections resulted in only a trickle of new Republicans being victorious as newly elected members in the House of Representatives. Many political pundits contended that the Republicans' failure to realize their tsunami predictions for a higher level of electoral success in the 2022 mid-term elections and Trump's loss to Joe Biden in the 2020 presidential election could, in part, be explained as a waning of support for Donald Trump and Trumpism.

Several factors contribute to concerns about the possible waning of Trump's political support. Commenting on this these concerns, David Smith, an independent political journalist, interjects an important question about Trump and Trumpism by asking the following: "Trump and Trumpism were fresh and new during the 2016 campaign. Has his fame fizzled?"

Instead of taking off like a rocket when he announced his candidacy for president of the United States in November 2022, Donald Trump's bid to win back the White House appeared to have blown up on the launchpad. The swagger of 2016 gave way to cautiousness in 2022. Opinion polls were grim throughout 2022. A run of dismal results in the 2022 midterm elections, culminating in another Republican loss in the Georgia December 2022 race for the Senate punctured Trump's aura of invincibility within the Republican Party.

Smith added the following assessment of Trump's increasing loss of invincibility in the following way: "Trump has performed astonishing acts of self-sabotage, from dining with anti-Semites to calling for the Constitution to be suspended. He avoided a widely anticipated spree of public rallies and instead remained largely out of the public gaze during much of 2022."

According to Allan Lichtman, a history professor at American University in Washington, DC, "It's not because Donald Trump is making mistakes. It's because Donald Trump is being Donald Trump. He was something new and fresh and interesting back in 2016. He presided over three disastrous election cycles for Republicans in 2018, 2020 and 2022 and he is the same old Donald Trump, caring only about himself, wrapped up in his own grievances and his own whining. It's just not playing anymore with the American people."

The results of the 2020 presidential election and 2022 midterm elections were wins for our nation's democracy. Of particular alarm for many members of the Republican Party is the fact that most of Donald Trump's endorsed candidates lost their elections in 2022 as well. While that is cause for celebration among persons supporting American democracy, the persistence and popularity among many supporters of Trump and Trumpism are reasons to be cautious and beg for continued conscientiousness in working to maintain our democracy in future elections.

The wisdom to be cautious in not writing off Donald Trump as the possible Republican nominee for the 2024 presidential election as well as the possibility of him winning that 2024 election is grounded in reasonable trepidations. As stated above, the first concern relates to the fact that the more than 74 million people voted for him in the 2020 election. That statistic is historic as it represents the second most votes ever cast for a presidential candidate in the history of the United States. Joe Biden was the only person to get more votes (more than 81 million votes) in any U.S. presidential election. The huge number of people who voted for Trump in 2020 is an eye-catching fact that continues to fuel Trump's political base including those Republican Party members who have begun to question Trump's future political viability.

A second concern emerged more recently. It involves the surprising rising popular support reflected in national surveys among those persons who express their ongoing support of Trump's presidential candidacy despite the numerous legal problems he experienced in 2023. During that year, Donald Trump was arrested in four different federal courts with a total 91 charges lodged against him.

It is generally accepted that any one besides Donald Trump who might be subjected to such serious legal charges would have his or her interest in being a politician ingloriously and expeditiously ended in disgrace. However, surprising to many journalists and political pundits, Donald Trump's popular support among Republicans substantially increased in surveys that calculated his popularity as the Republican Party nominee for the 2024 presidential election despite his arrests based on numerous serious criminal charges.

Summary

The first section of this chapter discusses who Donald Trump is as a human being. This section began by exploring both Trump's attributes and his deficiencies as viewed by his supporters and detractors. To facilitate this exploration, I utilize what psychologists and other mental health professionals refer to as the *alpha personality type* to garner data in my research into Trump as a human being. More specifically, I selected the concept of an alpha personality to generate this data as it is a useful framework in assessing Trump's attributes and deficiencies as a human being as viewed by his supporters and his detractors.

Secondly, this chapter describes why mental health professionals have published serious concerns about the danger Donald Trump presented during his presidency and continuing now as a candidate for the 2024 presidential election. Throughout this book I highlight those concerns as they represent the ethical responsibility mental health professionals have to warn communities and the nation at-large of real dangers that any individual might present to our country. This includes publicly expressing the psychological, emotional, and behavioral dangers any person might present in threatening our collective safety particularly by powerful persons and certainly the President of the United States.

Third, this chapter concludes with a detailed discussion of the meaning of *Trumpism*. Using research-based reports, this section addresses numerous factors that investigators point to in explaining what Trumpism is, why it has grown so rapidly, and what might be done if this toxic formation of anti-democratic ideas and related actions are sustained in our nation.

Among the factors discussed in this part of Chapter 5 include describing Trumpism as a movement, the emotional underpinnings of Trumpism, and the convergence of social media, familial bonding, emotionality and entertainment that represent increasing threats to Americans democracy.

The next chapter discusses the difference between Trump supporters and what is referred to as the Trump Cult. Among the topics covered in Chapter 6 include exploring what factors characterize Trump supporters. It also describes the criteria and meaning of a cult as described by mental health professionals who are respected experts in their research of cults.

CHAPTER 6

TRUMP SUPPORTERS AND THE TRUMP CULT

It is important to think about what exactly Trumpism is and how it came to be before presenting another potentially premature eulogy on his behalf. For critical observers of Trump and Trumpism, it has always been apparent that everything Trump offered the public came slathered in snake oil. That is either a statement about the willful blindness of the American public or a barometer of how many Americans view Trump's dangerous liabilities as assets.

William Jelani Cobb, a an American writer, educator, and Dean of the Journalism School at Columbia University

Over the past few decades, the U.S. has undergone what political scientists call "the great sort," culminating in a Democratic Party that enjoys dominant support from voters of color and those who live in cities and inner-ring suburbs and the Republican Party that is dominant among White Christians and persons in rural regions. As people's personal identity has become bound up in one's racial, geographical, and political identity, each party's supporters increasingly believe the other party supporters pose a threat to their way of life. Trump took these divisions to their logical end.

He convinced his supporters that the Democratic Party wants to destroy White, Christian America and that a violent coup was necessary to stop them.

Waleed Shahid, Director for Justice Democrats and Nelini Stamp, Director of the Strategy and Partnerships for the Working Families Party

Introduction

This chapter complements and extends information presented in Chapter 5. One of the goals for the preceding chapter was to explore Donald Trump as a human being with strengths and flaws like all of us.

To accomplish this goal, I reviewed numerous video-taped televised news reports including broadcasts by Fox News, CNN and MSNBC. I was also able to gather information from a broad range of publications that focused on different dimensions of Donald Trump and his leadership style. This literature review resulted in securing more than 100 publications, including articles published in professional journals in the fields of counseling, psychology, psychiatry, social work, religion and spirituality, economics, political science, education, and various publications secured from focused google searches.

The data I generated from these research methods enabled me to develop tentative classifications, including persons identified as Trump supporters versus those identified as his detractors. Persons in both of these groups articulated their thoughts and feelings about Donald Trump and his leadership style in recorded news broadcasts and in articles published in the fields listed above.

These innovative investigative methods enabled me to analyze and incorporate my findings throughout this book. The investigative strategies I employed resulted in successful outcomes in my efforts to present a multidimensional psycho-political analysis of Donald Trump and his leadership style.

As might be predicted, Trump's supporters consistently commented on what they perceive to be his positive attributes in televised news broadcasts and in numerous publications related to these issues. In contrast, persons identified as Trump's detractors consistently described his personal, political, and leadership behaviors in negative terms.

The research methods used in the above stated ways can be criticized from more traditional psychiatric, psychological, and counseling research strategies. Nevertheless, the data presented in the preceding chapter is intended to stimulate broader thinking of readers' perceptions of Trump's attributes and deficiencies.

This chapter extends the information presented in Chapter 5 in a number of important ways. First, the reader is presented with a plethora of research-based information generated by numerous studies conducted by Dr. Thomas Pettigrew, a highly respected social psychologist in the United States. Much of Pettigrew's work explores the psychology of Trump supporters and members of the Trump cult. Again, as stated in the Preface, an important goal in writing this book is to provide information that enables readers to become more knowledgeable of some of the psycho-political factors which are relevant in understanding Trump's supporters in general and persons comprising the Trump cult as well.

Second, readers will experience more in-depth ways of thinking about the variables that are attractive to the millions of Trump supporters in the United States. Investigative findings by other mental health researchers are intentionally provided in this section of Chapter 6 to support readers in acquiring a deeper psychological understanding of the factors that are thought to attract Trump supporters in general and persons falling in the Trump cult classification in particular.

Finally, I describe four groups of people that are distinguishable from each other as Trump supporters. These groups are referred to as *the insiders support group, the outsiders support group, the Trump cult,* and *advocates of Christian Trumpism.*

The Psychology of Trump Supporters

A Social Psychological Perspective

Social psychology scientists are keenly aware that the world is exceedingly complex. The process of human development and mental health are similarly complex as they are both driven by multiple variables. This chapter unpacks the complexity of some of these variables. It does so by discussing the psychology of Trump's supporters from a psycho-political perspective.

No one psychological factor can accurately describe Trump's supporters. However, Dr. Thomas Pettigrew, a social psychologist at the University of California in Santa Cruz, conducted research that unveils several factors relevant in understanding the psychology of Trump's supporters.

Among the factors Dr. Pettigrew found in his studies include Trump supporters' preference for *authoritarianism* and *social dominance, a high level of out-group prejudice, a lack of intergroup contact,* and a genuine sense of their *relative deprivation.* It is important to understand the meaning of these concepts as they are relevant in gaining a deeper understanding of the psychology of Trump's supporters.

Authoritarianism and Social Dominance Orientation (SDO)

Authoritarianism is an extensively studied psychological factor that is consistently manifested among Trump supporters as documented in Dr. Pettigrew's research findings. In measuring authoritarianism, political psychology researchers prefer to ask questions such as the following to assess a person's preference for authoritarianism: What is more important for children, respect for elders or children's independence? Is obedience more important than self-reliance? Is it more important to be a well-behaved or a creative person? Is it more important to have good manners or to be a curious person?

Social psychologists like Pettigrew prefer to use such statements as the following when measuring a person's preference for authoritarianism: Persons in authority should be obeyed because they are in the best position to know what is good for our country; and, Obedience and respect for authority are the most important virtues children should learn.

Both of these methodological approaches to studying authoritarianism are highly interrelated and both have proven useful in generating valid and reliable measures of these psycho-political variables. As Dr. Pettigrew indicates in his research endeavors, authoritarianism, as measured in the above stated ways, is a highly rated concept among Trump supporters.

A Social Dominance Orientation (SDO) is closely related to authoritarianism and a distinct variable in many people's psycho-political development. This factor features an individual's preference for what's referred to as the *societal hierarchy of groups and domination over lower-status groups*. According to Pettigrew, Trump supporters consistently scored high on the SDO factor, which represents a predisposition toward anti-egalitarianism. Individuals who score high in SDO are also described as commonly being dominant, driven, tough-minded, disagreeable, and often as relatively uncaring seekers of power. They believe in a dog-eat-dog worldview and report being motivated by self-interest and self-indulgence.

According to Pettigrew, "Although authoritarianism is found among some liberal and progressive-minded left-wingers, a preference for a combination of authoritarianism and SDO is more frequently manifested among right-wingers in our nation." Trump's speeches, studded with such absolutist terms as "losers" and "complete disasters," are classic authoritarian statements. "His clear distinction between groups on the top of society (Whites) and those 'losers' and 'bad hombres' on the bottom (immigrants, Blacks and Latinos) are classic social dominance statements."

Outgroup Prejudices

Pettigrew's research findings also found Trump supporters to score high on *outgroup prejudices*. Trump is less subtle in expressing prejudice for outgroups than most traditional candidates for office. This is noted in the many ways he repeatedly exhibited his unconcealed prejudice against outgroups ranging from "dangerous" Muslims to Mexican "rapists" to name a few. His dedicated followers loved his overt expression of such prejudice as it represents a breaking away from the so-called "political correctness" that Trump supporters typically resent.

Lack of Intergroup Contact: Numerous social scientists, including Dr. Pettigrew, reported that a major means of reducing intergroup prejudice is through intergroup contact. However, there is growing evidence that Trump's White supporters have experienced far less contact with racial minority persons than other Americans in numerous research findings. Rothwell and Diego-Rosell (2016) found that "the racial and ethnic isolation of White persons at the zip-code level is one of the strongest predictors of Trump support." This finding remains true for both non-Hispanic Whites in general and for the smaller subset of White Republicans."

Relative Deprivation: In studies that included many Trump loyalists, these research participants commonly expressed strong emotional and cognitive reactions to having lost their jobs to Mexico and China and were understandably angry. The conclusion researchers drew from these research findings was that many Trump supporters feel deprived relative to what they expected to possess at this point in their lives and to what they erroneously perceived other less deserving groups had acquired in their lives.

Additional research findings included comments by Trump supporters that highlighted how rapidly rising costs of housing and prescription drugs have aggravated their financial concerns. These persons further indicated that their savings often did not allow for the type of ideal retirements they had long envisioned. Trump supporters frequently indicated that their hopes for their children advancing beyond their own financial status and going to college are being dashed by rising tuitions (Pettigrew, 2017).

All of the above stated research findings are designed to stimulate foundational thinking about the psychology of Trump's supporters as a result of the work that Pettigrew and other researchers have done in this area. What follows is a discussion of the various factors that attract people to Trump.

What Attracts People to Trump?

Sociologist Charlie Hochschild states that the emotional themes in Trump's rhetoric and leadership style are fundamental in their likability of Trump. Among Hochschild's research findings include an acknowledgement that "the former president's speeches–evoking dominance, bravado, live clarity, national pride, and personal uplift–inspire an emotional transformation which leads to extreme loyalty, all of which are attractive to many people who support Trump."

To gain a deeper understanding of one particular answer to the above stated question comes from the work of Dr. Bandy X. Lee, a psychiatrist and expert in violence prevention. In her book entitled, *A Profile of a Nation: Trump's Mind America's Soul*, Dr. Lee states that, "The reasons for Trump's attractiveness are multiple and varied, but I have outlined two major emotional drives that significantly impact his popularity and attractiveness. The first emotional drive is what I refer to as *narcissistic symbiosis* and the second is called *shared psychosis*."

In providing more details about the meaning of these terms, Dr. Lee has the following comments:

> *Narcissistic symbiosis* refers to the developmental wounds that make the leader-follower relationship magnetically attractive. The leader, hungry for adulation to compensate for an inner lack of self-worth, projects grandiose omnipotence, while the followers, rendered needy by societal stress or developmental injury are in search of a parental figure in their lives. When such wounded individuals are given positions of power, they arouse a similar psychological pathology that creates a 'lock and key' relationship.

Trump's followers represent the lock and Trump serves as the key that unleashes a sense of fulfillment and inspiration among persons who are attracted to his leadership style and persona. This short-term sense of increased fulfilment and inspiration serve as a balm that temporarily relieves many Trump supporters from the wounded frustration many of them experience as a result of the relative deprivation described by other researchers (see the definition of relative deprivation in the above section).

One of the main problems with all of this is that Trump's pathological lying, while producing temporary relief from the psychological suffering many of his supporters' experience in their lives, is based on irrational thoughts that do not match the reality of the social-political challenges we face as a nation. According to Dr. Lee, this break from reality in conjunction with the *lock-key relationship* described above often results in a unique *shared psychosis*.

In the above sections of this chapter, I discuss various aspects of the psychology of Trump supporters as well as reporting on research findings that help to answer the following question, "What attracts people to Trump?" My own research into these issues resulted in identifying four different types of Trump supporters. Describing these different types of Trump supporters from a psycho-political perspective is useful in that it helps to avoid overgeneralizing and stereotyping his supporters. By increasing one's understanding of the unique psychological similarities and differences Trump supporters commonly manifest in their attraction to the former president, readers can uncover a more comprehensive and accurate understanding of the psychology of Trump supporters.

Four Groups of Trump Supporters

In conducting my research while preparing to write this book, I concluded that there are at least four distinct groups of Trump supporters. *This includes the Trump insiders support group, the Trump outsiders support group, the Trump cult,* and *avid advocates of Christian Trumpism.*

The Trump Insiders Support Group

The Trump insiders support group is comprised of persons who are a part of the Trump family, business, and political orbit. The Trump family-business-political orbit is smaller in size than the three other Trump support groups described in this chapter. The Trump insiders support group include persons who are directly related to Trump as well as other individuals whose role and function is to demonstrate loyalty and deference to the former president in various business and political endeavors.

In addition to his sons and daughter (Don Jr., Eric, and Ivanka), a partial list of persons identified as important members of the Trump insiders support group include: Michael Flynn (former United States National Security Advisor), Rudy Giuliani (a former Trump Attorney), Kellyanne Conway (Trump's former Campaign Manager), Steve Bannon (a former Chief Executive for the former president), Dan Scavino Jr. (Trump's former Social Media Director), Michael Pompeo (former Secretary of State), William Barr (former Attorney General), Ginny Thomas (wife of Supreme Court Judge Clarence Thomas), Kevin McCarthy (former Majority Speaker), Michael Lindell (the Pillow Man), and Roger Stone (a former Republican Operative).

Although the above listed persons come from diverse fields with various business and political backgrounds, they share commonalities that distinguish themselves from the Trump outsiders support group members, individuals comprising the Trump cult, and Christian Trumpism supporters; all of which are discussed below. In addition to the loyalty and deference noted above, Trump insiders support group members were expected to unquestionably demonstrate acceptance of Trump's authoritarian leadership style, a willingness to implement time and energy to promote Trumpism in their respective business/political endeavors, and back Trump's alt-reality narratives as well as publicly perpetuating his misinformation, lies, and unfounded conspiracy theories.

Additional persons, who also fall within the Trump insiders support group include political officials, the vast majority of whom are Republican Party members. These persons consistently and publicly articulate their overwhelming support for former president Donald Trump. An interesting finding emerging from my research of this group of Trump supporters was the frequency with which many of them would publicly go on record as being strongly supportive of Donald Trump while privately expressing disagreement with his leadership style.

Dr. Brian Klaas, an associate professor of global politics at University College in London, directed his research endeavors to studying authoritarianism and fascism as they relate to the psychology of Trump insiders support group members who are part of the power structure of elected officials in Washington, DC. As Dr. Klaas stated, "Republican Party Trump supporters are required to publicly idealize a single political figure in order to be fully accepted. Republican Party members are punished for refusing to publicly support lies on behalf of that figure, otherwise, things can get out of control."

The Trump Outsiders Support Group

Persons viewed as being a part of the *Trump outsiders support group* is a large segment of individuals who voted for former President Trump in the 2016 and 2020 presidential elections. One way to measure the number of persons that comprise the Trump outsiders support group is by reflecting on the final total votes cast for Donald Trump in comparison to the total votes cast for Joe Biden in the 2020 presidential election.

A final tally of those total votes indicated that Trump received 74,223,975, or 46.8 percent of the total votes, whereas Biden received 81,283,501, or 51.3 percent of the total votes in the 2020 presidential election. This resulted in Biden receiving 7 million more votes than Trump.

There are a number of common characteristics that underlie the motivation of many persons falling within the Trump outsiders support group. Among these commonalities include people, who operate from an awareness of what they believe is the urgency to ensure Trump's nomination as the Republican Party's nominee for the 2024 presidential election.

This awareness contributes to a strong motivation that will lead a large number of Trump supporters to vote for Trump in the 2024 election. For some (perhaps many) of these Trump supporters, they are also likely to go further by encouraging other persons to vote for the former president in 2024. The most enthusiastic of these Trump supporters may also volunteer time to support local, state, and/or national Trump campaign organizations. By volunteering time and energy with the Trump campaign, these behaviors can be viewed as representing the sort of grassroots political capital that contributed to Trump's upsetting victory in the 2016 presidential election.

Another common characteristic exhibited by many Trump outsiders support group persons is that they commonly share a heavy-duty dislike for as well as maintaining a durable disagreement with members of the Democratic Party. For other Trump supporters, their emotional reaction to members of the Democratic Party and their allies gets close to genuine distain and, at-times, overtly aggressive and hostile comments and behaviors.

Members of this segment of Trump's supporters are attracted to Trump's ability to effectively give voice to many of their concerns, interests, and hopes in Making America Great Again. This support is anchored in the perceptions and beliefs expressed by these supporters as to what needs to be done to achieve a psycho-political goal of Making America Great Again as mandated by Donald Trump.

It is also important to note that a number of Trump's outsiders support group members demonstrate their ability to exercise varying degrees of critical thinking. As a result, some of these persons are able to occasionally express disagreement with various aspects of Trump's brash and controversial leadership style while maintaining their loyalty and support for his overall leadership qualities. This latter characteristic distinguishes persons comprising the Trump outsiders group members from another distinguishing and large group referred to as the Trump cult.

The Trump Cult

American politics has always had its rock stars. Our very first president, George Washington, was so popular that his eight-day trip from Mount Vernon to New York City in April 1789 was a huge celebrity event. Theodore Roosevelt was such a popular figure that he would attract capacity crowds everywhere he went as he became a hero to progressives and conservatives alike.

John F. Kennedy, with his youth, vitality, and good looks, combined with the beauty, elegance, and grace of Jackie Kennedy, brought "Camelot" into the romanticization of the White House. Ronald Reagan, an actual movie star, became a venerated figure to millions of Americans and the gold standard for modern conservatism.

More recently, Barack Obama symbolized hope and change for millions of Americans, while demonstrating that intelligence and his sense of humor were not impediments to great leadership. Each of these presidents had what some writers called the *cult of personality*. Yet it could be argued that none of them had the sort of personality cult that Trump has and continues to have among his passionate, energetic, and committed following. The question to be addressed in the following section of this chapter is stated as follows: Would it be fair to label Trump's followers a cult?

Most of Donald Trump's outsider supporters were looking for someone to shake things up and provide them with a new political in-group to join. While some people do not believe that Mr. Trump and his followers comprise a cult, my research findings indicate that between 15 and 20 million persons who voted for Trump in the 2020 presidential election fulfill the criteria typically used in sociological, religious, and psychological circles when defining a cult.

Mr. Trump's most devoted followers are a large part of the U.S. electorate. To understand how Mr. Trump and a large number of his outsiders support group members manifest cult characteristics, it is useful to be cognizant of the psychological, emotional, and behavioral characteristics that define the meaning of a cult across disciplines. These characteristics are listed below.

- A cult is led by one charismatic leader who is perceived to be the sole authority on truth; only this leader decides or has the right to approve all policies and practices to be abided by the cult members;

- A cult is comprised of members who are zealous, protective, and unquestionably committed to the leader;

- Cult members regard the leader's beliefs and practices as truth; the leader affirms and enforces this idea;

- The cult leader and its members often use humiliation or punishment to suppress individualism and doubt in the cult leader;

- Criticism or jokes about the cult leader are taken very seriously, often resulting in disparaging and hostile reactions by cult members;

- A cult is typically elitist in the sense that its leader and members claim special religious, political, and/or social status;

- Cult leaders routinely use the pull of their personality to convince cult followers that they are part of something bigger than themselves. In Trump's case, he enhanced his outsider supporters' belief that they are part of an in-group of "real Americans" who can achieve a level of greatness they dream of and that only he can lead them to that mythical state;

- Cult members are fully expected to submit to the leader's beliefs, comments, and policies even if they do not agree with them. Unquestioning obedience is compulsory and cognitive dissonance is avoided and rejected;

- More extreme cults extend their behavioral boundaries, often precipitating tragic endings. This characteristic was reflected in the way many Trump cult members supported his order to "fight hard and if you don't fight hard, you will lose your country." This statement by Trump occurred during his early afternoon speech at the "Save America" rally on January 6, 2021, in Washington, DC. As reported by the investigative reports by the January 6 House Committee, Trump's articulation of these orders contributed to many cult members' failed attempt to overthrow the United States government via a violent insurrection in our nation's capital;

- Some cults result in renouncing and/or breaking off association with family members, friends, and/or colleagues who disagree with their leader's beliefs, values, and leadership style; and

- The teachings of the cult leader are repeatedly drilled into its members.

Christian Trumpism

Another influential group supportive of Donald Trump consists of persons who self-identify as Evangelical Christians. Researchers have reported that a large percent of evangelical Christians manifested many of the above stated cult characteristics as avid advocates of what is referred to as *Christian Trumpism*.

According to 2016 election exit polls, 26 percent of all voters self-identified as being White evangelical Christians. More than three-fourths of these persons expressed a *very strong approval* rating for Trump's leadership style in a 2017 Pew Research Center survey. Approximately two-thirds of non-white evangelicals supported Hillary Clinton in 2016, with 90 percent of Black Protestants voting for her even though their theological views are similar to evangelicals.

According to Yale researcher Philip Gorski, "The question is not why did evangelicals vote but why did so many White evangelicals vote for Trump?" Gorski's answer to why Trump and not an orthodox evangelical as the first choice among White evangelicals was simply "because they are also White Christian nationalists and reactionary supporters of White Christian Trumpism."

Theologian Michael Horton states that "Christian Trumpism represents the integration of three trends, namely Christian Americans exceptionalism, end-times conspiracy, and the prosperity gospel. Horton further asserted that Christian Nationalism became a popular narrative that "God specially called the United States into being as an extraordinary miraculous providence and end-times conspiracy referring to the world's annihilation due to some conspiracy of nefarious groups and globalist powers threatening Americans' sovereignty." Horton also asserted that the "cult of Christian Trumpism blends these three ingredients with a generous dose of hucksterism as well as promoting a personality cult."

Evangelical Christian and historian John Fea pointed out that the evangelical church was responsible for warning against the pursuit of political power for a long time. He also acknowledged that "many modern-day evangelical leaders, such as Trump advisor and televangelist Paula White, ignored these admonitions."

As a result, Fea offered his support and praise for those evangelical leaders who integrated traditional beliefs and values of this religious group with a calling to become political allies and supporters of Donald Trump. The result of this strategy led to an increase in the secular, religious, and political power of those evangelical leaders who became strong supporters of Trump and Trumpism. This led to a contagious transformation of many White Evangelical Christians, encouraging them to operate as cult members as reflected in the definition of a cult outlined above.

Additional support for this growing cult consciousness was fortified by televangelist Jim Bakker who praised prosperity gospel preacher White's ability to "walk into the White House at any time she wants to" and have "full access to the King." According to Fea, an increasing number of evangelical leaders followed suit by "devoting their careers to endorsing Trump-allied political candidates and Supreme Court Justices in an effort to restore what they believed to be the Judeo-Christian roots of the country."

Trump, in turn, called on Fea to explain to Christian evangelical leaders why he could be trusted in spite of his moral failings. These efforts resulted in Fea collaborating with numerous respected evangelical leaders including James Dobson, Franklin Graham, Johnnie Moore Jr., Ralph Reed, Gary Bauer, Richard Land, megachurch pastor Mark Burns, and Southern Baptist pastor and Fox political commentator Robert Jeffress.

The broad support Fea created from these outreach efforts resulted in the formation of unprecedented influential religious-political leadership among large numbers of evangelical Christians. Once created, this powerful religious-political base ensured that prominent evangelical Christians who failed to support Trump would lose any presidential access as well as encountering a substantial risk of public criticism and backlash from their followers.

The extraordinary success of the above-stated actions had two important consequences. This included galvanizing cult-like ways of thinking, feeling and behaving among large numbers of evangelical Christians as well as enhancing Trump's political capital before, during and after his presidential term.

Summary

Chapter 6 completes Part 1 of this book. Chapters 1–6 discuss a broad range of issues of relevance to the title of this book. In doing so, Chapter 1 explores the meaning of foundational terms and concepts addressed in all of the following chapters including a definition of the psycho-political perspective that is the center piece of this book.

Chapter 2 outlines a new and expansive definition of White racism and White supremacy in our country. It also provides a detailed description of a new theory of our multiracial/multicultural democracy entitled, the RESPECTFUL theory that is anchored in a new psycho-political perspective.

Chapter 3 presents a detailed discussion of the potential promise of the ongoing evolution of our multiracial/multicultural democracy when and if it is supported and sustained by a majority of people in the United States. In contrast, Chapter 4 discusses pitfalls that could undermine our country's fragile multiracial/multicultural democracy if a majority of people do not support and sustain the ongoing evolution of this democracy in the future.

Chapter 5 explores Trump's psychology and describes the meaning of Trumpism from a psycho-political perspective. Chapter 6 discusses some of the similarities and differences that characterize the different types of Trump supporters that have emerged during his 2015–2016 campaign and his 2017–2020 presidential term. This chapter directs particular attention to the meaning of the terms, *the Trump cult* and avid advocates of *Christian Trumpism*.

Part 2 is comprised of Chapters 7–15. Chapter 7 discusses the mental health crisis in the United States and the impact of Trump's presidency, Trumpism, and the Trump cult on the increasing mental health problems millions of people in the United States encounter in their lives.

Chapter 8 discusses a new psychological theory referred to as an *integral theory of mental health and human development from a psycho-political perspective*. This new theory highlights the meaning of *optimal mental health (OMH)* and its relevance for the new integral theoretical model.

Numerous new terms and concepts are introduced in this chapter as they relate to the mental health of our nation.

Among these new terms and concepts include discussion of the meaning of what a *sane society* looks like and the role and function of mental health professionals in fostering the development of a sane society in the United States. Additional new terms and concepts discussed in Chapter 8 include: the *Trump mass psychology, sharing psychosis, malignant normality,* and *the myth of normal.*

As stated in the Preface, this book is a call to mental health professionals, their professional organizations, and interested persons in the general public to direct more time and energy in addressing the impact of the meaning of the above stated terms among millions of people in our nation.

Chapter 9 predicts that there will be increasing calls for mental health professionals and their professional organizations to more substantially address psycho-political dynamics that are known to undermine the optimal mental health of large numbers of people in our country. It is further predicted that a failure to address such issues within the mental health professions will undermine the long-term credibility, relevance, and viability of our nation's mental health system.

In Chapters 10–15, I draw from the knowledge of numerous empirically-supported psychotherapy, counseling, and human development theories. This is done to assist readers in expanding their understanding of some of the psychological, emotional, behavioral, racial/cultural and neurological factors that are linked to Donald Trump's leadership style and Trump supporters, including those persons who comprise the Trump cult.

Also, as noted in the Preface, a primary goal in writing this book is to stimulate new thinking and imagination about what can happen *beyond the lies* that currently mark the serious psycho-political divisiveness in our nation. Among the questions addressed in Part 2 include the following: What will happen in our country's future? What will our nation's democracy look like in the future? How can interested persons support the evolving multiracial/multicultural democracy in the United States? What can be done to address the adverse impact of Trumpism on healthy human development? Why is it important to support efforts that assist large numbers of persons in diverse populations to realize and sustain optimal mental health from a psycho-political perspective?

With all of this in mind, let us proceed on this intellectual journey by exploring the ideas presented in Part 2. In doing so it is hoped that we can work together to not only effectively address the crisis in our country's mental health system, but to do so in ways that foster optimal mental health, peace, and justice for *we the people*.

PART 2

As noted above, Part 2 is comprised of nine chapters (Chapters 7–15). Information presented in Part 2 builds on the foundational psycho-political perspective presented in this book. Early in Part 1, I discuss the perilous times in which we live, the ongoing evolution of our nation's multiracial/multicultural democracy, and the importance of White people helping to support and sustain the fragile development of that democracy. This point is accentuated by the fact that our nation is undergoing an unprecedented transformation in its demography; a transformation that is and will continue to affect the thinking, feeling, and behaviors of all the people in our society.

The sort of political activism that is congruent with the new integral theory of mental health and human development from a psycho-political perspective includes an expanded obligation as mental health professionals to assist people and the communities in which they live, work, and study to realize their untapped potential for optimal mental health. To effectively achieve this goal, it is equally important (and I want to repeat the words *equally important*) for mental health professionals to place an equal footing in addressing the toxic ecological systems that are known to negatively impact healthy human development across the lifespan. This professional and ethical commitment is aimed at, not only assisting people to realize their untapped potential for optimal mental health, but to also work with others to stimulate the building of what Erich Fromm called a Sane Society in his important book with the same title.

Other concepts relevant for building a sane society and the reasons for implementing research-verified interventions known to achieve

Erich Fromm's goal to build a sane society is discussed in other chapters in Part 2. This includes exploring the meaning and relevance of what is referred to as the Trump *mass psychology, the collective conscious, the collective unconscious, the malignancy of normalcy, the myth of normal,* and *optimal mental health* for the new integral theory of mental health and human development presented in Part 2 of this book.

Clearly, the terms and concepts outlined above will be controversial for many mental health professionals. Such controversy is likely to be predictably enhanced as the psycho-political perspective outlined in this book calls for important changes in the role many mental health professionals play in their work with an emphasis on enhanced political activism.

Nevertheless, it is my hope that readers' open-mindedness will result in thoughtful analysis of the ways in which the theories and interventions discussed in Chapters 10 - 15 can result in addressing the mental health crisis in our nation while simultaneously supporting the ongoing evolution of our multiracial/multicultural democracy. Translating this hope into a reality requires a clear understanding of the perilous times in which we live and work from a psycho-political perspective. As briefly stated above, this understanding needs to focus on the mental health crisis in our nation as well as the impact of Trump, Trumpism, Trump's supporters and persons in the Trump cult all of which are eroding our country's mental health (See Chapter 7).

The final chapter in Part 2 (Chapter 15) discusses concrete re-search-supported strategies that foster the optimal mental health of both individual persons and the communities where they live and work. The essential goal in implementing such strategies is to promote and sustain optimal mental health and the ongoing healthy development of larger numbers of persons from diverse groups and backgrounds than mental health professionals have done in the past.

The knowledge that is included in the chapters that comprise Part 2 is also designed to promote vibrant discussions within and across the mental health professions that serves a fourfold purpose. First, such discussions can direct attention to the strengths of the psycho-political perspective presented in this book.

Second, interested readers, who take part in such discussions, would do well to seek support from leaders in their professional organizations to identify the types of organizational resources that would lead to the implementation of the new integral theory of mental health and human development from a psycho-political perspective in our professional training programs, individual and community assessment strategies, and clinical practices.

Third, to ensure professional accountability, it is important to develop assessment strategies to determine the degree to which the psycho-political framework outlined throughout this book is or is not helpful in addressing the mental health crisis in our nation.

Fourth, it is hoped that all of the points stated above, and the new knowledge presented in this book will lead White mental health professionals in particular to help support and sustain the fragile and ongoing evolution of the multiracial/multicultural democracy in the United States.

CHAPTER 7

OUR NATION'S MENTAL HEALTH CRISIS

Research shows that stress levels are the highest in memory in our country; actually higher than any time since World War I. If you think of all the crises that happened in that time period, we are actually in a worse state today. We know that anxiety levels are 70 percent higher than two years ago. This is according to research from the American Psychological Association and American Psychiatric Association.

We know that public mental health is deteriorating. This is shown by the drastically increasing gun violence and murder rates as well as the epidemic of suicides occurring in the United States. Unfortunately, a population becomes habituated to such things. We become more adaptive to stress levels. People become jumpy and more anxious and look for comfort.

The more the population is suffering, the more vulnerable people will be to the false points Mr. Trump propagates and more convinced that such false ideas are true. The rest of the population then becomes exhausted from having to deal with those people and catching up with Trump's lies and untruths.

Dr. Bandy X. Lee, psychiatrist and president of the
World Health Organization

Politics is a pervasive and largely unavoidable source of chronic stress that exacted significant health costs for large numbers of American adults between 2017 and 2020. The 2020 election did little to alleviate those effects and quite likely exacerbated them. Around 40% of Americans consistently identify politics as a significant source of stress in their lives. This includes about 5% of persons who say they have considered suicide in response to recent political developments.

Kevin Smith, Chair of the Political Science Department at
the University of Nebraska, Lincoln

Introduction

I have conducted research that focuses on America's mental health crisis from 2019 to 2022. What follows is a summary of my findings that amplify the depth of the ineffectiveness of the United States's mental health system.

After summarizing my research findings, I incorporate the results of other researchers, who convey the adverse psychological, emotional, and behavioral reactions large numbers of persons suffered, in part, as a result of Trump's leadership style in his 2015–2016 campaign and during his one-term presidency. Relevant to these points is an acknowledgement of the ways that many Trump supporters, and particularly persons in the Trump cult, manifested blind obedience and a lack of critical thinking, both of which contributed to their failure to realize their untapped potential for optimal mental health.

Analyzing Our Nation's Mental Health System Crisis From a Pre-Covid and Post-Covid Perspective

The main goal of our nation's mental health system is to address the psychological, emotional, and behavioral problems millions of people experience in their lives each year. Psychiatrists, psychologists, counselors, social workers, and other allied mental health professionals play important roles in addressing this goal. Over the past several decades, researchers have published the results of important studies focusing on these and related issues.

Among these important research findings include studies describing the efficacy of different counseling and psychotherapy theories (Ivey, D'Andrea, & Ivey, 2012). The results of these investigations contributed to the emergence of the empirically supported counseling and psychotherapy movement in the mental health professions during the 1990s and the beginning of the 21st century (Drisko, & Friedman, 2019).

Additional investigations describe the impact of multicultural counseling and social justice advocacy on the health and well-being of diverse client populations (Sue, Sue, Neville, & Smith, 2019). The collective impact of these research endeavors advanced new thinking about ways to address people's mental health problems (D'Andrea, 2020). Despite this new thinking, the mental health system in the United States has increasingly fallen into serious crisis. The following sections of this chapter draw from research findings that explain the depth and scope of this multidimensional crisis.

Exploring the *Big Picture*

The above-stated points illuminate how numerous research findings foster important knowledge related to the efficacy of various counseling and psychotherapy interventions. Other research findings underscore the importance of having mental health professionals acquire a broad range of multicultural counseling and psychotherapy competencies to work respectfully and ethically with persons in diverse populations.

In contrast to the results of these studies, there has been a dearth of investigations that describe our nation's mental health system from a *big picture* perspective. This perspective involves researching the degree to which our national mental health system provides services among millions of people in need of professional help every year (D'Andrea, 2019).

This is a critical area of inquiry as it can increase practitioners' understanding of the strengths and weaknesses of our country's mental health theories and practices. An enhanced understanding of these issues can lead psychiatrists, psychologists, social workers, counselors, other allied professionals, and their professional organizations to advocate for changes necessary to address weaknesses that define our nation's mental health crisis.

With this backdrop in mind, the following sections of this chapter address the ensuing questions:

1. What percentage of people identified in need of mental health services actually received professional treatment in 2019 (the pre-Covid era)?

2. What percentage of people in need of such help did not receive professional treatment in the United States during 2019?

3. What are some of the factors contributing to our national mental health system's failure to address the needs of millions of people during the pre-covid era?

4. What mental health problems increased during the post-covid era (2021) resulting in a need for expanded mental health services?

5. How did Donald Trump's leadership style and presidency adversely impact the mental health of large numbers of people in our society?

Defining the Meaning of Our National Mental Health System

Before addressing the five questions outlined above, it is important to define what is meant by our *national mental health system*. As used in this book, our *national mental health system* is defined as that macrosystem comprised of persons whose training is relevant in providing mental health services among persons identified as being in need of such help. This includes counselors, psychologists, human service workers, social workers, psychiatrists, and other allied professionals who receive training in mental health.

Research Findings Illuminating the Weaknesses in Our Nation's Mental Health System

A review of research related to our nation's mental health system resulted in a limited number of publications in this area. One of the few national mental health organizations that sponsors annual research aimed at assessing the percentage of people in need of mental health services compared to the percentage of persons who actually receive treatment in the United States is the National Institute of Mental Health (NIMH).

NIMH research findings confirm that mental health problems are common in our country, affecting millions of people each year. In 2018 and 2019, NIMH researchers estimated that one in five adults (20.6% of adults in this nation) between the ages of 18 and 65 years of age experience some form of mental health problems each year in the United States.

As discussed in this chapter, mental health problems include different conditions varying in degree of severity ranging from mild/moderate to severe conditions. The NIMH uses two categories when assessing the percentage of persons identified as being in need of professional treatment. This includes persons manifesting any mental illness (AMI) compared to individuals manifesting serious mental illness (SMI). The AMI category encompasses all recognized mental illnesses. The SMI category is a smaller and more severe subset of AMIs.

Using data generated by researchers with the NIMH, it was noted that 51.5 million Americans aged 18 or older were in need of professional services for mental health problems during 2019. As noted above, this represents 20.6% of all U.S. adults in our nation who were identified as being in need of mental health services (NIMH).

The prevalence of AMI was higher among females (24.5%) than males (16.3%). Young adults aged 18-25 years had the highest prevalence of AMIs (29.4%) compared to adults aged 26-49 years (25.0%) and persons aged 50 years and older (14.1%).

Persons manifesting AMIs were highest among adults reporting two or more races (31.7%), followed by White adults (22.2%), Hispanic or Latino (18%), and African Americans (17.3%). Further analysis revealed the number of persons experiencing AMIs was lowest among persons of Asian descent (14.4%) in 2019.

A further analysis of the NIMH data indicated a substantial difference between the 51.5 million adults in need of mental health services with only 23.0 million persons (44.8%) actually receiving mental health services in 2019. More females experiencing AMIs (49.7%) received mental health services than males (36.8%). The percentage of young adults aged 18-25 years with AMIs receiving mental health services (38.9%) was lower than adults with AMIs aged 26-49 years (45.4%) and persons aged 50 years and older (47.2%).

Differences between the percentage of persons in need of mental health services and the percentage of those actually receiving such services (44.8%; 23 million persons) address the first and second questions established for this chapter. Conversely, the statistics reported above indicate that the 55.2% (28.5 million persons) identified as being in need of mental health services did not receive such professional help in 2019. In other words, a majority of people in the United States in need of mental health services are not receiving such professional help on a regular basis.

Other NIMH research results indicate that the above stated statistical findings are similar to previous studies investigating these issues annually. The following sections of this chapter discuss (a) some of the factors that contribute to people in need of mental health services not receiving such services and (b) the rising mental health problems manifested during the covid (2019-2020) and post-covid (2021) eras.

Factors Contributing to People Receiving and Not Receiving Mental Health Services

Numerous factors contribute to the millions of persons in need of mental health services who do not receive professional help. Among these factors include people's lack of finances for the cost of such services, lack of insurance, lack of interest, and fear of negative stigmatization (Sue, Sue, Neville, & Smith).

Other researchers point to the continued overuse of individual counseling and psychotherapy as the primary mental health services provided by most professionals. The overuse of these traditional services contributes to the disparity between the total number of persons in need of mental healthcare (51.5 million adults in the U.S.) with only 44.8% (23 million of these persons) actually receiving professional help in 2019.

These research findings underscore the importance of balancing individual counseling and psychotherapy with more group-based, community-based, and population-based interventions that are culturally responsive, strength-based, and prevention-based as well as aimed at fostering and sustaining ongoing healthy human development (Lewis et al). Recommendations to establish a formal policy for mental health practitioners to operate from such a multi-service approach are increasing in our nation (Aldarondo, 2007; Lewis et al. 2011; McKnight-Eily, Okoro, Strine, Verlenden, Hollis, Njai, Mitchell, Board, Puddy, & Thomas, 2021). These issues are discussed in more detail later in this chapter.

The information presented above addresses the third question established for this chapter. It also represents a clarion call for mental health professionals to make a commitment to transform the existing mental health system in the United States (D'Andrea, 2019). The following section describes the rising mental health problems reported in a covid and post-covid era; these problems further highlight the need to address the failure of the current system to meet the needs and personal interests of much larger numbers of people than mental health professionals have achieved in the past.

Rising Mental Health Problems During the Covid (2019-2020) and post-Covid (2021) Eras

Elevated levels of mental health problems, including but not limited to depression, panic attacks, substance use/abuse, domestic violence, child sexual abuse, traumatic experiences, and suicidal ideation were reported by increasing numbers of persons during the Covid (2019-2020) and post-Covid (2021) eras. Researchers reported the prevalence of anxiety disorders in 2020 were three times those exhibited in 2019 (25.5% versus 8.1%). These researchers also pointed to the prevalence of depressive disorders in 2020 that were four times those reported in 2019 (24.3% versus 6.5%). Approximately one quarter (25%) of respondents reported symptoms of a trauma stress-related disorder (TSRD) during 2020 (Mason, Welch, Arunkumar & Feinglass, 2021).

Approximately one in 10 persons stated that they started or increased substance use/misuse because of the Covid pandemic in 2020. Twice as many adult respondents reported serious consideration of suicide in 2020 than in 2018 (10.7% versus 4.3%) (Czeisler et al, 2020).

The rising mental health conditions listed above disproportionately affect specific populations. This includes young adults, persons of Latino/Latina descent, African Americans, essential healthcare workers, unpaid caregivers for adults, poor persons, individuals receiving treatment for preexisting psychiatric conditions, and older adults (McKnight-Eily, Okoro, Strine, Verlenden, Hollis, Njai, Mitchell, Board, Puddy, & Thomas, 2021).

In one of the most comprehensive studies of the impact of racial factors during Covid-19, Mude and his colleagues found Black and Latinx persons experienced significantly higher Covid-related prevalence, mortality, and hospitalizations compared to Whites.

These racial health disparities illuminate the systemically entrenched disadvantages (social, economic, and political) experienced by many racial minority persons. Research in these areas underscores the need to address inequities in racial minority communities while simultaneously striving to promote social justice as a correlate for *optimal mental health*.

The fact that 55.2% of adults in need of mental health services did not receive such help in 2019 (the pre-Covid era) points to additional weaknesses in the design and delivery of traditional mental health services in our nation. The unprecedented increase in the post-Covid disorders reported in the above statistics translates into millions of persons being added to those who already were identified as being in need of professional services.

This statistical reality only exacerbates the serious crisis in our nation's mental health system. In short, the above-stated research findings clearly indicate that our nation's mental health system is a broken entity in need of much improvement.

Trump's Impact on Our Nation's Mental Health

Several mental health professionals and journalists raised questions regarding the degree to which Trump's personality and leadership style as manifested in his 2015–2016 campaign as well as in his actions throughout his one-term presidential term from 2017–2020, negatively impacted our nation's mental health. From the perspective of the new integral theory of mental health and human development from a psycho-political perspective, it is hypothesized that the unprecedented rise in mental health problems in our country outlined above were further heightened by stressors associated with Trump's personality and leadership style.

Chauncey Devega, a senior politics writer for the *Salon* magazine, comments on the above issues in the following manner:

Donald Trump's presidency and the destructive forces it unleashed have resulted in a mental health emergency as well as a public health emergency in general. As early as 2015, many mental health experts began to warn that a Trump presidency would lead to a mental and physical health disaster for Americans.

Dr. Kevin Smith, chair of the political science department at the University of Nebraska, Lincoln, suggests that the number of people in the United States who found Trump's leadership style and policies to be a torrent might actually be much larger than he initially considered. In linking political factors to the deterioration of the mental health of large numbers of people in our society, Dr. Smith stated the following in an article entitled, "Politics is Making Us Sick: The Negative Impact of Political Engagement on Public Health During the Trump Administration":

Politics is a pervasive and largely unavoidable source of chronic stress that exacted significant physical and mental health costs for large numbers of American adults during Trump's one-term presidency between 2017 and 2020. The 2020 election did little to alleviate those effects and quite likely exacerbated them.

Around 40% of Americans consistently identify politics as a significant source of stress in their lives. Shockingly, about 5% of these persons considered suicide in response to recent political developments and divisive dynamics.

Dr. Smith added the following points in his article after assessing approximately 800 research participants in his study on politics and mental health:

Forty percent of the participants in this study indicated they were stressed out about politics, one in five research participants reported losing sleep, being fatigued, or suffering from depression because of Trump's politics. As many as 25% of the respondents also reported they manifested self-destructive or compulsive behaviors, including saying and writing things they later regretted, making bad decisions, and ignoring other priorities in their lives.

Dr. Smith also indicated that his interest in investigating the linkage between politics and mental health was based on his thoughts and feelings about the disastrous state of Americans' mental health, which, as he indicated, is one of the overarching stories in the country right now. For all of the divisiveness in our nation's politics, Smith indicated that there is a pretty broad consensus that the country is, psychologically, in an awful place.

Additional research supporting Dr. Smith's conclusions includes the results of a 2022 USA Today/Suffolk University poll. The results of this poll indicated that almost 9 in 10 registered voters believe there is a mental health crisis in the United States. Based on the research participants comments, Smith pointed out that this crisis expresses itself in all sorts of ways, such as "in rising rates of youth suicide, record overdoses, random acts of street violence, months-long waiting lists for children's therapists, mask meltdowns, and the increasing popularity of QAnon."

Reverend John Pavovitz, an author and pastor, commented on the ways that the dark side of humanity has risen as a result of the combination of the Covid pandemic and Trump's leadership style and personality. Reverend Pavovitz asserted the following:

> For the first time in America's history, the latent ugliness of people was revealed, validated and celebrated by a sitting president–it was officially normalized. And what we're experiencing now is a staggering, insensitive posturing in the face of so many people suffering that is the late-ripening fruit of something which has been set into the bedrock of our nation. It is the malicious entitlement that MAGA was designed to nurture from the beginning.

> This quickly metastasizing moral cancer is something we have never experienced on this level in our lifetimes and is something we are going to have to reckon with regardless of the political outcomes. If the former president somehow takes that office again, these stories will surely grow exponentially, more violent, and more commonplace, but either way, the ugliness is here now.

Anna North, a journalist, editor, and senior reporter at *Vox* magazine, outlines additional points that complement and expand the above stated points in her 2020 published article entitled, "People are not okay: The mental health impact of the Trump era." As North states in that article:

Now, Trump has finally left office, despite his constant threats that he wouldn't leave. But the impact on the American psyche of four years of racist rhetoric, incitements of violence, and out-and-out chaos remains among many in the body politic. For many people, the past several years has been especially difficult, bringing with it a pandemic, the police killings of George Floyd, Breonna Taylor, and other Black Americans as well as the Trump administration's violent response to the racial justice protests that ensued. This has created an environment where many people are constantly in a state of fight-or-flight as a result of experiencing a lot of stress, anxiety, and feelings of being overwhelmed.

Some of those feelings have been reflected in nationwide surveys with a significant increase in stress about the country's future and current divisive political climate. In survey results from 2020, 68% of the American respondents said that the presidential election that year was a significant source of stress in their lives, up from 52% reported in 2016.

Like the impact of Trump's policies, the stresses noted above do not go away overnight, especially when the conditions that led to Trump's 2016 election, including but not limited to systemic racism, anti-immigrant paranoia, and the rampant spread of misinformation are still very much a reality in our nation today. The problems Trump brought to light – racism, xenophobia, and transphobia to name just a few, certainly did not start with him. But from the moment he announced his candidacy in 2015 in a speech maligning Mexican people as rapists and drug dealers, he made such racist attitudes more explicit than ever within the bounds of traditional party politics.

His rhetoric helped embolden a wave of hate crimes across the country targeting Muslim Americans, immigrants, and a number of other groups that he demonized. Meanwhile, his constant *all-caps tweeting*, his preference for staff who enabled rather than checked his worst impulses, and his return to campaign-style rallies shortly after his victory in the 2016 election all led to a relentless new environment that subjected Americans to the president's disjointed and frequently abusive thoughts multiple times per day.

In the first three years of his presidency, Trump completed more than 11,000 tweets that attacked various persons Trump disagreed with or did not like.

While Trump was able to energize a core of supporters with his mix of bravado, defiance, and racism, for many others, his presidency was quite simply, scary. In the American Psychological Association's 2016 Stress in America survey, 63% of Americans said the future of the country was a "significant source of stress," and 56% said they were stressed out by the current political climate. In the 2018 version of this survey, those numbers went up to 69% and 62% respectively.

Clinical psychologist Jennifer Panning even coined the term "Trump anxiety disorder" to describe the stress many people were feeling in the weeks and months following the 2016 election. According to other survey results, it was clear that many people experienced ruminations of what's going to be next as they waited for each new tweet or action by the president.

Of course, these mental health problems were not evenly distributed. While all of America had to put up with Trump's toxic tweets, many immigrants, LGBTQ people, Black Americans and Indigenous persons as well as other people of color experienced real threats to their families, their well-being, and their lives. Thousands of children were separated from their parents at the U.S. – Mexico border, with attorneys still unable to locate the families of more than 600 of these youngsters.

Trans people faced the onslaught of the Trump Administration's regulations stripping away their protections from discrimination in healthcare, housing, and education. In at least 41 criminal cases, including an assault on a Latinx man in Florida and threats against a Syrian-born man in Washington State, Trump's name was invoked in connection with these forms of violence and threats according to an ABC News analysis. In contrast, the network found no criminal cases with such direct connections to presidents Barack Obama or George W. Bush.

Although Trump is no longer president, his fascist MAGA movement continues to cause harm. There are clear conclusions that can be drawn from all of these investigative findings. The first conclusion to be drawn from the above body of research findings is that we are in dire need of making the types of structural, systemic, and political changes necessary to address the mental health crisis in the United States.

The second conclusion is the acknowledgement that the degree to which new systemic and structural changes will be implemented largely depends upon the political and professional will mental health practitioners and their professional organizations are willing to assert in addressing what is clearly a call to support a new paradigm shift in our nation's mental health system. Failure to make such changes will predictably result in our mental health system ultimately suffering from the long-term diminishment in its viability and relevance in the coming years (Ivey et al. 2012).

Recommendations to Rectify the Past Failures and Current Crisis Facing Our Nation's Mental Health System

The Need for a Unified Goal

Nelson and Prilleltensky (2005) emphasize that the starting point in making systemic changes in our mental health professions involves gaining broad-based support for an overarching and unifying goal among the members of these professions. These researchers emphasized the importance of developing such a goal for the work that needs to be done in making substantial multi-service changes in our current mental health system. Although gaining support for a primary unifying goal needs to be manifested by large numbers of mental health practitioners, it also needs to complement and expand the unique and diverse goals mental health practitioners are trained to achieve in their work (D'Andrea, 2020).

As a starting point, I offer the following initial draft of a proposed goal to be discussed with other mental health practitioners as we begin to work together in creating an acceptable primary goal that can be used to make the changes necessary to transform the mental health system in our nation:

The primary goal for mental health professionals is to foster and sustain the healthy development of larger numbers of persons from diverse groups and backgrounds than has been done in the past.

The highlights of this initial proposed draft goal are briefly described below.

First, the newly proposed unifying goal for addressing and transforming our nation's mental health crisis places a premium on the role practitioners can play in *promoting and sustaining healthy human development across the lifespan.*

Supporting this component of the proposed draft goal will require professional training programs to increase their curriculum requirements to include introductory and advanced training that focus on the content and process of human development and the realization of optimal mental health among larger numbers of persons from diverse groups and backgrounds than mental health professionals have achieved in the past.

Second, the previous chapters have highlighted the psycho-political impact of the unprecedented demographic transformation of our nation. This changing demographic reality demands mental health professionals to become increasingly competent in multicultural counseling and social justice advocacy.

With this point in mind, mental health practitioners and their professional organizations would be wise to encourage state licensure boards to increase their requirements for multicultural counseling and social justice advocacy competencies. These and related issues are discussed in greater detail in Chapter 13 entitled, the Multicultural/Social Justice Force in the Mental Health Professions.

Third, in addition to fostering healthy human development, the psycho-political perspective described in this book emphasizes the importance of mental health professionals operating in ways that *sustain* this development across the lifespan. One of the reasons for adding this *sustainability* concept to the proposed draft goal is anchored in research findings indicating that positive outcomes from individual counseling and psychotherapy are time limited. Drawing from research summarized by Klaus Grawe (2007), it is reported that between 60% and 80% of people who experience positive outcomes from individual counseling and psychotherapy exhibit a resurgence of the same symptoms which led them to seek mental health services two years after successfully achieving their therapeutic goals.

Fourth, to be successful in fostering and sustaining the healthy development of larger numbers of persons from diverse groups and backgrounds, it is important for mental health practitioners to receive more intensive training and supervision in areas that have and continue to be wanting in a number of key areas. An incomplete listing of some of the areas in need of greater attention in professional mental health training programs include institutionalizing educational and professional resources that assist 21st century practitioners to develop the knowledge and skills necessary to work effectively and respectfully when engaging in system change, community organizing, community development, prevention, and social justice advocacy interventions. From the perspective of the new integral theory presented in this book, these interventions need to be designed to simultaneously ameliorate our nation's mental health crisis and support the ongoing evolution of our multiracial/multicultural democracy.

Pragmatically speaking, the new integral theory of mental health and human development presented in this book is grounded in a realistic commitment to generate financial support to implement its non-fragmented, comprehensive, and truly holistic approach to mental health. The following section begins a discussion of the practical, professional, organizational, and political strategies necessary to secure such fiscal support.

Re-establishing and Expanding the 1963 Community Mental Health Center Act

Transforming our current mental health system requires the procurement of financial resources to more effectively address the mental health needs of increasing numbers of people in our society. The research findings reported in this chapter represent strong empirical evidence highlighting the failure of our nation's mental health system to meet the needs of a majority of persons experiencing psychological, emotional, and behavioral problems in the pre-Covid and Covid eras. Additional research findings outlined above further illuminate why the increased number of persons in need of mental health services in the post-Covid era beg for innovative structural changes in our nation's mental health system.

Given the serious mental health crisis facing the United States, it is recommended that mental health practitioners and their professional organizations use the current crisis as an opportunity to make substantial changes resulting in more effective, broad-based, and culturally responsive training, supervision, and clinical practices. As previously stated in the new integral theory, the goal in making such changes is to foster and sustain the mental health and ongoing development of larger numbers of persons in culturally/racially diverse groups than has been done in the past.

To be successful in achieving this goal, professional changes will necessitate political lobbying efforts by organizations like the National Institute for Mental Health, American Psychiatric Association, American Psychological Association, American Counseling Association, and the National Association of Social Workers to name a few. It is also suggested that this sort of unified national endeavor needs to include major lobbying efforts with state legislatures as well as the United States Congress to reestablish and expand the 1963 Community Mental Health Center Act.

This act was a centerpiece of President John F. Kennedy's domestic policy. It was designed to finance the building of more than two thousand community mental health centers across the United States in the early 1960s. These actions represented practical efforts to create a new mental health service infrastructure where counseling, psychotherapy, consultation, community outreach and prevention interventions could be provided across the country (Kennedy, 1963).

It is unfortunate that the lack of ongoing funding for President Kennedy's unprecedented vision of a new multi-service health system that placed mental health at the center of our national consciousness derailed the realization of this political policy. The final death blow to this vision came from President Ronald Reagan's administration which successfully cut federal funding for mental health services by 25% during the mid-1980s. This major fiscal cutback resulted in shifting federal funding for mental health services to substantially reduced state grants (Torrey, 2013).

Numerous researchers and social justice advocates then (and now) described the positive outcomes of comprehensive, non-fragmented, multi-service, prevention, and community-based mental health projects (Accordino, Porter, & Morse, 2001; D'Andrea, 2004, 1984;). These research findings represent compelling support for re-establishing and expanding the 1963 Community Mental Health Center model. It is especially important to restore and expand the visionary perspective underlying the 1963 Community Center Act given the current crisis of our national mental health system (D'Andrea, 2020; Lewis, 2013). Current political discussions regarding the need to re-define and revitalize our nation's overall infrastructure represent fertile terrain to advocate for the reestablishment and expansion of the 1963 Community Mental Health Center Act.

Digging Deeper to Address our Nation's Mental Health Crisis

In addition to outlining the above-stated recommendations to address the mental health crisis in the United States, my research endeavors led me to dig deeper to better understand new concepts of relevance in addressing the perilous political and psychological times in which we are situated. As I continued to dig deeper, I found the following terms and concepts particularly important to more fully understand the relevance of the new integral theory of mental health and human development from a psycho-political perspective when addressing our nation's mental health crisis and the perilous political times in which we live.

Among these new terms/concepts are those listed below, along with persons known to address each term and concept in their research findings:

1. The Sane Society (Fromm, 1955)
2. Optimal Mental Health (Seligman, 2002)
3. Mass Psychology in the Age of Trump (Jost & Hunyady, 2018)
4. Malignant Normality (Lipton, 2017)
5. Shared Psychosis (Lee, 2020)
6. The Myth of Normal (Mate, 2022)

Chapter 9 details the meaning of the terms and concepts listed above as well as discussing their relevance for awakening to the new integral theory of mental health and human development from a psycho-political perspective. This information represents another way to give away knowledge related to human development, psychology, and counseling theories among *We the People* as promised in the Preface.

Summary

This chapter opens Part 2 of this book. In doing so, it reports on research findings that describe details related to our nation's mental health crisis. The multiple analyses utilized in this research endeavor involved comparing and contrasting the percentages of persons who were identified as being in need of mental health services on an annual basis with the percentages of people who actually received professional help.

The percentages of persons in need of psychological/counseling services were compared in three-time phases. These comparisons were made during the pre-Covid era (2019), the Covid era (2020-early 2021) and post-Covid era (late 2021 – 2022).

Chapter 7 is also designed to answer five questions related to our nation's mental health crisis. This chapter continues by summarizing conclusions and outlining specific recommendations for corrective actions in ameliorating our nation's current mental health crisis.

The numerous recommendations made in this chapter represent practical suggestions to overcome the ongoing failure of our national mental health system by more effectively addressing the needs of the majority of persons manifesting psychological, emotional, and behavior problems. The first recommendation emphasizes the importance of developing and securing support for a unified goal to address weaknesses in our current mental health system. This proposed goal emphasizes the importance of psychiatrists, psychologists, counselors, social workers and other allied professionals working together to foster and sustain the healthy development of larger numbers of people from diverse populations than has been accomplished in the past.

An additional recommendation for counselors, psychologists, psychiatrists, social workers, and other allied professionals to consider involves the need to make a commitment to operate as a united front in calling for re-establishment and expansion of the 1963 Community Mental Health Center Act.

Research findings included in this chapter describe how and why an unprecedented upsurge in mental health needs will continue to be manifested in a post-Covid society. Based on these findings, it is asserted that maintaining the current mental health system will result in a predictable exacerbation of the inherent weaknesses in this human system. It is hoped that the information and recommendations outlined in this chapter lead to the initiation of concerted and unified efforts to build on the successes of our past struggles to promote mental health with new and innovative strategies which address the weaknesses in our country's current mental health system.

The final section in Chapter 7 discusses the need to direct our collective attention to new terms and concepts that are gaining increased interest among persons in multiple disciplines. These terms and concepts are detailed in the following chapter as they represent essential characteristics of the new integral theory of mental health and human development from a psycho-political perspective.

Let us continue our journey by thinking about what can and must be done *beyond the lies* (as asked in the title of this book) as we draw from the strengths of psychology, human development, and counseling theories in mounting a movement to realize our collectively untapped potential for the optimal mental health of ourselves and the communities where we live and work.

CHAPTER 8

THE INTEGRAL THEORY OF MENTAL HEALTH AND HUMAN DEVELOPMENT: A PSYCHO-POLITICAL PERSPECTIVE

The evolution that we learn about in school is the evolution of the physical form. We learned, for example, that the single-celled creatures of the oceans are the predecessors of more complex forms of life. A fish is more complex, and, therefore, more evolved from a sponge; a horse is more complex, and, therefore, more evolved than a snake; a monkey is more complex, and, therefore, more evolved than a horse, and so on, up to human beings which are the most complex, and. therefore, the most evolved life forms upon our planet. We were taught, in other words, that evolution means the progressive development of organizational complexity.

This definition is an expression of the idea that the organism that is best able to control both its environment and all the other organisms in its environment is the most evolved. *Survival of the fittest* means that the most evolved organism in a given environment is the organism that is at the top of the food chain in that environment. According to this definition, therefore, the organism that is most able to ensure its own survival, most able to serve its self-preservation, is the most evolved. We have long known that this definition of evolution is inadequate, but we have not known why.

Our deeper understanding tells us that a truly evolved being is one that values others more than it values itself, and that values love more than it values the physical world and what is in it. We must now bring our understanding of evolution into alignment with this deeper understanding. It is important that we do so because our current understanding of evolution reflects the phase of evolution that we are now leaving. By examining this understanding, we can perceive how we have evolved to now, and what we are now in the process of leaving behind. By reflecting upon a new and expanded understanding of evolution, one that validates our deepest truths, we can see what we are evolving into, and what that means in terms of what we experience, what we value, and how we act.

Gary Zukav, author of The Seat of the Soul

Donald Trump's presidency and the destructive forces it unleashed are a mental health emergency as well as a public health emergency in general. Trump may no longer be president, but his fascist political movement and the political party he controls continue to cause harm.

Chauncey Devega, senior politics writer for Salon

Introduction

This chapter builds on information presented in Chapter 7 which details the mental health crisis in these perilous political times. In doing so, a new comprehensive theoretical framework is presented, entitled the *integral theory of mental health and human development from a psycho-political perspective.* This new theory is detailed in this chapter.

The following information details four quadrants that constitute the non-fragmented, comprehensive, and truly holistic nature of the new integral theory discussed in this chapter. Key foundational concepts of the new integral theory are grounded in the earlier work of other integral theorists. This includes the theoretical work of Ken Wilber and Raúl Quiñones Rosado.

Ken Wilber and Raúl Quiñones Rosado's Integral Theories

Ken Wilber and Raúl Quiñones Rosado are recognized as two of the most respected integral theorists in our society. Ken Wilber's groundbreaking book entitled, *Integral Psychology: Consciousness, Spirit, Psychology, and Therapy,* published in 2000, provides an in-depth description of the rudiments of his original integral theory.

Raúl Quiñones Rosado's equally important book entitled, *Consciousness-in-Action: Toward an Integral Psychology of Liberation and Transformation,* extends and deepens one's understanding of Wilber's integral theory. It does so by spotlighting the relevance of cultural and social justice issues. Both of these authors emphasize the importance of evolving beyond the reductionist, fragmented, and non-holistic way of thinking that continue to dominate the mental health professions into a non-fragmented, multidimensional, comprehensive, and truly holistic consciousness.

The Integral Theory of Mental Health and Human Development: A Psycho-Political Perspective

The new integral theory of mental health and human development based on a psycho-political perspective is anchored in a threefold purpose. First, this new integral theory strives to increase readers' understanding of the multidimensional nature of our perilous times.

Second, it aims to expand readers' thinking about the implications of these times for the mental health crisis we face as a nation.

Third, the new integral theory is a response to the title of this book that explicitly asks what will happen *beyond the lies* that continue to be perpetuated among extreme right-wing MAGA movement supporters.

As noted above, this new theoretical model is comprised of four quadrants that illuminate numerous factors underlying this multidimensional helping framework. Each of these quadrants are described below.

The Individual Interior Perceptions and Meaning-Making Quadrant

The individual interior perceptions and meaning-making quadrant concentrates on people's interior psychological processes (e.g., conscious, subconscious, unconscious) and subjective constructions of one's life experiences. According to this integral theory, everyone is born with the proclivity to construct meaning of themselves and their life experiences. It could be said that this innate drive to construct meaning of one's life is part of our DNA.

Numerous human development theories published over the past several decades are helpful in understanding the different ways people construct meaning of themselves and their life experiences. Contributions by developmental theorists like Carol Gilligan (Moral Development, 1982), Allen Ivey (Developmental Counseling, 1986), Derald and David Sue (Racial/Cultural Identity Development and White Racial Identity Development, 2015), Robert Kegan (Social Maturity and Orders of Consciousness, 1982), Jane Loevinger (Ego Development, 1986), and Jean Piaget (Cognitive/Intellectual Development, 1963, 1965, 1985) are all helpful in understanding the diverse ways people construct meaning of their life experiences when operating at different lines and stages of human development.

In this section of Chapter 8, two specific developmental theories are discussed to increase the reader's knowledge and understanding of the individual interior perceptions and meaning-making quadrant. This includes a discussion of Jane Loevinger's ego development theory and Carol Gilligan's theory of female and moral development.

Before discussing the relevance of these two developmental frameworks, a couple of points are interjected below to clarify the meaning of the terms *theory* and *theories* as used in this book. The following comments about theories are aimed at increasing the reader's knowledge of the individual internal perceptions and meaning-making quadrant in the new integral theory of mental health and human development from a psycho-political perspective.

Definition of terms/concepts

A *theory* is a system of ideas intended to explain something; a set of principles upon which the practice of an activity is based; a plausible or scientifically acceptable principle or body of principles offered to explain phenomena.

As used in this book, *theories* of mental health and human development are ideas that are grounded in research findings by theorists who operate from their own personal and professional socialization. These socialization processes contribute to culturally/racially biased ideas about mental health and human development that are often inaccurately viewed as universal and objective truths.

Among the outcomes of viewing theories as objective truths is the degree to which they are often accepted as being relevant for a broad range of persons. This includes people who are socialized in different social-cultural-political contexts that result in different constructions of what mental health means and their understanding of the content and process of human development.

My own preference as a social scientist is to view such theories as stories about mental health and human development. I also view these theoretical stories as being helpful, but certainly not universal objective truths. Rather, I think of theories as valuable resources that enable us to consider patterns of our own and other people's cognitive/intellectual, emotional, behavioral, neurological, and cultural development within a specific social-political context during these perilous times.

I remain mindful of the importance of being tentative in our interpretations of mental health and human development. We can anchor this tentativeness in the realization that developmental and mental health theories are commonly modified as a result of the ongoing evolution of the mental health professions. This ongoing evolution emerges from new research findings that revise and, in some instances, contradict previous ways of thinking about mental health and human development.

The following sections of this chapter draw from two different theories of human development as they tentatively describe plausible and scientifically acceptable principles related to mental health and human development from a psycho-political perspective. The two developmental theories discussed below are relevant in expanding the reader's knowledge of the adverse impact of Trump's personality, leadership style, and his continuing political presence as well as the millions of people who persist in supporting him.

Based on the research findings presented in Chapter 7, it is apparent that new theories of mental health are needed to effectively address our nation's mental health crisis. Chapter 8 is designed to stimulate new thinking about the complexity of mental health and human development from a psycho-political perspective that fits the individual internal perceptions and meaning-making quadrant of the integral theory discussed in this book. This new thinking is advanced by learning more about a concept referred to as *optimal mental health* discussed in Chapter 9.

The reader's attention is now directed to a discussion of Jane Loevinger's ego development theory. This discussion is followed by a description of key points related to Carol Gilligan's female and moral development theory that illuminate an ethic of care. Several suggestions are also presented in this chapter and offered as conversation starters in responding to one of the main purposes of this book; to assess what our collective future will bring beyond the lies that continue to be promoted by Donald Trump, his supporters in general and members of the Trump cult in particular (See Chapter 6).

Jane Loevinger's Ego Development Theory

Jane Loevinger's theory is comprised of five stages or phases of self-development. I refer to the changes described in Loevinger's theory as a theory of people's consciousness development. They include the impulsive, self-protective, conformist, conscientious, and autonomous/integrated stages. A brief description of key characteristics related to these stages is presented below.

The Impulsive Stage – Persons operating at this stage of consciousness generally lack impulse control while simultaneously striving to have their interests, goals, and needs addressed as soon as possible. While this stage generally characterizes the development of young children, there are individuals whose cognitive processes, emotional reactions, and behavior patterns fit this stage well into adulthood.

The on-going manifestation of this developmental phenomenon is, in part, due to a neurological concept referred to as *developmental stagnation*. This concept is discussed in greater detail in Chapter 14.

The Self-Protective Stage – Persons operating at this stage have greater impulse control than persons at the preceding stage. However, they commonly exhibit a heightened motivation to satisfy their own ego-centric needs and drives by disregarding cultural norms of civility, mutual respect, organizational policies, and/or legal statutes. While this developmental stage is typically exhibited among youngsters in middle/late childhood and early adolescence, some persons continue to manifest characteristics of this developmental phase during adulthood due to *neurological stagnation;* a theoretical concept also described in greater detail in Chapter 14.

The Conformist Stage – At this stage of human consciousness development, people are less motivated by external rewards and punishments. They increasingly view the meaning of life and their personal happiness intertwined with the fate of a group or groups they have learned to self-identify.

Both conformity and loyalty to such groups are main characteristics manifested among people operating from this developmental stage of human consciousness. Research suggests that many adults stagnate at this developmental stage for extended periods of time as central characteristics of the conformist stage are reflected in their personal, interpersonal, work, and political lives.

The Self-Aware Stage – Individuals operating at this stage of consciousness exhibit less enthusiasm to conform to all of the norms, values, and beliefs of a group that had previously provided meaning and happiness in their lives. Realizing a greater level of cognitive complexity at this stage enables people to exhibit new moral reasoning and problem-solving skills that underlie one's reduced interest in group conformity.

Persons generally operating from this developmental stage commonly exhibit a greater level of authenticity, honesty, and self-reflection in their personal relationships. Research findings indicate that a majority of American adults operate from this developmental stage.

The Autonomous/Integrated Stage – As people progress to higher levels of consciousness development, they become interested in questions of a more philosophical nature. These persons demonstrate greater complexity in their thinking and heightened levels of impulse control and emotional regulation in their interpersonal interactions with other people, including persons operating at different developmental stages than themselves.

The following information provides new ways of thinking about Donald Trump's personality and leadership style as well as his supporters' loyalty by referring to Loevinger's developmental theory. For full disclosure, the information provided in the next section of this chapter is not designed to make a psychiatric diagnosis of Donald Trump or his supporters.

Making a diagnosis of someone without conducting a direct interview with that individual is a violation of professional ethics. On the other hand, I agree with the important points made by numerous mental health professionals about their ethical duty to issue warnings about persons who are a danger to their communities and our nation at-large (Lee, 2017).

Loevinger's Ego Development Theory, Trump's Personality/Leadership Style, and the Trump Cult

Numerous persons in different disciplines have commented on the many volatile emotional reactions Donald Trump routinely manifested as President of the United States. These impulsive outbursts represent examples of Trump's lack of emotional regulation, which is an important characteristic of Loevinger's impulsive stage of consciousness development.

Additional reports of Trump's failure to regularly demonstrate emotional regulation is further marked by consistent patterns of blaming other people for his insensitivities, directing demeaning and rude comments to journalists and political competitors as well as his persistence in referring to false hoaxes and conspiracy theories to explain his personal and political failures. These ways of thinking and behaving are consistent with the description of the self-protective stage of ego development.

Information presented in Chapter 6 points to the heightened and often unquestionable conformity many people, who self-identify as a part of Trump's MAGA movement, publicly and privately exhibit their support for and loyalty to Trumpism. This heightened conformity, which is driven by a lack of critical thinking and unquestionable loyalty to Donald Trump, are important characteristics of Loevinger's conformist stage. It is further asserted that the high level of unquestioned conformity and loyalty manifested by many Trump supporters, especially among members of the Trump cult, are not reflective of optimal mental health that is discussed further in Chapter 9.

Carol Gilligan's Moral Development Theory, Trump's Personality/Leadership Style, and the Trump Cult

Carol Gilligan is another developmental theorist whose extensive research resulted in the creation of a new theory of female and moral development. In her theory, Gilligan describes the developmental unfolding ethic of caring that is an important part of a person's moral development. This developmental unfolding is reflected in three distinct phases of moral consciousness.

As used in the new integral theory of mental health and human development described in this book and as adapted from Gilligan's moral development theory, three stages of people's moral consciousness development are referred to as: [1] the *me/selfishness consciousness stage,* [2] the caring for people like us consciousness stage, and [3] the caring for all of us consciousness stage of moral development*

The Me/Selfishness Level of Moral Reasoning

The me/selfishness level of moral reasoning is similar to Loevinger's impulsive and self-protective ego development stages. This moral development consciousness is marked by a dominant egocentricity and self-absorption as well as low levels of emotional regulation and a lack of empathy for other persons.

People operating from the me/selfishness level of moral development direct little attention to other people's thoughts and feelings. They also exhibit rigid thinking and a stubborn commitment to achieve one's goals, ambitions, and success over other people's needs and desires. Trump commonly exhibits characteristics associated with the me/selfishness level of moral development (See Chapter 5).

The Caring for People Like Us Phase of Moral Development

The caring for *people like us* phase of moral consciousness development is similar to Loevinger's conformist stage of ego development. At this point in one's consciousness, individuals are strongly motivated to demonstrate their caring for and conformity to a group that one personally identifies. People generally operating from this stage find meaning and comfort in being a part of something bigger than themselves with like-minded persons who are committed to similar values and beliefs. These developmental characteristics are detailed in an earlier discussion of the psychology of Trump's supporters and particularly persons identified as being part of Trump's cult (See Chapter 6).

The Caring for All of Us Consciousness: A Universal Moral Ethic

According to the new integral theory presented in this chapter, the process of people's moral development may potentially continue to unfold at a third level of human consciousness. This level of moral reasoning is anchored in a universal caring for persons in all human groups.

Realizing their potential to develop more complex aspects of one's capacity for increased moral consciousness, these persons manifest the sort of thinking, feeling, and actions that are linked to the third developmental level described above. This commonly results in these persons expressing authentic concern and caring for the impact individuals, societal organizations, political decisions, and professional groups have on the well-being of persons in local, state, national and global communities.

The three stages/levels of moral consciousness development along with Loevinger's stages of ego development are important components of the individual interior perceptions and meaning-making quadrant. That quadrant is an important component of the new integral theory discussed in this book. The following section directs the reader's attention to a second quadrant that adds to one's understanding of the comprehensive, non-fragmented, truly holistic nature of the new integral theory of mental health and human development from a psycho-political perspective.

The Neurological/Brain-Functioning Quadrant

The second quadrant in the integral theory directs attention to neurological/brain-functioning factors as they impact the way people think, feel, act, and develop. Advances in neuroscience are having an increasing impact on the mental health professions. Neuroscientists continue to add to the ever-expanding knowledgebase that increases our understanding of the relevance of neuroscience and brain functioning for people's mental health and ongoing development.

Given space limitations in this book, it is not possible to provide a detailed discussion of the many factors that are relevant in understanding how people's neurological system in general and brain-functioning in particular impact people's mental health and sense of well-being. Despite such limitations, the following information describes central factors that are designed to assist readers in acquiring an increased understanding of critical variables related to neurological development and brain-functioning processes from an integral perspective.

First, the reader's attention is directed to information that describes the evolution of the human brain. Second, readers will be presented with information aimed at expanding their knowledge of the meaning and importance of the *brain network differentiation* and *integration* for people's mental health and ongoing development. Additional information related to the neurological/brain-functioning quadrant is provided in Chapter 14 in a discussion of neuro-counseling theory and its relevance for addressing the mental health crisis in our nation.

The Evolution of the Human Brain

The evolution of the human brain was described by the American physician and neuroscientist Paul MacLean in the 1960s. According to Dr. MacLean, the evolution of the human brain resulted in the development of three major brain parts collectively referred to as the *triune brain*. The triune brain consists of the reptilian complex (the brain stem and basal ganglia), the paleomammalian complex (the limbic system), and the neomammalian complex (the neocortex).

The first evolutionary stage of the human brain comes from the reptilian complex and is responsible for primal instincts as well as the regulation of autonomic bodily systems. This includes the automatic regulation of our respiratory, cardiac, digestive, and immunological systems as well as maintaining our body temperature and blood pressure. As the title suggests, the reptilian complex represents the total brain of reptiles and, in a unique evolutionary way, connects us with the reptilian species.

The paleomammalian complex or limbic system is about the size of an almond. This brain complex is located approximately three inches from the top and center of one's skull. The limbic system is largely responsible for processing memories and regulating emotions. It is comprised of the hippocampus and amygdala.

The complete paleomammalian brain consists of the brain stem and basal ganglia as well as the limbic system. This evolutionary process resulted in the development of a brain stem, basal ganglia and a limbic system which, in another unique neurological way, connects us with other mammals.

The third evolutionary part of the triune brain consists of the development of the neocortex (the large grey matter covering the entire brain). This brain material includes the prefrontal lobe (directly behind our forehead) where higher cognitive functioning originates.

Brain Differentiation and Integration

In his book entitled, *A Pocket Guide to Interpersonal Neurobiology*, Dr. Daniel Siegel describes the importance of understanding how the processes of *brain differentiation* and *brain integration* are essential in fostering optimal brain functioning. From the perspective of the neurological/brain-functioning quadrant, a central component in the new integral theory, it is important to understand that optimal human brain development is marked by these two vital aspects of mental health.

The first of these processes involves an increasing differentiation of various brain networks. This brain network differentiation is necessary for people to realize their potential for optimal brain functioning. It begins in utero as the fetus manifests elementary brain networks during the mother's pregnancy. The formation of these differentiated brain networks is further developed during one's childhood, adolescence and adulthood.

A second critical neurological process that complements *brain differentiation* is *brain integration.* The neurological integration process is at the heart of interpersonal neurobiology, a new field developed by Dr. Siegel. Defined as the linkage of differentiated components of the brain system, *brain integration* is viewed as a core mechanism in the cultivation of mental health through advanced synaptic connections.

Siegel relies on his research findings to further indicate that the result of brain integration is "kindness, resilience, and health." His research findings led him to assert that such integrated linkages further "enable more intricate functions to emerge—such as insight, empathy, intuition, and morality." According to Siegel, sustained outcomes of the neurological integration process are a coherent mind, empathic relationships, and fuller brain network interconnections in multiple parts of the human brain.

In interpersonal relationships, neurological integration entails each person being respected for his or her autonomy and differentiated self, while at the same time being linked to others in empathic communication. Ongoing research findings contribute to increasing understanding of the ways that brain network differentiation and integration correlate with the manifestation of *optimal mental health;* an important component of the new integral theory and is detailed in Chapter 9.

The Cultural Quadrant

The third quadrant in the integral theory of mental health and human development from a psycho-political perspective provides readers with new knowledge regarding *cultural evolution.* While this section of Chapter 8 is designed to increase readers' understanding of the meaning of cultural evolution, it is useful to point out that this information is complemented by additional information related to *cultural/racial identity development theories.*

Mental health researchers and theorists, who self-identify as multicultural counseling and social justice advocates, have made major contributions in publishing journal articles, book chapters, and entire books that clarify the content and process of cultural/racial identity development theories. These contributions are summarized in greater detail in Chapter 13.

Compared to the existing knowledge related to cultural/racial identity development theories, there is a dearth of information related to the meaning and relevance of cultural evolution for the mental health professions. The lack of people's understanding of the relevance of cultural evolution for our nation's mental health is a potential barrier to more fully understanding the importance of this quadrant for the new integral theory.

Definition of Cultural Evolution

Cultural evolution is defined as changes in socially transmitted beliefs, knowledge, customs, skills, attitudes, and/or languages. This definition highlights the ways that this developmental process affects changes in people's way of thinking, feeling, and responding to life experiences. The people who supported the American Revolution against the King of England and the individuals who supported the Union in the United States's Civil War were involved in actions that contributed to the cultural evolution of American democracy and support for the eradication of slavery in our nation.

These evolutionary advances are anchored in new learning from members of their cultural groups through their imitation, teaching, and other forms of social transmission. At its most basic level, cultural evolution involves a noticeable shift from a simpler consciousness to a more complex and more accurate awareness and understanding of the ways that racial injustices impair millions of people's mental health as well as the unveiling of injurious contradictions to American democracy.

Building on the above definition of cultural evolution, the new integral theory acknowledges that people who self-identify with various racial/ethnic groups engage in unique forms of cultural evolution that have been impacted by historical events in general and the perpetuation of White supremacy and White racism in particular.

The ongoing cultural evolution in Black communities is manifested in many ways among persons of African descent. Such evolutionary endeavors persisted from the slavery era through the brief Reconstruction years (1866-1877); perpetuated during the Jim Crow era (1876–1965); and continuing in the civil and human rights movements from the 1960 to the present time.

Many Black religious/spiritual/political/racial justice leaders throughout the history of the United States contributed in many important ways to the ongoing cultural evolution of African American communities. A partial list of these evolutionary contributors include: Frederick Douglass, Shirley Chisholm, James Baldwin, Arthur Ashe, Medgar Evers, Bayard Rustin, Sojourner Truth, Fannie Lou Hamer, Rosa Parks, Angela Davis, Huey Newton, Bobby Seale, Fred Hampton, Mohammed Ali, Malcolm X, Hurricane Carter, Martin Luther King Jr., Jesse Jackson, James Brown, Aretha Franklin, and countless others who risked their own safety and well-being to stimulate evolutionary changes among their people. These cultural truth-tellers operate as stimulators in promoting the ongoing evolution of persons of African descent and the communities where they live and work.

It is readily acknowledged that race relations in our country have improved in a variety of ways over the past several decades. However, the resurgence and multidimensional nature of White supremacy and White racism reflected in Donald Trump's leadership style and the substantial popularity of Trumpism (reflected in the more than 74 million persons who voted for Trump in the 2020 presidential elections) has resulted in what I refer to as *White cultural devolution* (D'Andrea, 2017). Future national elections will help to determine the ongoing viability or demise of this White cultural devolution.

The ongoing cultural evolution among people of color combined with the increasing demographic transformation across our nation (See Chapter 1) both contribute to a rise in various forms of political activism, especially among Black and Brown persons. Given these evolutionary dynamics, many people (including the author of this book) predict that the continuing White cultural devolution will motivate persons in marginalized groups to expand their collective resistance to the authoritarianism and fascism that continue to persist in the Age of Trump.

All of the issues related to cultural evolution and cultural devolution described above will continue to have an important impact on these perilous times and the mental health of our nation. These issues are further discussed in the next quadrant of the new integral theory of mental health and development from a psycho-political perspective.

The Societal/Political/Professional Quadrant

Throughout this book, I intentionally report on numerous research findings and provide theoretical references that link the perilous political times in which we are situated to the mental health crisis in our nation. The combination of these psycho-political dynamics is leading many persons both in the general public and the helping professions to raise questions about the overall mental health of our nation. While many of these dynamics are detailed in Chapter 9, I provide a partial list of the social-political-cultural factors that contribute to our perilous times and the mental health crisis in the United States below:

- The unprecedented level of gun violence and mass shootings in our society are not indicative of mental health in general and optimal mental health in our society in particular;

- The perpetuation of poverty in the richest country in the world that strangles the developmental potential of millions of persons is a major factor contributing to the current mental health crisis in our country;

- The belief that there is no alternative except to maintain annual increased military funding to ensure peace in our world is not indicative of mental health in general and optimal mental health in our society in particular;

- The denial of climate warming and the overall global environmental crisis among Donald Trump and millions of his supporters despite the scientific evidence indicating that failure to implement major policies and actions to ameliorate these problems will result in the end of the long-term viability of the human species is not indicative of mental health in general and optimal mental health in our society in particular; and

- The rising threat of nuclear war, its total annihilation of our planet and the human species along with the failure of the United States to initiate efforts that result in the complete dismantling of all nuclear weapons in our world is not indicative of mental health in general and optimal mental health in particular.

The few examples outlined above are part of a broader gestalt of factors that fuel questions about the sanity and/or insanity of our society. This gestalt has also led to the development of new terms and concepts that expand our thinking about the meaning of optimal mental health from a psycho-political perspective.

Several new concepts, strategies, and interventions are discussed in this book to promote a more complex understanding of optimal mental health from a psycho-political perspective. This includes defining the meaning and relevance of such terms as a *mass psychology in the Age of Trump* as described by Jost and Hunyady, the meaning of the term *a sane society* as discussed by Erich Fromm, what Dr. Robert Lifton calls a *malignant normality*, what Dr. Bandy Lee refers to as a *shared psychosis*, and what Dr. Gabor Maté calls *the myth of normal* for the new integral theory of mental health and human development. Learning about the meaning and relevance of the above stated terms and concepts are important in understanding the diverse roles and functions people in the general public as well as mental health professionals can play in building a saner society by nurturing a greater level of optimal mental health in communities across the United States. Recognizing the importance of assisting readers to gain expanded thinking about the above listed terms and concepts, they are more deeply addressed in Chapter 9.

Emphasizing the Intimate Interconnections of All Four quadrants

There are numerous differences between the integral theory of mental health and human development from a psycho-political perspective and traditional psychology, counseling, and human development theories. These traditional theories are criticized for being fragmented, reductionist, and not truly holistic. Evidence supporting the latter point is reflected in the failure of many (perhaps most) mental health professions, faculty members, and practitioners to incorporate psycho-political factors when assessing the mental health of individuals and the communities where they live and work (Ivey, D'Andrea, & Ivey, 2012).

In contrast, the new integral theory operates with great intentionality and vigor to be a comprehensive, integrative, non-fragmented, non-reductionist, and a truly holistic approach to mental health and human development. These are all characteristics of the new integral theory that distinguishes it from traditional psychology, counseling, and human development theories.

My research indicated that psycho-political factors are infrequently included in traditional psychology, counseling, and human development theories. This is in sharp contrast to the numerous ways psycho-political factors are analyzed to more fully and accurately understand the impact of these factors on people's mental health and ongoing development.

The following section of this chapter illuminates the sort of intimate interconnections and interactions the four quadrants that comprise the integral theory have with one another. In the following case study, I use an integral approach to assess reactions Trump supporters typically experience when attending his popular political rallies.

A Case Study Using the New Integral theory

Recognizing his power as the charismatic leader of the MAGA movement, Donald Trump quickly begins his rallies by enthusiastically articulating the shared thoughts and feelings that bond attendees with himself. This approach reinforces the attendees' strong political meaning-making mechanism; a crucial characteristic of the individual internal meaning-making quadrant discussed above.

Remembering the important role emotions play in Trump's popularity (See Chapter 6), he intentionally and consistently stimulates specific emotions in his supporters with his charismatic verbalizations during his political rallies. These emotional reactions include but are not limited to his supporters' collective frustration, hostility, and anger over the political policies advanced by what Trump and his supporters identify as extreme socialist left-wing democratic politicians. These emotional reactions are activated neurologically in the limbic system (a fundamental characteristic of the neurological/brain-functioning quadrant).

In addition to this neurological activation, Trump's persistent use of negative descriptors when discussing persons in marginalized groups as well as his perceived political enemies can simultaneously reinforce new and/or existing negative cultural/racial beliefs and biases among Trump supporters. These reactions are grounded in the Cultural Quadrant of the integral theory of mental health and human development.

An awareness of the comprehensive, non-fragmented, integrative, and truly holistic nature of the new integral theory leads mental health professionals to include an assessment of the impact of the various factors that comprise the societal/political/professional quadrant and their impact on the individual internal meaning-making quadrant, the neurological/brain-functioning quadrant, and the cultural quadrant. This might include assessing how psycho-political factors such as structural racism, White supremacy, and the level of social justice advocacy services designed to ameliorate these societal cancers are or could be implemented as part of an integral assessment that leads to new treatment planning for individuals and the community at-large.

Addressing the Rise of Cultural Wars

Journalistic researchers have discussed how Trump and his supporters are promoting *cultural wars* in the United States. In doing so, the stakes in defending our country's democracy increase geometrically. However, what is often missing in researchers' findings about the rise of cultural wars is the failure to acknowledge how the anti-democratic nature of cultural wars is a continuation of the long history of White supremacy and White racism in our society.

Essentially, the rise of *cultural wars* in the United States is intentionally designed to replace our nation's democracy with Donald Trump's and Ron DeSantis's styled authoritarianism and fascism (See Chapter 1). Three major factors are described below to assist readers in expanding their thinking about the meaning of cultural wars at this point in the history of the United States.

The first factor energizing our country's cultural wars is the increasing awareness, fear, and anger related to the unprecedented demographic transformation of the United States (See Chapters 1 and 2). These reactions are magnified by the continuing immigration crisis at our country's southern border.

A second factor related to the rising cultural wars in the United States is the attacks by Republican Party leaders and Trump supporters who back the banning of thousands of books in our public school libraries and prohibiting teachers from teaching about Black history as well as issues related to gay, lesbian, bisexual, and transgender people in developmentally appropriate and respectful ways.

Third, throughout this book, it has repeatedly been noted that the toxic realities of White supremacy and White racism continue to be an inherent aspect of our national heritage and current threats to our democracy. The current manifestation of the different dimensions of the cultural wars is an extension of the racial injustices, oppression, and state-sanctioned violence that continue to be foundational principles among Donald Trump and his MAGA supporters. Thus, it is important to be aware that today's cultural wars are evidence of the historic sustainability of White supremacy and White racism in the United States in the 21st century.

The above-stated factors associated with cultural wars are particularly relevant for the cultural and societal/political/professional quadrants that comprise the integral theory of mental health and human development from a psycho-political perspective.

Additional discussions of the *cultural evolution* and *cultural devolution* in our country's history and the present time are, in part, activated by the way individuals construct meaning of the various psycho-political dynamics occurring in our society (a key aspect in the individual interior perceptions and meaning-making quadrant). The thoughts, feelings, and actions that result from cultural evolution and cultural devolution are anchored in the neurological/brain-functioning quadrant.

Summary

This chapter builds on many of the points made in Chapter 7. In the preceding chapter, research findings focused on the current mental health crisis in our nation. Chapter 7 includes suggestions for dealing with this crisis which were further defined in the integral theory of mental health and human development in this chapter. This discussion included a description of the four quadrants that comprise this new integral theory and their simultaneous intimate interconnections.

The first quadrant in this new integral theory is the individual interior perceptions and meaning-making quadrant. In that section of Chapter 8, two theories of human development are discussed with particular attention to the relevance of these developmental theories for the new integral theory. These developmental theories include a description of the stages of Jane Loevinger's theory of ego/personal development and Carol Gilligan's moral development theory. The information presented in this section of Chapter 8 is used to assess Trump and his supporters' personal and moral development.

The second quadrant focuses on the relevance of neurological and brain-functioning processes for people's mental health and development during the Age of Trump. Specific attention is directed to discussing the evolution of the human brain as well as brain differentiation and integration as these two neurological processes relate to people's mental health and ongoing development.

The third quadrant, the cultural quadrant, introduces the relevance of two new terms and concepts as well as their relevance for the new integral theory. These concepts are referred to as *cultural evolution* and *White cultural devolution*.

The fourth quadrant, the societal/political/professional quadrant is presented in the latter part of this chapter. This quadrant introduces a number of new terms and concepts of particular relevance in expanding readers' understanding of these perilous times and the mental health crisis in the United States.

The new terms and concepts introduced in this section of Chapter 8 and more thoroughly unpacked in the ensuing chapter include: descriptive information related to differences between a sane and *not-so-sane society;* the meaning of a *mass psychology in the Age of Trump;* clarification of the definition of a *malignant normality,* a discussion of the meaning of a *shared psychosis,* and a concept that Dr. Gabor Maté calls *the myth of normal* (2022).

The new integral theory of mental health and human development based on a psycho-political perspective is different from other traditional theories of mental health and human development in several ways. The continuing dominance of traditional theories of counseling, psychology, mental health, and human development are criticized for being reductionist in their explanation of mental health problems and fragmented in their theoretical assumptions of human development despite asserting being holistic in their assessment and intervention strategies.

In contrast, the new integral theory of mental health and human development from a psycho-political perspective is intentionally grounded in comprehensive, non-reductionistic, non-fragmented and more fully holistic principles. In addition to these distinguishing characteristics is the importance of ensuring that the factors comprising the four quadrants operate in intimately harmonious and complementary ways. The final section of Chapter 8 details the intimate interconnections that all four quadrants have with each other.

The next chapter begins with the view that the perilous times and threats to our democracy are subsiding at least for the time being. Data supporting this view is anchored in the election losses for Trump and Republican Party candidates supportive of the MAGA movement during the 2020 presidential and 2022 midterm elections.

Over 1000 persons participating in the January 6, 2021 violent insurrection aimed at overthrowing the U.S. government have been charged with various federal violations. A growing number of these persons have been found guilty of different charges resulting in lengthy prison terms. These judicial actions are particularly important in holding persons accountable for violating laws aimed at protecting our nation's democracy.

The House Committee report on the January 6, 2021 insurrection resulted in over 1500 interviews as well as a series of nationally televised public hearings and the publication of a final 850-page report detailing the Committee's investigative findings. Survey polls taken during and after these public hearings resulted in increasing numbers of persons indicating they believe Trump played a major role in rousing his supporters to participate in the violent insurrection.

Increasing research publications are emerging that are authored by respected mental health professionals in both professional and public news outlets. All of these endeavors are evidence that new ideas and suggestions for dealing with the nation's mental health crisis have entered into mainstream discussions.

Chapter 9 discusses the emergence of a new *awakening* in our society and its relevance for these perilous times, the ongoing threats to our democracy, demographic changes occurring in our society, and in new suggestions to address the mental health crisis in the United States.

CHAPTER 9

AWAKENING

Nothing is more common than the idea that we, the people living in the Western world of the 20th century, are eminently sane. Even the fact that a great number of individuals in our midst suffer from more or less severe forms of mental illness produces little doubt with respect to the general standard of our mental health. We are sure that by introducing better methods of mental hygiene we shall improve still further the state of our mental health, and as far as individual mental disturbances are concerned, we look at them as strictly individual incidents, perhaps with some amazement that so many of these incidents should occur in a culture that is supposed to be sane.

Many psychiatrists and psychologists refuse to entertain the idea that society as a whole may be lacking in sanity. They hold that the problem of mental health in a society is only that of the number of "unadjusted" individuals, and not that of a possible adjustment of the culture itself. This book— The Sane Society— deals with the latter problem; not with individual pathology, but with the pathology of normalcy, particularly the pathology of contemporary Western society.

Erich Fromm, The Sane Society, 1955

Human beings are malleable creatures. We adjust to many different kinds and levels of pathology. Why? We actually live in a pretty violent world. As such we are very adaptable. This is how a society can have an immense amount of pathology and many different kinds of atrocities can occur— and yet the population adjusts. As a person or society falls into a more pathological state, an individual or populace starts to actually feel that things are not that wrong. Our ability to recognize that something is a problem starts to diminish, as a person or society falls ever more deeply into the pathology and collective sickness of an insane society.

Dr. Bandy X. Lee, president of the World Mental Health Coalition

Introduction

This chapter builds on a number of points made in Chapter 8. It does so by opening a discussion of the perceived degree to which most people believe our society is a sane society. It also describes numerous ways our society fails to meet the definition of sanity. In the past, this concept has been researched and discussed by a relatively small number of mental health researchers and practitioners. This includes the work of Theodor W. Adorno, Elise Frankel-Brunswik, Daniel Levinson, and Nevit Sanford in the 1940s as well as Erich Fromm in the mid-1950s.

A growing number of mental health professionals have more recently focused on issues related to the failure of our own nation to operate as a sane society and the negative implications of this phenomenon for people's mental health and ongoing development. A partial list of these professionals includes John Jost and Orsolya Hunyady (2018), Robert Lipton (2017), Bandi Lee (2020), and Gabor Maté (2022) to name a few. Contributions made by these persons are stimulating new awakenings within the mental health professions as well as among increasing numbers of persons in the general public.

This observable lack of sanity in our society is further sustained by a toxic psycho-political process referred to as *cultural wars*. As briefly stated in the preceding chapter, the term, *cultural wars*, is increasingly used in discussions about the social-psychological-emotional-political divisiveness that marks our nation's interests, values, goals, and discussions. As used in this chapter and elsewhere in this book, cultural wars is defined as cultural/racial conflicts manifested between social groups (See Chapter 8).

These conflicts are often perpetuated by persons vying for the dominance of their social-political values, beliefs, and practices. The opposite of cultural wars is when people from different cultural/racial groups strive to communicate in respectful ways, learn from one another, and demonstrate a genuine commitment to support the ongoing evolution of our multiracial/multicultural democracy as we build a saner society.

Erich Fromm's Sane Society

Erich Fromm's 1955 book entitled *A Sane Society* is one of the most *frequently referenced resources* related to this topic. The following points taken directly from his book provide an overview of central points related to Fromm's view of a sane society.

> While modernity has increased the material wealth and comfort of the human race, it has also wrought major wars that killed millions, during which every participant firmly believed that he was fighting in his self-defense, for his honor, or that he was backed up by God. In a sentiment of chilling pertinence today, after more than half a century of alleged progress has drowned us in mind-numbing commercial media and left us to helplessly watch military budgets swell at the expense of funding for the arts and humanities.

> What is so deceptive about the state of mind of the members of our society is the *consensual validation* of their thinking about mental health. It is naively assumed that the fact that the majority of people share certain ideas or feelings proves the validity of these ideas and feelings.

> Nothing is further from the truth. Consensual validation as such has no bearing whatsoever on reason or mental health… The fact that millions of people share the same vices does not make these vices virtues, the fact that they share so many errors does not make the errors to be truths, and the fact that millions of people share the same forms of mental pathology does not make these people sane.

In offering a recipe for creating a sane society, it is important to get out of the rut in which we are moving, and to take the next step in the birth and self-realization of humanity. The first condition in realizing this aspect of a sane society is the abolishment of the war threat hanging over all of us now and paralyzing faith and initiative. We must take the responsibility for the life of all people, and develop, on an international scale, what all great countries have developed internally, a relative sharing of wealth and a new and more just division of economic resources. This must lead eventually to forms of international economic co-operation and planning to forms of world government and complete disarmament.

In the political sphere, it is important to return to town hall meetings by creating thousands of small face-to-face groups, which are well informed and whose decisions are integrated in a new social order.

Man can protect himself from the consequences of his own madness only by creating a sane society which conforms with the needs of man, needs which are rooted in the very conditions of his existence. A society in which man relates to man lovingly, in which he is rooted in bonds of brotherliness and solidarity; a society which gives him the possibility of transcending nature by creating rather than by destroying, in which everyone gains a sense of self by experiencing himself as the subject of his powers rather than by conformity, in which a system of orientation and devotion exists without man's needing to distort reality and to worship idols.

Like all of us, Erich Fromm was a product of the socialization processes of his time. It is hoped that the reader will understand his gender-biased language as he uses the terms "man, he, him, his" throughout his writing, emerges from Fromm's gender socialization.

Beyond this critique of his socialized writing style, Fromm outlines a number of important factors in describing his recipe for a sane society. These suggestions are important to discuss with other mental health professionals as well as any person in the general public interested in learning about the promise and pitfalls of a multiracial/multicultural democracy in our nation (See Chapters 3 & 4).

Building on Erich Fromm's Concepts of a Sane Society

In the early part of the 21st century, I was involved in researching the work of Erich Fromm and other individuals listed above. All of these authors have explicitly written about the importance of building a sane society to foster the mental health and ongoing development of larger numbers of persons from diverse groups and backgrounds than mental health professionals have done in the past.

These efforts resulted in infusing many of the research findings reported by these professionals throughout this chapter. They also resulted in an article entitled, "Can Americans Build a Sane Society?" that was published in the American Counseling Association's monthly magazine, *Counseling Today* (D'Andrea, 2002). Key points drawn from this publication are presented below as they are aimed at building on concepts published by Erich Fromm and other mental health professionals who studied issues related to a sane society and their relevance for the new theory of mental health and human development discussed throughout this book.

As outlined in the 2002 publication, it is asserted that there are numerous factors in our contemporary society which arguably confirm the ways that societal dynamics, political policies, and interpersonal interactions fall short in a sane society. These factors are summarized below.

- A society falls short in operating in a sane manner when it spends more money building weapons of mass destruction than it does on preschool education programs, feeding hungry people, or providing assistance to secure the basic needs of homeless children, adolescents and adults;

- A society has lost its moral bearing when it allows corporations and manufacturing industries to release massive toxic chemicals in our environment. These corporations and industries do so to such an extent that it not only causes physical harm and emotional concern to millions of people across the country, but also compromises the long-term viability of our planetary ecosystem in the process;

- When a society creates a justice system that treats individuals differently according to their racial background and economic class standing, incarcerates more than 2 million of its citizens in prisons that do little to rehabilitate people, and allows the government to execute a disproportionate number of people of color, that society falls short in operating as a sane society;

- When a nation has nine times more animal shelters in comparison to shelters for women victimized by domestic violence, that society has lost much of its capacity for rational compassion and sanity;

- The continuing epidemic of gun violence, in which the United States leads all other countries in the deaths and wounds from the rampart accessibility of guns in our society, is an indicator of the lack of sanity in our society; and

- When mental health practitioners continue to direct most of their efforts helping individuals adjust to the ecological systems which they are a part without directing equal time and energy to foster positive changes to toxic and unjust ecological conditions, these professionals have become part of the problem and not part of the solution in creating a sane society.

Noam Chomsky, a professor emeritus in linguistics at MIT, respected social justice and peace advocate, and author of over 100 books highlights another important factor reflecting the lack of sanity in our society. This factor involves the failure of our nation to address the continuing threat of nuclear war. Chomsky repeatedly discusses the irrationality underlying even the consideration of using nuclear weapons in modern warfare in his recent writings and public appearances.

Despite the irrationality of this threat to our global civilization, President Trump dismantled the Reagan-Gorbachev INF (Intermediate-Range Nuclear Forces) Treaty during his presidential term. He proceeded to discuss the possibility of restarting the testing of nuclear weapons with his military advisers despite the fact that such testing has not been done since 1992.

Before the end of his presidential term, Trump indicated that he was not thinking about signing a new Start Strategic Arms Reduction Treaty with Russia or Iran. From the perspective of the new integral theory of mental health and human development described in this book, the refusal of elected leaders in the United States to initiate serious discussions with all countries that have developed nuclear weapons is another example of how our society is not operating in a sane manner.

Some readers may assert that the above listed factors are primarily political issues and should not be included in the purview and responsibility of mental health professionals. In contrast, this book introduces a new integral theory that embraces a *psycho-political perspective.* This perspective is, in part, aimed at assessing insane threats such as those described above to foster a saner society while simultaneously promoting mental health and human development in our nation.

Early in this book, the term, *psycho-political perspective,* was defined as an understanding of the dynamic interaction between mental health, human development, and politics. It denotes the psychological, emotional, and behavioral impact of politics and political structures, policies, expectations, and governance on human development for better or worse (See Chapter 1).

The above listed factors are variables that undermine our country's ability to realize its full potential as a sane society. This point is a cornerstone of the new integral theory of mental health and human development from a psycho-political perspective.

Two additional points are made here. The first point is that the new integral theory is consistent with the importance of mental health professionals conducting a truly comprehensive and holistic assessment of all the factors that impact people's mental health. This includes assessing the impact of various psycho-political experiences on people's mental health and development.

The second point is the ethical need to use a comprehensive and holistic assessment approach when implementing interventions aimed at stimulating healthy human development. This necessitates understanding the meaning and relevance of people's *collective consciousness, mass psychologies,* and *malignant normalcy* from the perspective of the new integral theory.

What is the Meaning of a Collective Consciousness?

Collective consciousness is defined as a sociological and psychological concept that refers to common ideas, attitudes, beliefs, and knowledge shared amongst a social group, organization, or society at-large.

This shared understanding of societal norms serves as a key foundation for an individual's sense of personal identity and self-worth within a broad psycho-political context. It was first described by sociologist Emile Durkheim who sought to assess how and why individuals form groups or societies with one another.

Durkheim came to believe that, at the societal level, people's beliefs, values, and knowledge are psychologically linked together to form a *collective consciousness*. Durkheim defined this concept as a shared way of thinking or understanding the world. He also believed that societies exist due to individuals developing a collective consciousness.

Durkheim further explained how a collective consciousness is manifested in all societies throughout the world. This is because social interactions occur in every society and such interactions foster the development of a collective consciousness.

The first major theoretical force in the mental health professions is the psychodynamic theory of mental health and human development. Sigmond Freud and Alfred Adler were two of the creators of psychodynamic theory that expanded Durkheim's description of the collective consciousness. Freud and Adler's contributions in this area are detailed in Chapter 10.

Mass Psychologies in the Age of Trump

The description of the *collective consciousness* described above results in the formation of different types of *mass psychologies*. John Jost, a professor of psychology and politics at New York University and Orsolya Hunyady, a psychoanalyst in private practice in New York City, worked together to describe two distinct *mass psychologies* manifested during the Age of Trump.

The first mass psychology described by Jost and Hunyady is anchored in a well-established philosophy based on historic beliefs about White supremacy and White racism. The pervasive nature of the different forms of White racism and White supremacy that continue to be perpetuated in our nation fosters a socialization process that effects many White people's collective consciousness.

This aspect of the socialization process is central in fostering an *authoritarian mass psychology* during the Age of Trump. In addition to the historic racist roots of this collective consciousness, Donald Trump's leadership style has been effective in activating a MAGA movement among people who are susceptible to this aspect of the socialization process.

Pointing to Trump's authoritarian leadership and the rising fear, anger, and anxiety described above, Jost and Hunyady make the following points in their article entitled *Mass Psychology in the Age of Trump*:

Even before Donald Trump was elected President, many worried that his campaign style signaled a sea change in American politics—a new danger that right-wing authoritarianism would finally triumph at home. Other Republicans had been accused of dog-whistle politics, using coded language to cue subtle racial biases. But Trump makes comments that come off as overtly, unabashedly racist, sexist, and xenophobic.

For many citizens, these comments are taken as evidence of Trump's authenticity—a breath of 'fresh air' and principled opposition to 'political correctness.' To others, it has been shocking to see a successful candidate for President using such crass language and defending violence.

According to Time magazine, Trump said he would 'like to punch protesters in the face' and offered to pay the legal fees of supporters who did. His rallies were punctuated by this roar 'Get them out!'—when a dissenter began chanting or raising an anti-Trump sign at his rallies. Whatever the psychological causes, we are witnessing the rebirth of an extreme right-wing political movement that thrives under anxiety.

To gain a greater understanding of the characteristics underlying this authoritarian mass psychology, Jost and Hunyady encourage readers to explore the work of Theodor Adorno. Adorno was one of the 20th century's leading philosophers and social critics. He rose to prominence in post-war Germany in the late 1940s, producing a vast body of research findings that encompassed a range of subjects including authoritarianism.

According to Jost and Hunyady, Adorno's research findings uncovered nine characteristics comprising what he called the *authoritarian syndrome*. These psychological characteristics complement Jost and Hunyady's description of *authoritarian mass psychology*. They are also cornerstones in understanding the new integral theory of mental health and human development from a psycho-political perspective.

The nine points Adorno generated in his research endeavors as they relate to an *authoritarian mass psychology* include: (1) aggression against persons who deviate from the beliefs and norms of authoritarianism; (2) submission to idealized moral authorities; (3) uncritical acceptance of the mass psychology group's values; (4) mental rigidity and a proclivity to engage in stereotypical thinking; (5) a preoccupation with toughness and power; (6) exaggerated sexual concerns; (7) a reluctance to engage in introspection; (8) a tendency to project undesirable traits onto others; and (9) cynicism about the process of healthy human development.

The second mass psychology described by Jost and Hunyady is characterized by what is referred to as *liberalism*. As described by Jost and Hunyady:

> *Liberalism* is an ideology and system of values. The distinctive ideological contents of liberalism are openness to social change (or progressivism) and the promotion of social, economic, and political equality. If a conflict arises for liberals but not for conservatives, it is probably because liberalism prioritizes equality above all else.
>
> The liberal call for diversity (and, by extension, pluralism) is, among other things, a call to treat different values equally–to avoid elevating one over others in terms of status and respect. This applies even to conservatism.
>
> On some abstract level, liberals feel compelled to proclaim that conservative intuitions are equally acceptable, equally valuable, and equally valid to their own intuitions.
>
> At the same time, when it comes to the specific content of conservative opinions (on affirmative-action, universal healthcare, Social Security, gun control, climate change, gay rights, and so

on), liberals are convinced that conservatives are dead wrong. Strictly speaking, this conflict is not resolvable and is manifested as genuine ambivalence.

Liberals struggle to separate Trump and his actions from the people who elevated him to power, and in doing so, they retain the ability to be empathic and critical. Do conservatives engage in similar contortions of a political psychological nature? No, because their philosophy (and their psychology) does not require it.

Liberals, therefore, face a special conflict that they are especially ill-equipped to resolve: Between tolerance and the *tolerance of intolerance*. If the conflict is unavoidable, and ultimately unresolvable, one can commit to one side only at the expense of the others.

If the liberal decides that openness and acceptance matter above all, that we should never treat anyone as *the other*, and that we always need to listen, this inevitably comes at the expense of achieving progressive political goals.

In their description of *liberal mass psychology*, Jost and Hunyady explain why many adherents to liberalism become overcome with anger and extreme indignancy with Trump and his supporters. From an integral theory perspective, the roots of such anger can be traced to liberals' foundational belief in and value of equality in a democracy (the individual interior perceptions and meaning-making quadrant of the integral theory).

It is further acknowledged that maintaining openness and acceptance above all, even at the expense of progressive political goals, results in a unique and paradoxical dissonance. Resolving this dissonance has the potential to unfold new ways of thinking about the interconnections between democracy, mental health, and human development. In the process of resolving such dissonance, it is predicted that changes in the current mass liberal psychology would need to occur.

The new integral theory of mental health and human development from a psycho-political perspective supports these potential changes in ways that foster *optimal mental health* and address our nation's mental health crisis in the process. Numerous mental health professionals have written about the dangers that are associated with repeated toxic political events that become acceptable and normalized in our society. Dr. Robert Lifton refers to this phenomenon as *malignant normality*.

Malignant Normality

In describing the concept of *malignant normality*, Dr. Robert Lifton states the following:

> Our situation as American psychological professionals can be summed up in just two ideas–we can call them themes or even concepts: First, what I call *malignant normality*, which has to do with the social actuality with which we are presented as normal, all-encompassing, and unalterable; and second, our potential and crucial sense of ourselves as *witnessing professionals*.

> Concerning malignant normality, we start with an assumption that all societies, operating at various levels of consciousness, put forward ways of viewing, thinking, and behaving that are considered desirable or "normal." Yet, these criteria for normality can be affected by the political and military currents of a particular era. Such requirements may be fairly benign, but they can also be destructive to the point of evil.

> I came to the idea of malignant normality in my study of Nazi doctors. Those assigned to Auschwitz, when taking charge of the selections in the overall killing process, were simply doing what was expected of them.

> True, some were upset, even horrified, at being given this task. Yet with a certain amount of counseling—one can call it perverse psychotherapy— offered by more experienced hands, a process that included drinking heavily together and giving assurance of help and support, the great majority could overcome their anxiety sufficiently to carry through their murderous assignment.

> This was a process of *adaptation to evil* that is all too possible to initiate in such a situation. Above all, there was a *normalization of evil* that enhanced this adaptation and served to present participating doctors with the Auschwitz institution as the existing world to which one must make one's adjustments.

There is another form of malignant normality, closer to home and more recent. I have in mind the participation in torture by physicians including psychiatrists, psychologists, and other medical and psychological personnel. This reached its most extreme manifestation when two psychologists were revealed to be among architects of the CIA's torture protocol in Iraq. More than that, this malignant normality was essentially supported by the American Psychological Association in its defense of the participation of psychologists in the so-called "enhanced interrogation" techniques that spilled over into torture.

I'm not equating this American behavior with the Nazi example but, rather, suggesting that malignant normality can take different forms. And nothing does more to sustain malignant normality than its support from a large organization of professionals.

There is another kind of malignant normality, one brought about by President Trump and his administration. Judith Herman and I, in a letter to the *New York Times* in March 2017, stressed Trump's dangerous individual psychological patterns: his creation of his own reality, and his inability to manage the inevitable crises that face an American president. He has also, in various ways, violated our American institutional requirements and threatened the viability of American democracy.

Yet, because he is president and operates within the broad contours and interactions of the presidency, there is a tendency to view what he does as simply part of our democratic process—that is, as politically and even ethically normal. In this way, a dangerous precedent becomes normalized, and malignant normality comes to dominate our governing (or, one could say, our anti-governing) dynamic.

Lifton insists that this situation does not mean we are helpless as mental health professionals or as citizens of the United States. He emphasizes that we remain part of a society with considerable openness, with institutions that can still be life-enhancing and serve the truth.

The integral theory of mental health and human development is anchored in a psycho-political perspective which emphasizes the importance of acknowledging that mental health professionals, in particular, are capable of confronting the malignant normality created by Trump and his supporters in our society. To do so, Lifton (2017) adds, that "we (mental health professionals) need to combine our sense of outrage with a disciplined use of our professional knowledge and experience to address our nation's *mental health crisis*" (p. xviii).

Lifton (2017) discusses how mental health professionals failed to address another form of political insanity by supporting the malignant normality that marked the nuclear threat during the Cold War with the USSR in the following manner:

> It is not generally known that during the early Cold War period, a special governmental commission chaired by a psychiatrist and containing physicians and social scientists, was set up to help the American people achieve the desired psychological capacity to support U.S. stockpiling of nuclear weapons, cope with an anticipated nuclear attack, and overcome the fear of nuclear annihilation.
>
> The commission had the task of helping Americans accept *malignant nuclear normality*. There have also been parallel examples in the recent history of professionals who have promoted equally dangerous forms of normality in rejecting climate change.

The integral theory of mental health and human development from a psycho-political perspective agrees with Lipton when he asserts that mental health professionals do not have to serve these forms of malignant normality. As Lifton further asserts: "We are capable of using our knowledge and technical skills to expose such normality, to bear witness to its malignancies—to become witnessing professionals." In doing so, mental health professionals are able to join increasing numbers of people in our country who are experiencing a social-political awakening during these perilous times; an awakening that is similar to the social-political-cultural revolution of the 1960s.

A Psycho-Political Awakening

Upon looking up the definition of the term *awakening*, I found a number of points that were used to define this word that are helpful to keep in mind. The first item used to define awakening is, "An act of waking from sleep." Additional definitions of awakening include: "an act or moment of becoming suddenly aware of something, coming into awareness."

Based on the above definitions of awakening and as used in the new integral theory presented in this book, there is evidence to conclude that increasing numbers of people in our nation are being awakened by numerous factors discussed in this chapter. This includes:

- being concerned about the lack of sanity reflected in Trump's leadership style and his continuing popularity among his supporters;
- an increased understanding of the unhealthy aspects of our nation's socialization process that results in many people acquiring a collective consciousness marked by racial biases, frustrations and hate;
- gaining an awareness of the different mass psychologies impacting people's mental health and ongoing human development in the United States; and
- a growing cognizance of the meaning and relevance of the *malignant normality* on people's mental health and ongoing development.

At the same time, it is important to acknowledge that many Trump supporters exhibit a different kind of awakening. This awakening is largely based on:

- a growing awareness of the implications of the demographic transformation of our nation;
- an attraction to and support for the sort of authoritarian leader Donald Trump manifests as he successfully builds on his MAGA movement;
- concerns about the immigration crisis in our nation; and
- an increasing commitment to maintain the 2nd amendment as it relates to people's rights to bear arms without legal impairments.

The term *optimal mental health* has been used throughout this book. There are a number of factors that have led to the inclusion of this concept in the new integral theory of mental health and human development from a psycho-political perspective.

In addition to the detailed research findings reported in Chapter 7, the following information summarizes additional investigative findings relevant for the present discussion. These research findings are designed to extend the reader's understanding as to why it is important to awaken to the meaning of *optimal mental health* as used in the new integral theory of mental health and human development.

The first in a series of research reports focuses on increased levels of stress, anxiety, and depression linked to political-related dynamics in our society. This includes emphasizing specific research findings related to the negative impact of Donald Trump's authoritarian leadership style and other political dynamics supportive of White supremacy and White racism as well as efforts to undermine the ongoing evolution of multiracial/multicultural democracy in our nation.

Among these research findings include those published by the Associated Press-NORC Center for Public Affairs Research survey (AP-NORC) in 2021. The AP-NORC was created in conjunction with political science experts at the University of Chicago and journalists affiliated with the Associated Press.

The results of the most recent AP-NORC national survey indicated a significant increase in people's stress levels as they relate to the future and the current political climate of the United States. The AP-NORC specifically reported that, during the 2020 presidential election, 68% of Americans surveyed said the election was a significant source of stress in their lives, up from 52% in 2016.

Additional AP-NORC survey results specified that increased moderate-to-severe anxiety was expressed by a large number of adults during Trump's presidency. During that time, reports of moderate-to-severe anxiety jumped to 37.3% among survey respondents, up from 6.1 percent in 2015.

In the American Psychological Association's 2016 Stress in America survey, 63% of Americans said the future of the country was a significant source of stress and 56% stated that they were stressed by the current political climate in our nation. In the 2018 version of this survey, those numbers went up to 69% and 62% respectively.

The Commonwealth Fund implemented a study in 2020 comparing mental health issues among people in the United States with other persons in comparable high-income countries. A summary of the results of this study is presented below:

- About one-quarter of U.S. adults reported having a mental health diagnosis such as anxiety, depression or emotional distress. This is one of the highest rates among 11 high-income countries.

- While U.S. adults are among the most willing to seek professional help for emotional distress, they are among the most likely to report access and/or affordability barriers in their efforts to secure professional help for their distress.

- The United States has some of the worst mental health-related outcomes, including the highest suicide rate and second-highest drug-related death rates among comparable high-income countries.

- The U.S. has a relatively low supply of mental health workers, particularly psychologists and psychiatrists. Just one-third of U.S. primary care practitioners include mental health professionals on their teams, compared to more than 90% in the Netherlands and Sweden.

Lifepoint Health is an organization that focuses on a broad range of health issues and outcomes. In a 2022 report that draws from the results of a national survey conducted by CNN and the Kaiser Family Foundation, Lifepoint Health describes additional aspects of America's mental health crisis. It does so by addressing the following question: Where do we stand as a nation in terms of our country's mental health? As highlighted by the Lifepoint Health organization:

- 90% of Americans believe there is a mental health crisis in our nation. Nearly 50% of those who believe there is a crisis also noted there was a severe mental health crisis in their own families;

- The survey went on to ask respondents what factors they think have contributed to this growing crisis. A majority of the respondents stated that the opioid epidemic, mental health issues in children and teens, and severe mental illness in adults are among the most prominent factors;

- The survey results also reflected a growing need for behavioral health treatment for children, teens and adults with a majority of the respondents expressing frustration that they don't have access to prompt and effective treatment;
- 55% of the respondents stated there is not enough mental health providers;
- 62% are afraid of the stigma attached to having a behavioral health issue;
- 80% indicated the high cost of receiving mental healthcare was a major barrier; and
- 63% say there are not enough mental health providers who take insurance.

With all of the research findings reported in Chapter 7, along with the statistics presented in this chapter, five important comments can be accurately asserted about our nation's mental health system.

First, there are serious problems in our mental health system.

Second, most of the people in the United States are aware that there are serious problems in our country's mental health system.

Third, most mental health professionals are aware of various factors that contribute to our mental health crisis.

Fourth, mental health practitioners and their professional organizations have not effectively addressed the multidimensionality of this nation's mental health crisis.

Fifth, the term *optimal mental health* not only relates to the health of individuals, but is expanded to include the health of entire communities where people live, study, work, engage in social activities, and are impacted by political dynamics in their local, state, and national communities.

What is Optimal Mental Health?

Several mental health professionals and their professional organizations have offered definitions of *optimal mental health*. What follows is a synthesis of significant points utilized in traditional definitions of this important concept.

Optimal mental health has been defined as a person's state of emotional and psychological well-being. Mental wellness and mental health are terms that have and continue to be used in the definition of optimal mental health. These traditional terms emphasize the importance of understanding optimal mental health as it encompasses both an individual's emotional and physical health as well as his or her spiritual self.

People who exhibit optimal mental health are typically productive at work, loving with family members, and kind as well as being helpful to others. Conversely, people who do not manifest optimal mental health may be overwhelmed with life responsibilities or find themselves caught in unhealthy patterns of thought (e.g., worry) or behaviors (e.g., substance abuse).

For some people, seeking professional help for their mental health is the best way to restore balance and wellness to capture the essence of optimal mental health. For others, making smaller changes within everyday routines may be enough to promote the sort of positive thinking and behaviors inherent to the concept of optimal mental health.

After conducting an extensive review of the professional literature in counseling, psychology, and psychiatry, the following suggestions were made to achieve optimal mental health.

1. Exercise
2. Eat well/get the proper nutrition
3. Avoid toxic people in your life
4. Get outside
5. Volunteer in your community
6. Practice mindfulness and meditation
7. Try something new
8. Discover your intrinsic need for meaning and significance
9. Set realistic goals that are helpful in staying grounded with achievable expectations
10. Keeping a journal can be helpful in realizing one's *optimal mental health* as it helps to process one's thoughts and feelings
11. Self-care, including anything from taking time for yourself to making sure you get enough sleep and exercise.

The suggestions listed above are typically recommended by many (perhaps most) mental health professionals when asked for help by people interested in achieving optimal mental health. It is reasonable to assume that the percentage of persons who implement these suggestions would experience optimal mental health to some degree in the general population.

However, a study implemented by a U.S. government organization entitled "Healthy People 2020," estimated that only 17% of adults in the United States are considered to be in a state of optimal mental health. The integral theory of mental health and human development from a psycho-political perspective considers this to be an unacceptably low percentage of adults who experience optimal mental health as a result of implementing suggestions outlined by mental health professionals listed above.

The integral theory presented in this book points to research findings that describe ways to increase the level of optimal mental health among larger numbers of persons from diverse populations than has been achieved in the past. Increasing the percentage of adults who realize their potential for optimal mental health will require changes to traditional ways of implementing mental health services in our nation.

There is another reason for making changes in the traditional ways of implementing mental health services. This involves understanding the lack of sustainability and lasting long-term positive outcomes resulting from counseling, psychotherapy, and other related mental health services.

Klaus Grawe, a respected neuroscientist, is one of the few researchers who reports on the sustainability of positive changes resulting from successful counseling and/or psychotherapy in his book entitled, *Neuropsychotherapy: How the Neurosciences Inform Effective Psychotherapy*. Grawe reported that between 60% to 80% of clients who experience positive outcomes upon completing successful counseling and/or psychotherapy manifested the same symptomology that led them to seek professional assistance in the first place two years after receiving help from mental health practitioners.

The above listed points related to the low percentage of adults operating from optimal mental health as well as the lack of sustainability of positive counseling and psychotherapy outcomes represent additional evidence supporting the need for substantial changes in our nation's mental health system. As used in the integral theory of mental health and human development from a psycho-political perspective, the meaning of *optimal mental health* is more comprehensive, holistic, and complex than the definitions traditionally used in describing the meaning of this term. What follows is a summary of key changes mental health service providers and their professional organizations would do well to achieve in their efforts to promote optimal mental health when addressing the mental health crisis in our country.

Promoting optimal mental health is an aspirational goal. As used in the new integral theory described in this book the term, *aspirational* refers to a person and/or a community that strives to be ambitious, desiring success, expressing a hope or intention but not creating a legally binding obligation. The concept of *aspirational* is often appealing to people who aspire to accomplish such a goal. What follows is a synthesis of key points made in the integral theory of mental health and human development from a psycho-political perspective. These points are particularly relevant in promoting optimal mental health among individuals and their communities.

First, it would be wise to continue discussions with interested readers about the concrete ways mental health professionals could use the integral theory in their own local communities. The final section of Chapter 15 provides specific information that is designed to continue engaging interested readers in discussions about the nuts and bolts of implementing the information presented throughout this book.

Second, promoting optimal mental health requires mental health practitioners to expand their thinking about their professional responsibilities. This includes not only viewing individual clients as the recipients of their professional services, but equally important by viewing the communities in which clients are situated as equal entities in realizing *optimal community mental health*. Chapter 15 details ways to utilize community counseling and community psychology theories to effectively meet the needs of individual clients, people in the general public interested realizing their own optimal mental health, and stimulating the overall health and well-being of their entire communities.

Third, there are six major theoretical counseling and psychology forces that have and continue to shape the work mental health professionals do in the field. These include: the psychodynamic force (Chapter 10), the cognitive behavioral force (Chapter 11), the existential-humanistic force (Chapter 12), the multicultural and social justice force (Chapter 13), the neuroscience/neurotherapy force (Chapter 14), and the community counseling/psychology theoretical force (Chapter 15). Key aspects of community counseling and psychology theories are presented to integrate the information presented in Chapters 10–14 in the final chapter of this book.

Fourth, it is important for mental health professionals to make a commitment to work with the *natural helpers* in their communities in ways that lead to an increased level of optimal mental health among individuals and the communities in which they are situated. These natural helpers include but are not limited to parents, public school educators and administrators, athletic coaches, elected officials, religious/spiritual leaders, political activists, and anyone else interested in helping to promote optimal mental health in their communities.

Fifth, it is important for mental health professionals and natural helpers to incorporate the knowledge and skills necessary to implement prevention interventions intentionally aimed at fostering and sustaining mental health and human development across the lifespan.

Sixth, mental health professionals and natural helpers are encouraged to work together with elected officials and other policymakers to lobby for the re-establishment and expansion of the Community Mental Center Act that was initiated in 1963. More details about this important strategy are outlined in Chapter 15.

Seventh, mental health professionals and natural helpers are encouraged to promote optimal mental health by initiating community-based psychoeducational events intentionally designed to promote multicultural competence among all persons interested in developing the knowledge and skills necessary to be more effective during the unprecedented demographic transformation in our nation.

Eighth, given the adverse impact that White supremacy and White racism have in realizing optimal mental health in our society, organizing town hall meetings that address these social justice issues as a part of the new integral theory is vital in addressing the mental health crisis in our nation. Such community-based town hall meetings can be convened in schools, churches, synagogues, mosques, and universities, to name a few locations.

Summary

This chapter illuminates numerous factors associated with an increasing *awakening* occurring in our society in general and the mental health professions in particular. In an effort to explore various factors associated with this awakening, this chapter discusses the concept of a sane society that has been discussed by numerous mental health professionals and particularly as defined by Erich Fromm.

Additional factors are discussed in this chapter to expand readers' understanding of the different variables that are relevant for the awakening process unfolding in our society. For instance, the reader is introduced to the concept of the *collective consciousness* which results from a socialization process resulting in two distinct *mass psychologies* in our society. These mass psychologies include the *mass authoritarian psychology* and the *mass liberal psychology*.

These concepts were followed by a discussion of *malignant normality*. Here the work of Dr. Robert Lipton along with other mental health professionals is discussed with a focus on their relevance for the new integral theory discussed throughout this book.

Finally, a summary of concepts and recommendations that can be used to more effectively promote the optimal mental health of individual persons as well as their communities are discussed with a more detailed description of these issues outlined in the final chapters of this book (Chapters 10–15). Key components of each of the theoretical forces and their relevance for the new integral theory of mental health and human development are discussed in these final six chapters.

CHAPTER 10

THE PSYCHODYNAMIC FORCE

Don't let the past remind us of who we are not now.

Crosby, Stills and Nash lyrics in the song
entitled "Suite: Judy Blue Eyes"

Not all those who wander are lost.

J.R.R. Tolkien

Introduction

The psychodynamic frame of reference represents the first major theoretical force that helped to shape the mental health professions. The genius of the psychodynamic perspective can be traced to the pioneering work of Sigmund Freud, Carl Jung, and Alfred Adler in the early 1900s.

While Freud's psychoanalytic theory has had a profound effect in shaping the work many mental health practitioners do in the field, it is often viewed as being an antiquated and an irrelevant perspective by some persons today. This is unfortunate because various aspects of this rich theoretical framework can be helpful in understanding people in diverse groups and backgrounds as well as Trump and his supporters.

There are three important theoretical points Freud incorporated in his psychodynamic theory. These theoretical points are relevant for the new integral theory of mental health and human development from a psycho-political perspective. These relevant theoretical points include the impact of early life experiences on a person's adult development, the role and function of people's unconsciousness, and Freud's discussion of the purpose of unconscious defense mechanisms.

The Impact of Early Life Experiences

According to Freud's psychodynamic theory, it is important to make interpretations about the way unresolved conflicts and anxieties from the formative years in one's childhood and adolescence affect a person's functioning in adulthood (the individual perceptions and meaning making quadrant in the new integral theory).

Michael Kruse, a journalist with *Politico* magazine reported on his investigation of Trump's early development based on the first psychodynamic concept noted above. In doing so, Kruse describes how Trump's childhood and adolescent experiences impacted his adult development. These points are highlighted below and taken from Kruse's 2017 publication:

> Nearly a year into his presidency, Trump's behavior—as much as, or more than any policy he's advanced—stands as the subject of consternation, fascination and speculation. Psychology experts read and watch the news, and they have the same basic curiosity reflected in the following question: What makes somebody act the way Trump acts?

> None of these persons evaluated Trump in an official, clinical capacity as Trump is pretty consistently anti-shrink. Nonetheless, it is possible to consider answers to this question from afar, tracking back through his 71 years, searching for explanations for his belligerence and his impulsivity, his bottomless need for applause and his clockwork rage when he doesn't get it, his failed marriages and his ill-tempered treatment of women who challenge him.

> And they always end up at the beginning. With his parents. Both of them. Trump might focus on his father, but experts say the comparative scarcity of his discussion of his mother is itself telling.

'You don't have to be Freud to interpret this,' says Dr. Mark Smaller, past president of the American Psychoanalytic Association.

Patrice Taddonio, an investigative journalist with *Frontline* shared additional information about the impact of Donald Trump's childhood on his later development. She also discusses the impact of Trump's early adolescent experiences when he was sent to military school at the age of 13. The following comments were made in an article written by Taddonio and published by *Frontline* on September 22, 2020, entitled, "Trump the Bully: How Childhood & Military School Shaped the Future President."

> From a very young age, Donald Trump was taught there were only two kinds of people in this world: winners—or "killers"—and losers.

> It was a lesson imparted by his father, Fred, a stern and demanding real estate developer. Donald was determined to end up a "killer."

> 'I strongly suspect that he had a relationship with his father that accounts for a lot of what he became,' stated Tony Schwartz, who co-authored *The Art of the Deal* with Trump.

> Fred Trump decided to send Donald at age 13 to military school, where the lessons in how to dominate would reach another level.

> Trump would emerge from military school with a blueprint for leadership by force and ridicule.

> Donald Trump's relationship with his mother, Mary, was formative in a different way. She had become seriously ill for a time when Trump was two-and-a-half years old.

> 'Donald, who at a critical point in his development as a child, was essentially abandoned by his mother,' reported Mary Trump, Donald Trump's niece, and a psychologist.

> 'When you ask him about how she showed her love, he has nothing to say,' Mary Trump stated. That left more room for Fred Trump's lasting influence on his son.

John Bowlby and Mary Ainsworth worked together as social scientists by committing their longstanding careers to validating and expanding Freud's theoretical points about the impact of childhood and adolescent experiences on people's adult interpersonal styles. Based on their research, it is hypothesized that Trump's childhood and early adolescent experiences with his mother and father contributed to his adult interpersonal style.

Bowlby and Ainsworth's attachment theory enables one to see the fit between Trump's adult interpersonal style and the characteristics of what attachment theorists refer to as *acting out* and *avoidant interpersonal behaviors*.

Freud's Personal Unconscious

The second key point of relevance for the integral theory of mental health and human development from a psycho-political perspective relates to Freud's description of people's *personal unconscious*. Psychodynamic helping methods in general and Freud's psychoanalytic theory in particular can be thought of as *uncovering therapies*. This is because the focus of these therapies is on helping people become more conscious of their present ways of thinking, feeling, and behaving. Some of a person's unconscious content may be recalled into what Freud referred to as a person's preconscious, but others cannot and are truly unconscious.

As emphasized in Chapter 9, much of the new integral model directs attention to the importance of awakening to the perilous times we face in general and the importance of increasing our awareness of the mental health crisis in the United States in particular. The new integral theory presented in this book defines the *personal unconscious* as consisting of everything subliminal, forgotten, and repressed in an individual's life.

Early in this book a comprehensive description of the multidimensional nature of White racism was presented (See Chapter 2). This included a discussion of overt intentional, overt unintentional, covert intentional and covert unintentional White racism. The integral theory of mental health and human development from a psycho-political perspective finds Freud's concept of the personal unconscious to be relevant for many White persons who unconsciously perpetuate White racism in overt unintentional and covert unintentional ways.

It is important to add that, according to Freud, all of us possess a personal unconscious that impacts our thoughts, feelings, and behavior. It might be interesting for readers to consider for a moment the degree to which your own individual personal unconscious works in such a way as to make different interpretations of the points made in this book; interpretations that may be very different than the intent of the author.

Freud's original concept of people's personal unconscious has been expanded to include the multidimensional nature of the unconscious. Other theorists have included the family unconscious (Nobles, 1998; Taub-Bynum, 1984) and a collective cultural unconscious (Akbar, 1994; Parham, et al., 1999) to Freud's original theory. The new integral theory encourages mental health professionals and other persons in local communities interested in addressing these perilous times as well as helping to rectify the current crisis in our national mental health system to be aware of the three types of unconscious listed above when thinking about the persons we interact with in our communities.

Unconscious Defense Mechanisms

The third major component of Freud's psychodynamic theory relevant for the new integral theory involves his notion of *unconscious defense mechanisms.* Based on Freud's psychotherapy theory, it is acknowledged that stresses manifested in people's lives commonly lead to much of the anxiety people experience in their lives.

From the new integral theory and as stated in previous chapters, research findings from multiple sources note that the genesis of much of this stress and anxiety is the growing awareness of the unprecedented demographic transformation of our nation. As stated previously, this unprecedented demographic transformation will result in our nation becoming a minority majority population which is distressing for many White people in the U.S.

According to Freud's theory of human development, stress and the ensuing anxiety are universal human characteristics routinely experienced by all people. Many persons can and do consciously identify some of the sources of their anxiety with the unprecedented demographic transformation noted above. Psychodynamic theory also asserts that we all experience some degree of *free-floating anxiety* which is not always consciously understood in our personal lives.

Most people experience this free-floating anxiety along with other forms of stress-based unease. When people are unable to develop a rational explanation for the source of their anxiety, they may experience uncomfortable and threatening thoughts and feelings. To deal with these uncomfortable experiences, Freud asserted that individuals commonly use various *unconscious defense mechanisms*. Some of the more commonly known defense mechanisms include repression, denial, projection, displacement, and sublimation.

There are a couple of reasons why the above information is relevant for the new integral theory of mental health and human development from a psycho-political perspective. First, although Freud may be right in saying that unconscious defense mechanisms are universal, the new integral theory emphasizes that the specific manifestations of these unconscious psychodynamic processes are exhibited in culturally relevant ways.

Second, the following description of the more common unconscious racial defense mechanisms utilized by large numbers of people, particularly those who self-identify as Trump supporters, include the following:

a. **Repression:** A general concept of all defense mechanisms is that some of our behavior, thoughts, and actions are repressed from our consciousness. The mechanism of repression often stems from adverse developmental experiences during childhood and adolescence. To cope with the discomfort of these unresolved childhood and adolescence experiences and memories, people unconsciously repress such memories from their consciousness.

From the perspective of new integral theory grounded in a psycho-political perspective, large numbers of White persons, who self-identify as White nationalists and/or White supremacists, are likely to employ the unconscious defense mechanism of repression. The function in doing so is to ensure that they will not be put in a position where any information about racial equality and justice would call into question their inaccurate thinking about racial issues.

b. **Denial:** Some adherents of psychoanalytic theories suggest that *denial* is the most difficult and troublesome defense mechanism to deal with. Many people continue to deny recognizing and acknowledging the perilous times that we live in, the authoritarian nature of Trump and his supporters, and/or the perpetuation of various forms of White supremacy and White racism underlying much of the White anxiety given the unprecedented demographic changes in our society.

c. **Projection:** When people refuse to recognize or are unable to acknowledge behaviors or thoughts that reflect their various forms of White racism and White supremacy, they may project these behaviors and thoughts onto someone else; which is the essence of projection. This unconscious defense mechanism is manifested with increasing frequency as White persons argue that political policies, practices, and the continued call for greater racial equality and justice represent forms of reverse-racism against White people in our nation.

The new integral theory recognizes that all three of the above defense mechanisms; repression, denial, and projection are difficult to overcome in one's lifetime. Efforts to foster even incremental liberation from such unconscious defense mechanisms often requires therapeutic intervention with a mental health professional. Despite the different views mental health practitioners have about the impact of people's past history on present psychological functioning, it is apparent that this fundamental psychodynamic principal has gained much acceptance in the general public as well as in the mental health professions.

One of the goals of this book is to explore how we can respond to other colleagues, students, friends, and perhaps family members who have strong alliances with Donald Trump, his authoritarian leadership style, and people who continue to support Trump and the MAGA movement.

An important question raised by the integral theory of mental health and human development from a psycho-political perspective is to what degree should readers engage in political discussions with Trump supporters who manifest strong resistance to any anti-Trump perspective (See Chapter 1). This includes political discussions we might find ourselves being called into with colleagues, friends, family members, and other persons in the communities where we live and work.

When encountering persons who demonstrate a strong inclination to manifest the sort of unconscious racist defense mechanisms described above and sensing that they are not likely to consider alternative ways of thinking about White supremacy and White racism in our society, it is important to ask ourselves if it is possible that such discussions could serve to strengthen negative racial stereotypes and misinformation that such persons operate from? This question is again addressed using advances made in neuroscience related to neuroplasticity and brain functioning issues discussed in Chapter 14.

Alternatively, the integral theory suggests that a more effective use of one's time and energy could instead be directed to working with other anti-racist allies to discuss how issues related to racial injustice could be addressed in their communities. This could include working to develop community-based and school-based psychoeducation interventions to promote a broader understanding of White supremacy and White racism during these perilous times and simultaneously addressing our nation's mental health crisis.

The second reason why it is important to learn about the relevance of Freud's *personal unconscious* is that it can help to expand our understanding of how the psycho-political perspective in the new integral theory adds to more accurate and effective ways of thinking about and responding to the complex and multidimensional nature of White racism and White supremacy. Based on my decades of research into White supremacy and White racism, I have concluded that there is a unique collective consciousness and unconsciousness operating among White people as a result of a socialization process that continues to perpetuate various forms of cultural/racial biases.

The new integral theory presented in this book strongly advocates for the implementation of a broad range of services designed to increase readers' awareness of the current socialization process and its adverse impact on race relations in the United States. This raises the important question as to if and when the mental health professions will make a commitment to raise the level of prevention interventions by using anti-racist and social justice psychoeducation strategies with the same frequency as traditional psychiatric, counseling, and psychotherapeutic interventions continue to be overused in our society.

The research findings reported throughout this book illuminate how the pervasive and malignant cancers of White racism and White supremacy are perpetuated in our collective socialization. Given these realities, the new integral theory asserts that the time has well-passed the point when the mental health professions can afford to continue denying and repressing the centrality of these psycho-political dynamics as they poison the soul of humanity in the United States.

Alfred Adler's Psychoanalytic Theory: Social Interest

Alfred Adler is another important founder of the psychoanalytic perspective. His interest in this theoretical perspective began in the early 1900s when he decided to study psychiatry in his doctoral training program. This interest was increased when Adler was invited to join Sigmund Freud's inner circle of psychodynamic theorists in 1907.

His close association with Freud led Adler to thoughtfully reflect on his psychoanalytic perspective. This resulted in Adler developing an alternative perspective on the Freudian view of mental health and human development. Like the above discussion describing important concepts of Freud's theory that are relevant for the integral theory of mental health and human development, the following section focuses on terms/concepts that mark Adler's theory and their relevance for the new integral theory.

The development of Adler's psychological theory was impacted by his participation in World War I (a factor associated with the societal/professional quadrant in the integral theory). During Adler's participation in this military conflict, he served as a physician in the Austrian army, first on the Russian front and later in a children's hospital.

As a result of these experiences, Adler saw firsthand the damage that war does. His thoughts turned increasingly to the concept of what he referred to as *social interest*. He felt that, if humanity is to survive, it had to change its ways with greater time and energy directed to addressing the *social interests* of a democratic society.

According to Dr. Gerald Corey, the above-stated life experiences also led Adler to become:

> ... a politically and socially oriented psychiatrist who showed great concern for the common person. Part of his mission was to bring psychotherapy to the working class and translate psychological concepts into practical methods for helping a varied population meet the challenges of life.

Dr. Gerald Corey's comments about Alfred Adler and his psychodynamic theory represent the essence of the new integral theory of mental health and human development from a psycho-political perspective. According to Corey, Adler's unique psychodynamic views on *bringing psychology to the people* gained acceptance from mental health professionals in Europe in the early 1900s. However, these views are much slower in coming to the attention of psychological practitioners in the United States.

Differences between Alfred Adler's theory and Sigmund Freud's psychodynamic framework resulted in a split between these two intellectuals in 1911. Adler's perspective of mental health and human development represented a major shift in thinking from Freud's theory. As noted in Adler's theory (which he called *individual psychology*), his worldview is distinguished from a Freudian perspective in several fundamental ways. Among the differences noted between Adler's and Freud's theories, the following are illuminated below.

First, while Freud emphasized the important role the unconscious plays in a person's psychological functioning, Adler placed greater value on people's consciousness in their development. From an Adlerian perspective, consciousness rather than unconsciousness is the primary source of one's ideas, values, and sense of psychological health. This important premise in Adler's theory is reflected in the new integral theory, which embraces the notion that people's conscious understanding of their lives and problems is critical in fostering mental health and human development. This Adlerian principle falls within the individual perceptions and meaning making quadrant of the integral model (See Chapter 9).

Adler agreed with Freud's assessment of the important impact that biological factors and early childhood experiences have on one's personality development. He did not, however, share the same convictions as Freud about the way these factors were thought to determine an individual's personality development.

While Adler agreed that biological, sexual, and aggressive drives as well as one's childhood experiences increase the probability that people have a propensity to develop in certain ways, he placed a much greater emphasis on people's creative ability to realize their personal goals and live purposeful lives. These Adlerian principles represent important aspects of his individual psychology theory and fall within both the individual perceptions and meaning making quadrant and the neurological/brain-functioning quadrant in the integral theory (See Chapter 9).

Perhaps the most important similarity between Adler's theoretical perspective and the new integral theory is his description of *social interest* as a critical barometer in people's mental health and ongoing human development. Adler's highlighting of the strong correlation between people's social interest, mental health, and ongoing human development has been expanded in the new integral theory discussed throughout this book. This conceptual expansion is reflected in the way the integral theory centralizes social justice as central in promoting the ongoing evolution of our nation's fragile multiracial/multicultural democracy, in addressing the challenges of these perilous times, and ameliorating the serious crisis in the mental health system in the United States.

Summary

This chapter builds on several concepts discussed in Chapter 9. It begins by providing an overview of Sigmund Freud's psychodynamic theory and its relevance for the integral theory of mental health and human development from the psycho-political perspective. Chapter 10 shines a spotlight on the relevance of three of Sigmund Freud's key theoretical concepts for the new integral theory.

The first important theoretical concept addressed in this chapter focuses on the impact of childhood and adolescent experiences on adult development. This discussion highlights the ways that psychodynamic principles used in the creation of John Bowlby and Mary Ainsworth's *attachment theory* are relevant when reflecting on the impact of Trump's childhood and adolescence experiences has had on his adult development.

From an attachment theory perspective, it is suggested that Trump's childhood and adolescent experiences contributed to his controversial interpersonal style. The new integral theory acknowledges the relevance of Bowlby and Ainsworth's use of the terms *acting out* and *avoidant interpersonal behaviors* as they fit much of Trump's adult interpersonal style.

The second key Freudian concept addressed in this chapter focuses on the concept of the *personal unconscious*. The relevance of this concept for the new integral theory links Freud's concept of the *personal unconscious* with the perpetuation of overt unintentional and covert unintentional White racism as described in Chapter 2. The perpetuation of these forms of White racism and White supremacy are often manifested by good hearted and well-meaning White persons who are genuinely unconscious of their complicity in supporting unintentional forms of White racism in our nation.

The third important Freudian concept discussed in this chapter involves the relevance of unconscious defense mechanisms when used to legitimize White power in maintaining control over the political rights and responsibilities of persons of color in our nation. The three unconscious defense mechanisms discussed in this regard include *repression, denial,* and *projection of blame.*

The reader's attention is then directed to the innovative work of Alfred Adler in introducing new psychoanalytic concepts that extend and differentiate his theory of individual psychology from critical Freudian concepts. These efforts resulted in the first time the concept of *social interest* is identified as a barometer of people's mental health and ongoing human development.

It is also noted that this early psychoanalytic concept is greatly expanded by the new integral theory with its emphasis on social justice as a critical factor in promoting the mental health and ongoing human development of larger numbers of people in diverse groups than mental health professionals have achieved in the past. The integral theory's emphasis in stimulating a greater level of social justice from a psycho-political perspective correlates with the ongoing evolution of our nation's fragile multiracial/multicultural democracy in addressing the challenges of these perilous times and ameliorating the serious crisis in our nation's mental health system.

The following chapter discusses the second major force in the mental health professions referred to as *cognitive behavioral theory* (CBT). As discussed in Chapter 11, the CBT force provides a very different way of thinking about mental health and human development. Details related to this new force and the relevance of CBT for the integral theory of mental health and human development from a psycho-political perspective are detailed in the following chapter.

CHAPTER 11

COGNITIVE-BEHAVIORAL THERAPY THEORY (CBT)

Whatever a person frequently thinks and reflects on, that will become the inclination of their mind.

Gautama Buddha

Emancipate yourselves from mental slavery
None but ourselves can free our minds.

Bob Marley, musician, songwriter, social–political activist

Introduction

Currently, the most frequently used mental health theory is cognitive behavioral therapy (CBT). CBT has undergone considerable research in diverse settings. Although CBT has been criticized for failing to describe the specific multicultural competencies necessary to use this theory in culturally and racially diverse situations, its effectiveness with diverse populations attest to its wide-ranging effectiveness.

CBT constitutes the second major theoretical force in the mental health professions. This force is grounded in a worldview significantly different from the psychodynamic perspective described in Chapter 10. What follows is a brief description of popular assumptions that distinguish CBT from other theories used in the mental health professions.

- Supporters of CBT direct primary attention to observable behaviors persons demonstrate in response to their life experiences and not on a person's unresolved past conflicts, which many CBT mental health professionals believe cannot be meaningfully defined;

- CBT is grounded in the belief that people are born as *blank slates* and whatever people learn to do (meaning all of their behaviors) depends on their interactions and experiences with their environment;

- CBT supporters follow the *law of effect*. The law of effect was initially defined by Thorndike (1911) as "behavior that is followed by satisfying consequences will be more likely to be repeated than behavior that is followed by unsatisfying consequences which will be less likely to be repeated"; and

- CBT embraces a concept referred to as *associative learning* (Wolpe, 1982). Associative learning occurs when people engage in events and behaviors with other people that stimulate new ways of thinking, feeling, and behaving in our society.

More detailed discussions of the above assumptions are presented later in this chapter. To help readers gain a better understanding of the integral theory of mental health and human development, the following points are made to briefly explain the relevance of the above CBT assumptions for the new integral theory.

Given the perilous times that threaten our democracy, the integral theory of mental health and human development emphasizes the importance of directing attention to behaviors that people implement to address the perilous psycho-political times we face as a nation. This is contrasted with people who contribute to ongoing threats to our nation's democracy.

It is also noted that the new integral theory shares the value of CBT supporters when it comes to assessing a person's mental health and well-being by directing attention to specific behaviors people manifest in an effort to support or dismantle our democracy. Minimally, demonstrating one's commitment to voting at local, statewide, and national levels are concrete examples of the shared values and behaviors manifested among advocates of the new integral theory presented in this book.

Political Apathy is Not an Option

It might be said that political apathy during these times is not an option when talking about the mental health of our country. I am not alone in asserting that political apathy needs to be a factor which mental health professionals direct their attention during these perilous times.

In the early 2000s there was a concerted effort to address the issue of political apathy within the context of what is now referred to as *optimal mental health* in our democratic society. At that time, Dr. Jeffrey White opened discussions on this issue with other mental health professionals. These discussions led to the publication of an article entitled, "Political Apathy Disorder: Proposal for a New DSM Diagnostic Category" in the *Journal of Humanistic Psychology* (White, 2004).

The abstract for this article provides an overview of Dr. White's rationale in focusing on this issue and reads as follows:

Political apathy disorder (PAD) is proposed as a new DSM diagnostic category for the failure to develop a social conscience. The essential feature is a pervasive pattern of failing to help reduce human suffering in the world combined with overconsumption of society's limited resources. Those suffering from PAD fulfill the basic DSM criteria of a mental disorder: distress, disability, and increased risk of suffering death, pain, disability, or an important loss of freedom. It is proposed that the failure to achieve the characteristics necessary to live a constructive moral life that benefits society should be considered grounds for inclusion in the diagnostic nomenclature.

Like CBT, the new integral theory of mental health and human development grounded in a psycho-political perspective shares a common value grounded in the belief that people are born as *blank slates*. Consequently, whatever people learn to do (meaning all of their behaviors, including political behaviors) depends on their interactions and experiences with their environment.

The new integral theory asserts that people, who are engaged in volunteering time at the polls for different elections, those who are involved in voter registration in their communities, and those who work with schools and universities to have voter education events, all of these behaviors fall under the category of the *optimal mental health* as discussed in this book. It should be added that these political behaviors are consistent with Alfred Adler's innovative incorporation of the concept of *social interest* in his discussions about mental health and human development (See Chapter 10).

The new integral theory also affirms the *law of effect* that is a centerpiece in CBT. With that similarity in mind, this new theory utilizes the law of effect by describing and implementing political strategies that can be employed in local communities, which result in satisfying outcomes among interested persons participating in such community-based strategies. This is an important aspect of the new integral theory drawn from Thorndike's definition of the law of effect, defined as behaviors more likely to be repeated when addressing the ongoing threats to our democracy and our nation's mental health crisis.

The Evolution of CBT

To understand the emergence of the second force in the mental health professions, one needs to be knowledgeable of the four historical phases that mark the development of this major theoretical force. The first three phases highlight behavioral aspects of CBT. These are referred to as classical conditioning theory (Pavlov, 1927; Watson, 1923), operant conditioning theory (Skinner, 1953, 1969), and social learning theory (Bandura, 1962, 1975, 1997).

The evolutionary process of CBT includes theoretical offshoots that focus on specific learning and training outcomes. These outcomes serve as ways to prevent mental health problems from occurring as well as being incorporated into helping interventions provided to people already experiencing psychological stresses and disturbances.

A partial list of some of these innovative mental health services include: relaxation training, biofeedback and self-regulation training, interventions that focus on ways to change faulty thought patterns, learning activities aimed at promoting people's emotional regulation, psychoeducational interventions designed to help people learn to control negative automatic thinking, stress management training services, life skills training, assertiveness training, and relapse prevention services to name a few. These innovative mental health services are largely aimed at helping people learn to cope with their environmental conditions in different ways.

Given space limitations, the reader's attention is now directed to one of the most popular and effective CBT theories. This theoretical framework was created by Dr. Albert Ellis and referred to as rational emotive behavior therapy (REBT).

Albert Ellis and REBT

Albert Ellis's interesting childhood and early adolescent experiences are relevant in understanding the development of his REBT framework. Born into a Jewish family in Pittsburgh, Pennsylvania on September 17, 1913, Albert Ellis was the eldest of three children. Ellis's father had limited success in a series of business ventures and did little better in expressing affection toward his children.

Ellis described his mother as a self-absorbed woman with a bipolar aspect - "a bustling chatter box who never listened" (Ellis, Abrams, & Abrams, 2005, p. 1). As emotionally unavailable as his father was, Ellis's mother was often still asleep when he left for school and frequently not at home when he returned. Additional insights into Ellis's childhood experiences are described below:

> Instead of feeling bitter about his parents' lack of emotional responsiveness, Ellis took on the responsibility of caring for his siblings. He purchased an alarm clock with his own money and woke and dressed his younger brother and sister. Despite his parents' emotional paucity, his family had very little privation until the Depression. That historical event necessitated Albert and his brother and sister to seek work to assist the family.

> Young Albert was a frail young man who suffered numerous health problems throughout his youth. At the age of five, he was hospitalized with a kidney ailment. He was also hospitalized

with tonsillitis shortly thereafter, which led to a severe infection requiring emergency surgery.

He reported that he had eight hospitalizations between the ages of five and seven. One of those hospitalizations lasted nearly a year. His parents provided little or no emotional support for him during these years. Ellis stated that he wanted to confront his adversaries, but then developed a growing indifference to their dereliction (Ivey, D'Andrea, & Ivey, 2012).

Ellis's Early Training

Ellis attended City University of New York in the mid-1920s, majoring in business. Upon graduating from this institution, he briefly tried to secure a business career only to find that this was not his life's calling. During these early adult years, Ellis explored his literary capacities by writing fiction. Although he discovered that he was not an effective fictional writer, he did learn that he had a talent for nonfiction.

Much of his early nonfiction writing focused on a broad range of issues related to human sexuality. Since there were few mental health professionals who were experts in human sexuality at the time, Ellis soon developed a respected reputation for his expertise in this area. He was increasingly called on to counsel individuals experiencing various sexually related problems and concerns.

Due to his success in providing these counseling services, Ellis decided to enroll in the clinical psychology doctoral program at Columbia University in 1942. It was here that he received training in the psychoanalytic tradition. After acquiring his doctoral degree in 1947, Ellis began working full time in private practice. While working as a clinical psychologist, Ellis continued to receive psychoanalytic training supervision from Robert Hulbeck, a leading training analyst at the Karen Horney Institute.

Karen Horney, a psychoanalytic leader in her own right, was a very influential force in Ellis's professional development. It was Horney who introduced Ellis to a number of other psychodynamic leaders, including Alfred Adler, Erich Fromm, and Harry Stack Sullivan – all of whom influenced his early thinking about counseling, psychotherapy, mental health, and human development.

While Ellis's extensive training and personal involvement in psycho-analysis led him to develop a sound understanding of the psychoanalytic worldview (See Chapter 10), it also resulted in him becoming disgruntled with various aspects of this helping perspective. His increasing disagreement with many of the central tenets of the psychoanalytic perspective resulted in the formation of his own theory of counseling and therapy.

Ellis's New Approach

Ellis formulated what he originally referred to as rational-emotive therapy (RET) in the mid-1950s as he became increasingly aware of the ineffectiveness of psychoanalysis to produce lasting change among his clients. Although he had an extremely successful private psychoanalytic practice, he was dissatisfied with the results he was obtaining. Gradually, Ellis found himself taking a more active role in therapy, attacking his clients' logic, and even prescribing behavioral activities for clients to follow after they left therapy.

As his own thinking about counseling, psychotherapy, mental health, and human development evolved, Ellis increasingly found it useful to link clients' irrational thoughts with their ineffective behaviors. As a result, Ellis can be credited with pioneering a method of cognitive-behavior therapy that is connected to classic behavioral theories and methods.

In the revision of his classic *Reason and Emotion in Psychotherapy*, Ellis (1995) changed the name of his 40-year-old therapeutic method from rational-emotive therapy (RET) to rational emotive behavioral therapy (REBT). According to Ellis:

> RET is a misleading name because it omits the highly behavioral aspect that rational emotive therapy has favored right from the start. RET has always been one of the most behaviorally-oriented of cognitive-behavior therapies. In addition to employing systematic desensitization and showing clients how to use imaginal methods of exposing themselves to phobias and anxiety-provoking situations, it favors in vivo desensitization or exposure. It is more behavioral than the procedures of other leading cognitive-behavioral therapies. RET has really always been rational emotive behavioral therapy (REBT) (Ellis, 1995, pp. 86-89).

Ellis's Key Theoretical Constructs of REBT

Ellis's REBT theory focuses more on dysfunctional thoughts than do other theories of counseling and psychotherapy. REBT also emphasizes the centrality of a person's emotional reactions to life's events and challenges. The REBT view that people often make themselves emotional victims by their own distorted, unrealistic, and irrational thought patterns is another centerpiece of Ellis's REBT theoretical model (Ellis, 1999).

Ellis takes an essentially optimistic view of people in general and counseling/therapy in particular, but criticizes some humanistic helping approaches as being too soft at times. These criticisms include acknowledging that humanistic counseling approaches frequently fail to address the fact that people can virtually self-destruct through irrational and muddled thinking. Consequently, Ellis emphasizes that the task of the REBT therapist is to correct clients' thought patterns by minimizing irrational ideas while simultaneously helping them change their dysfunctional feelings and behaviors.

Emotion is central in Ellis's CBT work (Ellis, 2000). According to Ellis, unless the "E" in REBT is present, change is unlikely to occur. Ellis is often seen personally as a highly rational and logical person. Yet, awareness of others' emotions and constructions of reality are essential in his theory of mental health.

Ellis distinguishes REBT from other cognitive-behavioral theories in the way it is driven by unique philosophic perspectives (Ellis, 1994). Of course, all CBT theories emphasize cognitive processes, but they generally do not have a philosophic emphasis like REBT does. REBT emphasizes that humans are born (as well as reared) as philosophers and they are natural scientists, creators of meaning, and users of rational means to predict the future. One of its main goals, therefore, is to help people make profound philosophic changes that will affect their future as well as their present emotions and behaviors (Ellis, 1995).

From the perspective of the integral theory of mental health and human development from a psycho-political perspective, the perilous times in which we live, the threats to our nation's democracy, and the crisis in our mental health system all beg mental health professionals to help people develop their untapped potential in becoming more responsible citizens. At a basic level this involves assisting people in our communities learn to work with other persons to address these four challenges.

For some (perhaps many) people, this may necessitate them to make philosophic changes that will affect their future as well as their present emotions and behaviors from a political perspective. The above stated CBT value in facilitating psychological/emotional changes is relevant in adopting the integral theory of mental health and human development perspective in our professional practices.

One of the central constructs of REBT relates to a person's *belief systems*. Belief systems are organized ways of thinking about reality and one's personal experiences in life. Ellis emphasizes the importance of assisting people to move beyond the irrational beliefs that are often nurtured by environmental experiences. Multicultural and social justice counseling advocates acknowledge the importance of this process when working to promote what is referred to as *psychological liberation* (Aron & Corne, 1994). The integral theory of mental health and human development is embedded in a belief system that strongly values psychological liberation; a concept that is advanced by multicultural counseling and social justice mental health advocates (See Chapter 13).

From a REBT perspective, mental health practitioners assist people in moving beyond the irrational beliefs that are often nurtured by environmental experiences. Thus, the integral theory embraces the REBT position on this important point.

As noted in Part 1 of this book, many Trump supporters (especially those identified as part of the Trump cult who participated in the violent insurrection on January 6, 2021) (See Chapter 6), have freely bought into the irrational, oppressive, and unjust racist policies embedded in Trump's MAGA movement. In his REBT theory, Ellis discusses the importance of people's free will as it relates to their mental health and ongoing human development. The integral theory incorporates the concept of people's free will as a counter factor to what some people may think is the controlling factor in a person's consciousness development via our society's socialization process.

Ellis (1994) believes in free will, pointing out that people create their own emotional disturbances by strongly believing in irrational beliefs. Ellis further asserts that people can actively choose their belief systems and philosophies, but all too often they choose a philosophy that is irrational and causes them cognitive and behavioral difficulties. Consequently, REBT represents an attempt to bring people's irrational views into a more rational consciousness and effect positive behavioral changes (Ivey et al., 2012).

According to Ellis, people need to accomplish four goals that are vital in REBT. First, people have to examine the ways that they construct meaning in their lives. Second, people need to understand the irrational beliefs that underlie many of their mental constructions. Third, people need help in reconstructing more rational cognitions that transcend previous environmental conditioning. Fourth, Ellis asserts that people need to use their free will to commit themselves to make behavioral changes based on new and more rational constructions of themselves and the world in which they operate. The preceding points fall within the individual perceptions and meaning making quadrant, the neurological/brain-functioning quadrant, and the societal/professional quadrant that comprise the new integral theory presented in this book.

The above points are relevant for the new integral theory for a number of reasons. First, the integral theory recognizes that we are all susceptible to developing irrational beliefs in various ways from childhood through adulthood.

Second, the new integral theory emphasizes the importance of being aware of the similarities in the meaning of Ellis's concept of *irrational beliefs* and the meaning of the term, a *false consciousness*. Zoe Baker is a historian and author of numerous publications on consciousness-related issues. She has specifically written about the meaning of false consciousness. In doing so, she draws from the work of Lorna Finlayson in her book entitled, *An Introduction to Feminism* and distinguishes between five different kinds of false consciousness that are relevant in understanding the new integral theory.

The following five distinguishable forms of *false consciousness* are presented below to expand the reader's understanding of: [1] Ellis's concept of *irrational beliefs*, [2] their similarities to Finlayson's *false consciousness*, [3] CBT in general, and [4] the relevance of CBT concepts for the integral theory of mental health and human development from a psycho-political perspective.

Irrational Belief #1. This represents a false belief about the world. For example, a worker who thinks capitalism does not oppress them or a misogynist who believes that women are innately bad at mathematics.

Irrational Belief #2. An inaccurate representation of the world. For example, a woman who looks in the mirror and sees herself as ugly and larger than she actually is.

Irrational Belief #3. An emotional response that is inappropriate to the situation. For example, a victim of abuse who blames themselves for their abuse and venerates their abuser.

Irrational Belief #4. The failure to notice relevant truths. For example, a White person who does not notice racism and thinks they live in a *post-racial society*.

Irrational Belief #5. The failure to experience a certain emotional state. For example, a capitalist who doesn't feel empathy for their employees or a trans-person who does not love themselves because of internalized transphobia (Finlay, 2016, p. 18).

A Case Study of Michael Fanone and Danny Rodriguez

Another goal for this chapter is to increase the reader's understanding of how Albert Ellis's REBT is relevant in different work settings that do not involve mental health professionals. The specific material I am using in the following case study comes from information provided in a book written by Michael Fanone and John Shiffman. This book is entitled, *Hold the Line: The Insurrection and One Cop's Battle for America's Soul*. It describes the brutal assault on Officer Fanone during the January 6, 2021 insurrection in our nation's capital. One of the four persons arrested for the violent assault on Michael Fanone is Danny Rodriguez of Fontana, California.

The following section describes how REBT concepts can be used with people experiencing psychological and/or emotional problems by individuals other than mental health professionals. Upon reading the description of the interrogation two special agents with the FBI had with Mr. Danny Rodriguez, it was apparent that the investigative interviewing strategies these two special agents used were similar to the skills typically implemented when mental health professionals employ the REBT in their work.

This case study includes some of Officer Fanone's reactions to the video of Danny Rodriguez's interrogation. After Officer Fanone watched the video of the interrogation, he stated that the FBI interview did not disappoint him. He continues his comments by suggesting that Rodriguez's interrogation could itself be offered "as a case study in the Cult of Trump." He added the following comments that not only reflect his insight into the cult of Trump, but does so in ways that validate the integral theory's description of the characteristics of this cult (See Chapter 6).

With all of these points in mind, it is particularly relevant for this discussion to note how Fanone's analysis illuminates ways the skills and strategies associated with Ellis's REBT theory might be employed by law enforcement persons. With this backdrop in mind, the following section highlights Officer Fanone's assessment of the interventions utilized by the two special FBI agents in their interrogation of Danny Rodriguez.

In fact, it (Danny's interrogation) offered a case study in the Cult of Trump. It revealed the feeble-mindedness of a typical zealot. If we want to understand what we're up against, we need to grasp what drives people like Rodriguez, a failed drug dealer so desperate for a sense of belonging that he became an easy mark for a cult. After being bullied in high school and later by fellow drug dealers, Rodriguez fell in with Trump diehards who welcomed his support. He told the FBI agents that they made Danny feel proud and important. The Trump diehards gave him a sense of purpose.

On page 143 of his book, Michael Fanone describes his familiarity with the manner in which many arrested persons, who are guilty of crimes, begin to explain themselves to law enforcement personnel conducting investigative interviews. As Fanone stated: "Like most guilty people under arrest, Rodriguez dodged and evaded at the onset of his FBI interview, offering warped logic and pathetic excuses."

Rodriguez claimed to be brainwashed by years of listening to conspiracy peddler Alex Jones on InfoWars." InfoWars is an

American far-right conspiracy and fake news website owned by Alex Jones which was founded in 1999 and operates under Free Speech Systems LLC.

From an REBT perspective, these comments fit Ellis's theoretical framework as Rodriguez implicitly acknowledged his behavior was largely the result of irrational beliefs he developed as a result of spending countless hours listening to Alex Jones articulate irrational and unfounded beliefs for his own financial and career benefit.

At the early stage of his interview, Rodriguez begins crying profusely when talking about his violent actions during the failed insurrection of our government. This emotional reaction was highlighted in statements Rodriguez made in the interview, including the following quotations and follow-up comments by both FBI Special Agents conducting this interview:

As Danny started sobbing, he stated, "No sense in crying... I don't know what's wrong with me."

Comments by the special agents: "Take a breath. I feel like you want to get it off your chest," one of the special agents stated. These comments are consistent with the emphasis Ellis makes about the importance of building a relationship with people like Rodriguez. It seems that these statements were made by the special agent as a way to encourage Rodriguez to self-disclose more information about the specific ways he brutally assaulted Michael Fanone during the January 6th insurrection.

Such comments are consistent with mental health professionals, who use REBT in their work with persons like Rodriguez. Such relationship building efforts resulted in Rodriguez continuing to talk about the role he played in violently assaulting Officer Fanone.

Rodriguez proceeded to regress as he tried to irrationally legitimize his irrational and violent behavior. Officer Fanone pointed out how Rodriguez did this by stating the following on page 148:

Rodriguez offered a ridiculous rationalization. As he stated: 'The founding fathers would have understood what we did on January 6. When we talk about 1776, we see there was a lot of violence.

We had to go against the government and people died. Something good came out of that... I didn't think I was going to be the bad guy... I'm so sorry... I didn't know we were doing the wrong thing. I thought we were doing the right thing. I thought it was going to be awesome.'

Mental health professionals using REBT are familiar with persons, who begin to acknowledge the sort of irrational beliefs that drive their inappropriate and/or illegal behaviors, only to have them regress as Rodriguez did towards the end of his interview. This regression indicates that a person like Rodriguez continues to be a threat for future violence as he maintains his ongoing *false consciousness*. For this reason, it would be important to make sure that he is not a threat to society by ensuring his incarceration according to the legal statue relevant to Rodriguez's case.

The new integral theory emphasizes the importance of making reforms in our nation's jails and prisons. These reforms need to be driven by our increasing understanding that more than 50 percent of the people in this country's prisons and jails are in need of mental health services.

It is important to make sure people like Danny Rodriguez are subjected to incarceration that keeps our communities and law enforcement professionals like Officer Fanone safe. At the same time, mental health professionals would do well to advocate for substantial reforms in our jails and prisons as part of our nation's responsibility to address the current mental health crisis. This issue is discussed in more detail in Chapter 15.

It is hoped that this case study, the information provided in Fanone and Shiffman's book, and the information presented in this chapter on CBT theories in general and Albert Ellis's rational emotive behavioral therapy in particular increase the reader's understanding of some of the complex psychological dynamics that contributed to the violent insurrection on January 6, 2021. Perhaps more importantly, it is hoped that this information will stimulate more discussions about ways to prevent such atrocities in the future. The next section of this chapter discusses criticisms raised by multicultural advocates as they relate to REBT.

REBT and Multicultural Factors

Despite the advanced thinking and tolerance Ellis demonstrated in the 1950s and 1960s about issues related to individuals' sex roles and identity, his REBT approach to counseling and psychotherapy has been sharply criticized by multicultural counseling advocates. These criticisms focused on Ellis's failure to advocate for environmental changes that would help eradicate the adverse impact of social injustices on clients' lives (Rigazio-DiGilio, Ivey, & Locke, 1997).

This criticism of Ellis's work includes his failure to elaborate on the different ways irrational beliefs are manifested by persons who come from diverse cultural groups and backgrounds. He also failed to discuss the importance of having practitioners acquire a broad range of multicultural counseling competencies as outlined by the American Counseling Association (ACA) before mental health practitioners use his theory with culturally and racially different persons (D'Andrea, 2000).

Debate over these concerns grew and were evident in discussions on these topics during the 1999 ACA National Conference. The primary focus of this debate was on the ways that practitioners could make CBT and REBT more relevant for the various contextual challenges and cultural worldviews that characterize clients from diverse populations.

Clearly, more discussion of these issues needs to occur if mental health practitioners are to learn how they can work more effectively and ethically in a culturally diverse 21st-century society. Rigazio-DiGilio and her colleagues (1997) have written about the lack of cultural and contextual relevance in Ellis's theory, suggesting that, like other forms of cognitive-behavioral therapy, REBT would have a greater impact if practitioners were to direct attention to doing more than helping clients learn to change their inner thoughts and emotions as key goals in counseling and psychotherapy. It has been further noted that an expansion in REBT's cultural-contextual purview needs to include intentional efforts to help people learn "new behaviors that have an ameliorating effect within their own personal sphere while also interrupting constraining interactions that may exist in the wider social-cultural and social-political context" (p. 236).

Ellis actively participated in a series of public discussions during the late 1990s. These public discussions highlighted the need for counseling and psychology to become more sensitive and responsive to situational and cultural factors influencing people's lives. In doing so, Ellis modeled the type of professional leadership that is needed to promote changes in our thinking about CBT and REBT - changes that will increase the cultural and contextual relevance of these powerful theoretical helping frameworks. Ellis (2000) later wrote, "Personally, I favor REBT counselors taking this kind of social and social-political stand" (p. 100).

Ellis expressed an even clearer commitment to having his REBT theory become more culturally and contextually relevant during his last public debate about these issues at the 1999 American Counseling Association's annual conference in San Diego, California. At that event, Ellis agreed to include the "C" (contextual/cultural) factor in REBT. This resulted in moving his cognitive-behavioral theory from REBT to REBCT (rational emotive behavior contextual therapy). In doing so, Ellis demonstrated his own growing understanding of the need to incorporate contextual considerations into his theoretical model of counseling and therapy.

It is important to recognize that the new integral theory is deeply committed to multicultural competence, social justice advocacy, and supporting the ongoing evolution of our multiracial/multicultural democracy. From this theoretical perspective, the three values of multicultural competence, social justice advocacy, and supporting the ongoing evolution of our multiracial/multicultural democracy reflect the meaning of promoting *optimal mental health* in the United States.

Linking Neuroscience With REBCT

The neuroscience/brain-functioning quadrant is an important component in the integral theory of mental health and human development from a psycho-political perspective. Recent research findings in neuroscience complement and extend our thinking of the positive outcomes that can occur when using REBCT approaches to reduce people's feelings of frustration and anger.

A neuroscience perspective helps us to understand that emotions are regulated by a complex neural circuitry involving several brain parts. These include the prefrontal cortex, the cingulate system, and several subcortical areas (the amygdala, hippocampus, thalamus, and parts of the basal ganglia). These cortical and subcortical areas are intricately and extensively interconnected (See Chapters 7 & 14).

When operating normally, the amygdala, hippocampus, thalamus, and basal ganglia alert people to dangers in the environment through a fight-or-flight-or freeze response. When overly activated, these cortical areas result in aggressive, angry, and/or frustrated thoughts, feelings, and behaviors.

The normal functioning of the prefrontal cortex (and specifically the orbital-frontal cortex, an area within the prefrontal cortex) as well as the cingulate system promote rational cognitive processes. Such rational processes include, but are not limited to, a person's long-term goalsetting, abstract thinking, and perspective-taking abilities. Under activation of these executive functioning brain parts reduces an individual's capacity to analyze life experiences in more accurate, objective, and rational ways.

Recent research by Bufkin and Luttrell (2005) affirmed the work of other investigators by describing how the normal functioning of the prefrontal cortex (and the orbitofrontal cortex in particular) keeps negative thoughts, emotions, and behaviors in check by regulating the activation of the cortical areas listed above (the amygdala, hippocampus, and basal ganglia).

Additional values driving the new integral theory involve a commitment to promoting the sort of neurological/brain-functioning regulation that activates cortical areas which enhance positive thoughts, emotions, and behaviors in people's lives. The research by Bufkin and Luttrell described above is very relevant for the integral theory and its commitment to promoting mental health and human development from a neurological and psycho-political perspective.

Neuroscience researchers have pointed to several ways to foster the proper activation of all of the above stated brain regions known to regulate aggressive, angry, and frustrated thoughts, feelings, and behaviors. Research findings also affirm that the proper functioning of all of the brain networks listed above can be stimulated by nutritional dietary habits. Regular exercise is another factor that contributes to the normal functioning of the prefrontal cortex, orbital-frontal cortex, and cingulate system in particular.

Various medications are designed to stimulate the production of neurotransmitters such as acetylcholine and serotonin. These neurotransmitters support the optimal functioning of the prefrontal cortex, orbitofrontal cortex, and cingulate system and help regulate the activation of the amygdala, hippocampus, thalamus, and basal ganglia as well as the negative emotions, thoughts, and behaviors associated with these brain systems. Supporters of the new integral theory are knowledgeable of the various life skills and medications that stimulate the brain-functioning changes discussed above.

Although neurological research has not been conducted to assess the specific biological impact of using Ellis's REBCT theory with different groups of people, it is reasonable to hypothesize that efforts to promote people's rational thinking capacities are likely to stimulate prefrontal cortex, orbitofrontal cortex, and cingulate system functioning and the positive psychological/emotional/behavioral outcomes of these neurological processes.

It would be useful for future research endeavors to study the different neurological reactions people have when manifesting the sort of automatic negative thoughts that Amen (1998) describes in his neuroscience theory as they relate to people's mental health and development. These are all important areas for future investigation to further substantiate the therapeutic benefits of REBCT.

Summary

This chapter focuses on the second major force in the mental health professions referred to as cognitive-behavioral therapy (CBT). To increase the reader's knowledge of CBT, the opening section of this chapter describes key assumptions that drive CBT. That discussion is followed by a description of the evolution of CBT. Among the characteristics that mark the evolution of this theoretical force include what is referred to as classic conditioning, operant conditioning, and social learning theory, all of which move into a greater emphasis on cognitive factors.

Focusing on a popular form of CBT, the reader's attention is then directed to Dr. Albert Ellis and his rational emotive behavior therapy (REBT). The opening discussion on REBT describes key theoretical constructs related to this form of CBT. Ellis emphasizes the importance of exploring with people the irrational thoughts that have developed through the client's socialization process. This is followed by understanding the importance of intentionally working to build a relationship with people who acknowledge their irrational thoughts in order that they can emotionally and cognitively respond to this therapeutic process. To achieve these ends, Ellis explores the important concept of people's *free will*.

This chapter moves on to discuss a concept that is similar to one of the cornerstones of Ellis's REBT; *irrational beliefs*. This complementary concept is reflected in the *false consciousness* people develop across the lifespan.

A case study is then utilized to further assist the reader in understanding key REBT concepts. This case study draws from parts of a book entitled, *Hold the Line: The Insurrection and One Cop's Battle for America's Soul*.

Presenting this information in a case study format is aimed at further expanding the reader's understanding of REBT as demonstrated in the interrogation of one of the four persons arrested for brutally assaulting Officer Michael Fanone during the January 6th failed insurrection. Particular attention is directed to the skills the FBI special agents used in their interrogation of Mr. Danny Rodriguez, who was convicted and sentenced to 12 years in prison for his assault on Officer Fanone. Although the special agents were not trained in CBT, they demonstrated skills commonly used by REBT practitioners. This latter point is highlighted to demonstrate how untrained persons can effectively use REBT skills and other counseling and psychotherapeutic strategies in a variety of work settings.

Towards the end of this chapter, criticisms of Ellis's REBT were presented by numerous multicultural counseling and social justice advocates in the mental health professions. The results of these criticisms led Ellis to demonstrate the ethical leadership necessary to illuminate the importance of employing multicultural competencies when working with people from diverse groups and backgrounds. As a result of the new insights Ellis gained from these criticisms, he publicly announced he was changing the term rational emotive behavioral therapy (REBT) to Rational Emotive Behavioral Contextual Therapy (REBCT) during the American Counseling Association's 1999 national conference.

Neuroscientific research findings that are relevant for the REBCT are discussed in the final section of this chapter. A number of possible hypotheses for future investigative endeavors are outlined for consideration by researchers in the mental health professions. The next chapter discusses the third theoretical force in the mental health professions. This force is referred to as the Existential-Humanistic tradition.

CHAPTER 12

THE EXISTENTIAL-HUMANISTIC FORCE

All human beings are caught in an inescapable network of mutuality in a single garment of destiny. Whatever affects one directly affects all indirectly. I can never be what I ought to be unto you are what you ought to be and you can never be what you ought to be until I am what I ought to be.

Dr. Martin Luther King Jr., in a sermon entitled,
"The Man Who Was a Fool"

Freedom isn't free. It shouldn't be a bragging point that 'oh, I don't get involved in politics,' as if that makes someone cleaner. No, that makes you derelict of duty in a Republic. Liars and panderers in government would have a much harder time of it if many people didn't insist on their right to remain ignorant and blindly agreeable.

Bill Maher, social analyst and critic

Introduction

The existential-humanistic worldview is the third major force in the mental health professions. This worldview focuses on men and women as people who are empowered to act on the world and determine their own destiny. A person's locus of control and decision to lead a more satisfying and productive life is viewed as laying within the individual rather than in his or her past history or environmental determinants.

At the same time, the humanistic aspect of this tradition focuses on people in relationship to one another. The existential-humanistic worldview emphasizes respect for people and the importance of their relationship with others, which gives this theoretical framework its long-lasting strength.

Later in this chapter, attention is directed to the ways that the political divisiveness and violence (as reflected in the January 6, 2021 insurrection) adversely impact people's ability to demonstrate the respect that is a key aspect of the existential-humanistic theory as well as the new integral theory presented in this book. The integral theory denies that there is a moral equivalency in the diverse psycho-political perspectives asserted by different people in the United States. This important issue is discussed later in this chapter as well as its relevance for the implementation of the integral theory. Next, the reader's attention is directed to the history of the existential-humanistic force in the mental health professions.

The History of Existentialism

Søren Kierkegaard was a Danish philosopher in the 1800s who is considered the father of existentialism. He believed that individuals must give meaning to their own lives rather than receiving it from society or religion. Kierkegaard additionally focused on human emotion, particularly the anxiety that comes with making choices and discovering meaning and value in life.

Other early existential philosophers include Friedrich Nietzsche and Fyodor Dostoevsky. Dostoevsky, in particular, wrote about the psychological importance of creating one's own identity to give meaning to each person's existence. The inability to identify meaning in one's life causes anxiety, known as an *existential crisis*.

What Is Existential Therapy?

The German psychoanalyst Otto Rank is considered the first therapist to practice existential therapy. He emphasized present feelings and thoughts rather than focusing primarily on one's past experiences or a person's subconscious.

Existential therapists believe that anxiety comes from uncertainty about the changing nature of the meaning of life and uncertainty about existing in the world. This uncertainty is often linked to our relationship with ourselves, the relationship we have with other people, and our relationship with the broader world in which we are situated.

An existential therapist will help people confront anxiety about their existence, such as fear of death, fear of loneliness, fear of making the wrong choices with the freedom they have, and the fear of living a life without meaning. When confronting these fears, one typically experiences psychological distress.

An existential therapist also helps people focus on one's personal responsibility for making decisions. Mental health professionals that use an existential-humanistic approach in their work aim to help people develop insight into the reasons why they make their decisions and make future choices based on the value and meaning they identify for themselves.

All of the above stated points related to the existential-humanistic force are integrated into the integral theory presented throughout this book. The following section describes another key existential-humanistic principle also integrated into the new integral theory.

Being in the World

The notion of *being in the world* is regarded as one of the fundamental concepts of existentialism. From this viewpoint, we act on the world while the world simultaneously acts on us. Attempts to separate ourselves from the world alienate us and promote a false consciousness (See Chapter 11).

According to existential theorists and philosophers, human alienation results either from the separateness from other people and the world or from one's inability to choose and act in relationship with the world. The central task when using existential-humanistic principles to promote mental health is to enable alienated people to see themselves in relationship to the world and choose and act in accordance with their own self-evaluated standards and beliefs.

Integral Theory Challenges

Mental health professionals implementing the integral theory in their professional practices are challenged to address the toxic ways many Trump supporters and members of the Trump cult demonstrate unique forms of close-mindedness and uncritical thinking about their loyalty to Trump. This not only makes these persons challenging to work with in counseling and psychotherapy but results in a less than optimal prognosis for therapeutic success.

Based on my professional experiences working with Trump supporters and Trump cult members, I consistently found these individuals to become increasing rigid in their thinking as well as manifesting a lack of emotional regulation and a frequent use of unconscious defense mechanisms (See Chapter 10) when discussing the impact of psycho-political factors in counseling and therapy sessions. It is hypothesized that a distinct form of *neurological stagnation* is helpful in explaining these reactions (See Chapter 14). The related concept of *developmental stagnation* is discussed earlier in this book (See Chapter 8).

The manifestations of these forms of developmental and neurological stagnation represent unique challenges for mental health professionals. To repeat a point made above, the defensiveness and resistance manifested by members of the Trump cult, in particular, results in a negative prognosis for positive psychological and developmental outcomes in counseling and psychotherapy.

Recognizing the need to address such poor prognosis, the integral theory offers the following information to expand the reader's thinking about some of the research-supported psychosocial techniques and strategies that can be helpful when working with defensive and resistant Trump supporters. Numerous researchers have reported that building a positive relationship with all clients, especially individuals resistant to change, is necessary in promoting positive mental health and developmental outcomes. Theories of existential-humanistic counseling emphasize the importance of encouraging people to gain new insights into different types of relationships that mark their lives.

The integral theory is strongly anchored in the value of fostering positive relationships in the work mental health professionals do in the field. The following section addresses these issues in greater detail. In doing so, mental health practitioners are encouraged to consider implementing the existential-humanistic techniques described below to promote mental health and ongoing human development when working with resistant Trump supporters, and, particularly members of the Trump cult.

Exploring Four Different Types of Relationships From An Existential-Humanistic and Integral Theory Perspective

Mental health practitioners, who employ existential-humanistic theories in their work, commonly explore four different types of interconnected relationships in counseling and psychotherapy settings. By exploring these different relationships with other people, the new integral theory asserts that a person's mental health can be enhanced as people gain new insights into the strengths and/or areas for improvement in the following four relational domains.

Many existential-humanistic practitioners embrace the importance of exploring people's relationships as a starting point in this consciousness raising process. From an existential-humanistic and an integrally-informed perspective, people, who consistently express positive experiences in their personal relationship with themselves, is viewed as an indication of their mental health. Conversely, the lack of positive comments related to one's relationship with oneself tends to correlate with mental health issues in need of being addressed.

A second relationship that warrants appraisal from an existential-humanistic and integral theory perspective involves exploring a person's relationship with other people in their lives. People who consistently express having positive relationships with other people are indicators of mental health from an existential-humanistic and integral perspective. In contrast, an appraisal, which suggests that a person is consistently experiencing negative outcomes in her or his relationships with other people, is often a barrier to more fully realizing one's untapped mental health potential.

A third relationship that is important to explore involves assessing people's relationship with the world at-large. From an existential-humanistic and integral perspective, people who express having a positive relationship with different aspects of the world at-large are indicators of mental health and human development. People expressing negative experiences in their relationship with the world at-large might benefit from existential-humanistic and/or integral counseling that focus on this relational area.

Clemmont Vontress and other existential-humanistic theorists (Vontress, 1995, 1999) have more recently emphasized the importance of exploring a fourth relational area. This exploration focuses on a person's relationship with spirituality and religion when working to promote her or his mental health and development.

According to Vontress, spirituality and religion represent additive factors that commonly result in many people experiencing a greater sense of connection and community with others while simultaneously reducing one's sense of alienation and meaninglessness in their lives. Vontress's perspective can potentially provide a gateway to address other existential issues that many people face in our society, including various forms of personal alienation and anxiety.

The process of addressing the existential-humanistic relationships described above requires people to explore and reflect on the various experiences people have with themselves, other people, and the larger world in which they operate as well as people's spiritual beliefs and values. As a result of examining the meaning or lack of meaning of these personal, interpersonal, worldly, and spiritual relationships, it is believed that people are better positioned to realize their untapped potential for mental health and ongoing development.

Intentionality

Intentionality is another key existential construct. This concept asserts that people can move forward in their development by consciously acting on the world in which they are a part. However, existential philosophers encourage people to temper their understanding of the importance of acting with intentionality in the world by remaining cognizant of the ways that the world constantly acts on them as well. Consequently, the existential notion of intentionality provides a bridge to humanism that is full-blown in the theoretical writings of Carl Rogers.

Carl Rogers's Theoretical Worldview

Carl Rogers has done much to link existential-humanistic concepts to people's mental health and ongoing human development. In doing so, he emphasizes the value and dignity of all persons. This emphasis represents an important contribution to the existential-humanistic tradition, which recognizes opportunities for personal growth and healthy development that may be realized from one's relationships in life.

Basic to this philosophy is understanding and acknowledging one's responsibility for the many choices people make in life and then consciously accepting the responsibility to act in positive and intentional ways to realize untapped dimensions of their mental health and ongoing development (Ivey et al., 2012). Advocates of these existential-humanistic principles use the term *self-actualization* when discussing the goal of these developmental processes.

The word *self-actualization* is now a part of North American culture. The popularity of this term can be traced to the influence of several persons, most notably Carl Rogers and Abraham Maslow. This aspect of Rogers's worldview, now commonplace in counseling and therapy as well as in our contemporary society, is a radical departure from the psychodynamic and cognitive-behavioral traditions. Whereas psychodynamic and cognitive-behavioral theories view humankind as an unknowing pawn of unconscious forces and environmental contingencies, existential-humanistic psychology (particularly as interpreted by Rogers) stresses that the individual can take charge of life, make decisions, and act positively on the world.

At the heart of Rogers's worldview is the faith that people are generally positive, forward moving, basically good, and ultimately self-actualizing. *Self-actualization* may ultimately be defined as experiencing one's fullest humanity. Self-actualizing people enjoy life thoroughly in all its aspects, not only in occasional moments of triumph.

From Rogers's perspective, the fundamental task of mental health practitioners is to assist people in attaining the intentionality and development that are natural components of self-actualization and one's inner authentic self. According to Rogers, as a person becomes truly in touch with his or her inner self, the individual will move to positive action and personal fulfillment (Ivey et al., 2021). All of the above mental health characteristics are highlighted in the optimal mental health concept put forth by the integral theory of mental health and ongoing human development discussed throughout this book.

Abraham Maslow's Self-Actualization

Self-actualization is at the pinnacle of what the American psychologist and advocate of the human potential movement, Abraham Maslow, defined as a hierarchy of human needs. In this hierarchy, lower needs must be met before higher human development potentialities emerge. Physiological needs are primary in Maslow's hierarchy. The need for food, water, clothing, sleep, and shelter are the bare necessities for anyone's survival.

Maslow suggested that if an individual is starving or near starving, he or she is essentially defined by that hunger. In most cases, an individual with extreme hunger will not strive to address higher needs, such as love and belonging, unless the body's need for nourishment is satisfied.

Once physiological needs are met, the next level of need - safety - immediately rises to consciousness and begins to drive one's behavior. The need for food may be forgotten or suddenly seem trivial compared with the need for physical protection, provided the individual continues to have a steady food supply. This cycle of need fulfillment occurs at every stage of Maslow's hierarchy of needs.

Maslow asserted that average adults in affluent, organized societies have few safety needs under typical conditions. Most have little need to worry about physical attacks or fires. Maslow further noted that safety needs drive individuals' thoughts, emotions, and behaviors in less stable conditions, such as those living in low socioeconomic conditions or under wartime situations.

Love and belonging needs are next in Maslow's hierarchy. These include friendship, family, and sexual love as well as the desire to be accepted by peer groups and receive affection from others. To meet a person's love and belonging needs, individuals must be positioned to give and receive love. Maslow, like many theorists, psychologists, and psychiatrists, suggest that the failure to fulfill love and belonging needs are at the root of much of modern psychopathology.

This aspect of Maslow's theory is particularly relevant for the new integral theory of mental health and human development from a psycho-political perspective. Gun, physical, and emotional violence perpetuated by gang members and other persons in our society can (from Maslow's theory) be traced, in part, to the failure to experience authentic and respected belonging within many of the institutions and daily encounters that mark their lives.

Similarly, as articulated in the integral theory of mental health and human development from a psycho-political perspective, the unprecedented demographic transformation of our nation is stimulating forms of existential anxiety, frustration, and anger. These negative reactions can be explained by White people's loss of a sense of belonging as the dominant racial group in our society which is being replaced with a majority of persons of color as a result of the demographic transformation occurring in our nation and discussed throughout this book.

From the perspective of existential-humanistic theories, the anxiety, frustration, and anger manifested among increasing numbers of White persons during these unprecedented perilous times represent barriers to their ability to experience their own self-actualization. The integral theory further asserts that these barriers not only represent a developmental and neurological stagnation in White people's moral development, but often result in a regression in this important dimension of human development.

Near the top of Maslow's hierarchy are esteem needs. These needs include the desire to realize a person's competence, self-regard, self-respect, and respect for others. The realization of these needs lead to feeling a sense of personal strength and general self-worth. If these needs are not met, people frequently become deeply discouraged or develop maladjusted methods for coping with feelings of inferiority, meaninglessness and worthlessness. According to Maslow, only after these collective needs—physiological, safety, love/belonging, and esteem needs - are met can an individual be motivated by the drive for self-actualization. As Maslow stated:

> To be truly happy, painters need to paint, writers need to write, musicians need to play. This is self-actualization. However, even if all other needs are met, self-actualization does not emerge as

a motivator in all cases. When it does, it can take many forms, depending on a person's cultural identity, talents, and values. Often the self-actualizing urge is creative as in the case of artists or writers. It might also take the form of maximizing the quality of one's relationships or perfecting one's physical form through athletics and good health.

Maslow noted that self-actualization is one of the least studied and understood needs in human development. This is largely due to its relative rarity. Realizing one's full capacity for self-actualization is the exception rather than the rule in most people's lives.

He also pointed out that there are numerous examples of individuals living in states of racism, poverty, loneliness, and low self-esteem who nonetheless seem to self-actualize through their work. Examples include Vincent van Gogh, whose life and suicide suggest a deep well of unmet needs, and Anne Frank, whose universally acclaimed diary was written in conditions of extreme danger.

The Pathology of Normal: A Critique of Maslow's Self-Actualization

William Berry is a practicing psychotherapist in private practice and a faculty member at Florida International University. Dr. Berry published a critique of Maslow's self-actualization theory. This critique is described in an article entitled, "The Psychopathology of Normal." The following section describes Berry's meaning of the *psychopathology of normal* as it relates to Maslow's theory of self-actualization.

In opening his critique of Maslow's theory, Berry uses a direct quotation from Abraham Maslow which reads as follows:

"What we call normal in psychology is really a psychopathology of the average, so undramatic and so widely spread that we don't even notice it ordinarily." This quote by Maslow is made by the theorist who gave us the idea of the *hierarchy of needs* and *self-actualization*.

According to Berry, Maslow's point is that being *normal*, being average, although normally perceived as okay, is pathology. Pathology can be defined as disease or sickness. The dictionary's definition of psychopathology is the *study of the origin, development, and manifestation of mental or behavioral disorders*.

Berry continues by noting that, 'Most people would be offended if someone were to say they were average. Yet by definition, most people are. Average in psychological terms is a huge category, encompassing the majority of our national population.'

As Berry explains further, those who are not average are thought to be *outliers*. *Outliers* are the small percentage of people at either end of the bell curve. They are either well below the average or well above. Average in this sense doesn't have much to do with not being an individual. You can be an individual yet fall well within the average.

Maslow's intention was to highlight that the ultimate goal of what it means to be a human being is to self-actualize, to become all that a person can become in a lifelong process of self-improvement. He also contended that all humans have this potential. But before that can happen, other needs which are positioned below self-actualization must be met. These include physiological needs, needs for safety, needs for love and belonging, and the need for esteem. Not striving toward being all you can be is a major feature in the psychopathology of normal (Berry, 2011).

Research findings suggest that most people in the United States have the lower needs met on a regular basis. Most have enough food, water, and shelter. Most do not feel threats to their safety. And, hopefully, we feel loved and have a sense of belonging in our lives. With these needs met, we can move toward feeling esteem.

The manifestation of having esteem for oneself encompasses self-confidence, feeling competent, and believing at least some other people hold us in high esteem. It seems reasonable that readers of this chapter have these needs met as well. This is not to say you feel this way all the time. There are always flare-ups of self-doubt. But it is understood that generally, and most of the time, people feel confident in themselves and their abilities. So, with all of these important needs met, Berry raises the following important question: "Why aren't more people becoming self-actualized?"

Berry shares a simple answer to this question in the following manner:

People become complacent with the lower, but important needs being met. Then, instead of working towards self-actualization, people become consumers: keeping up with the Joneses, being the first on our block to have the newest gadget, overindulging in entertainment needs (movies, television, trips) and otherwise trying to fill the yearning for a higher purpose with purchases, rather than self-improvement.

Perhaps what is keeping the majority of people from self-actualizing is that they are misinterpreting their yearning for self-actualization as a need for more of something else: more love, more things, more fun. Therefore, the solution is to cease filling the void with things and instead, focus on yourself and what you can become. What are you doing that is creative? What are you doing to exercise your mind? What are you doing to make the planet (and your fellow human beings) better? What are you doing to be happier with yourself, rather than your possessions? Answer these questions and the movement toward self-actualization begins.

If a person has trouble getting started or maintaining progress in moving towards self-actualization, Berry suggests that it is possible that there are unconscious forces that lie within a person that keeps one in a state of developmental stagnation (See Chapters 8 & 10). Another point Berry asserts is that it may be useful for a person in developmental stagnation to enter therapy so he or she can discover these unconscious blocks, remove them, and get back on track to realizing one's untapped potential for self-actualization.

Making the unconscious become more conscious is one of the most beneficial aspects of existential-humanistic theories and the integral framework discussed in this book. Many people view therapy simply as a place to vent or get some direction with life problems. But at its best, therapy is geared towards stimulating new insights, toward understanding oneself on a deeper level, and becoming self-actualized.

The meaning of developmental and neurological stagnation is initially discussed in Chapter 8. They are also detailed in Chapter 14 in a description of the ways that neuroscientific research findings increase our understanding of how and why these two forms of stagnation exist and their relevance for the new integral theory of mental health and human development.

Expanding the Concept of Self-Actualization

There are two major psycho-political factors that emerge when discussing a person's responsibility for realizing one's untapped potential for self-actualization. On one hand, there are people who believe that individuals are solely responsible for addressing the various needs that precede self-actualization and then follow through in addressing the challenges needed to realize their self-actualization.

This perspective is a very individualistic view that emphasizes the responsibility of each person to realize and maintain her or his potential for self-actualization. From a psycho-political perspective, the new integral theory acknowledges that not all right-wing Republicans fall among this group of persons who operate from a very individualistic perspective in achieving and maintaining self-actualization.

Research findings provide evidence indicating that many people in the Republican Party who support former President Donald Trump and back the MAGA Movement believe that each person who tries his or her hardest can achieve success in our society; and, from a psychological perspective, achieve and maintain self-actualization. Numerous social scientists have studied this psychosocial perspective and refer to it as the *Myth of Meritocracy* (Cooper, 2015; Markovits, 2019; Reich, 2019).

On the other hand, there are people in our society who believe that the government has a responsibility to facilitate healthy human development. It does so by providing resources that enable people in general and disadvantaged persons in particular to have opportunities to meet the lower needs in Maslow's hierarchy for self-actualization.

This includes providing support to address basic needs like food (through governmental-supported food stamp programs), enabling the Environmental Protection Agency (EPA) to oversee clean water in urban and rural areas, providing subsidized and safe housing for elderly persons and people with disabilities, supporting community-based childhood and adolescent interventions to address the needs for love and belonging, and providing life skills training services to address people's esteem needs to name a few. These supports represent a collectivistic consciousness that are cornerstones in the integral theory of mental health and human development from a psycho-political perspective.

The personal responsibility and governmental responsibility perspectives stated above often result in antagonistic beliefs that are debated, voted on, and financially supported or subjected to cutbacks in governmental spending. The integral theory emphasizes the importance of having mental health professionals and people in the general public engage in political activism that support increased governmental financial support for mental health services and resources that are intentionally designed to assist people in need to realize their untapped self-actualization potential.

People's Search for Meaning

Additional concepts that existential-humanistic mental health professionals operate from include exploring and understanding the meaninglessness in many people's lives. This includes meaninglessness in people's interpersonal interactions, a loss of a sense of belonging, and living a life without conscious purpose. One of the offshoots of existential-humanistic approaches to mental health and human development that address these toxic conditions was developed by Victor Frankl and referred to as *logotherapy*.

Viktor Frankl's Early Years

Viktor Frankl grew up in the early 1900s in Vienna, Austria. He was raised by a disciplined father and a tender-hearted, pious mother. Frankl is described as being a precocious child who at the age of four announced to his family that he knew he wanted to be a physician in the future (Ivey et al., 2012).

Frankl's interest in psychosocial-political issues began to be manifested during his adolescence when he became actively involved in the local Young Socialist Workers Organization in high school. Although he had taken a keen interest in local, national, and world politics during his youth, Frankl was increasingly attracted to the study of philosophy and psychology. Upon finishing his high school studies, he had an article published in the International Journal of Psychoanalysis, which led him to have regular correspondence with Sigmund Freud.

Frankl attended medical school in Vienna in the early 1920s. It was there that he had the opportunity to personally meet Freud. In studying Freud's psychoanalytic theory, Frankl accepted his concept of the unconscious. However, Frankl asserted that the will to create meaning in one's life is stronger and more fundamental than the unconscious pleasure drive Freud espoused.

Despite his interest in Freud's work, Frankl became more attracted to Alfred Adler's theory of Individual Psychology (see Chapter 10). It was around this time that Frankl received professional training in Individual Psychology directly from Adler. As his interest in the psychoanalytic tradition and Adler's theory increased, so too did his efforts to develop his own existential-humanistic theory of human development; a theory he would call *logotherapy* during a public lecture in 1926.

Personal Tragedy

During the Nazi occupation of Austria, Frankl was made head of the neurological department at Rothschild Hospital. This was the only hospital for Jews in Vienna at the time. Frankl made many false diagnoses of his patients to circumvent the new Nazi policies requiring euthanasia of the mentally ill. It was also during this period that he began his manuscript called, *The Doctor and the Soul*.

Frankl married in 1942. In September of that same year, he and his wife, father, mother, and brother were all arrested and brought to the concentration camp in Bohemia. His father died there of starvation; his mother and brother were killed in Auschwitz in 1944; and his wife died at Bergen-Belson in 1945. Of his immediate family, only Frankl's sister survived (she had immigrated to Australia a short time earlier).

Frankl continued to develop his theory of *logotherapy* while imprisoned in Nazi concentration camps from 1942 through 1945. Unlike Freud's psychodynamic theory, which emphasizes the impact of past events on a person's development, *logotherapy* focuses on the future, that is to say, on the meanings to be fulfilled in one's future (Frankl, 1984).

This fundamental theoretical premise was severely tested in Frankl's personal triumph over the unimaginable trauma he experienced in Nazi concentration camps. When he was moved to Auschwitz, his manuscript of *The Doctor and the Soul* was lost in the concentration camp's disinfection chamber.

Frankl's Search for Meaning

After his liberation from the German concentration camps in April 1945, Frankl completed his book, *The Doctor and the Soul*. Shortly thereafter, he dictated his most famous work, titled *Man's Search for Meaning* which details the development and central concepts of his *logotherapy* theory. This scholarly endeavor was completed in only nine days.

Frankl was able to reframe his life situation while in a Nazi concentration camp and find positive reasons for living in the midst of unimaginable negative circumstances. He faced the existential dilemma of his meaning of life under the most extreme conditions.

Frankl's view of the human condition reflects a lifetime of struggle to find the positives in humankind. In his highly popular book, *Man's Search for Meaning,* Frankl relates his experiences in German concentration camps during World War II. Although Frankl describes the horrors of the concentration camps in great detail, the book is more a testimony to the power of the human spirit and its capability of survival under the most inhumane conditions.

Central Theoretical Constructs of Logotherapy

In coining his theory of *logotherapy*, Frankl used the Greek word *logos* which can mean "study, spirit, God, or meaning." It is this last definition (meaning) that Frankl focused on, although the other concepts are never far off in his writings. Comparing himself with Freud and Adler, Frankl explained that Freud essentially postulated a will to pleasure as the root of all human motivations, and Adler a will to power and social interest.

Logotherapy, in contrast, postulates a will to meaning. Consequently, the task for the logotherapist is to help people find meaning and purpose in life - and then to support them in acting on those personal meanings.

Logotherapists are interested in carefully learning how a person constructs meaning of the world. Once they have this understanding, they can move forward to more actively promoting mental health and human development with their clients.

Many persons, who seek existential-humanistic interventions, suffer from day-to-day problems that, from Frankl's perspective, are fundamentally linked to their inability to find positive meaning in their lives. How does one make sense of a meaningless job, learn to cope with a less-than-satisfactory personal relationship, or relate to difficult parents or in-laws?

The integral theory described in this book agrees that helping people find positive meaning when addressing the above questions is not a technical helping skill. There is no formula that can be easily applied to any one person or group of people who are in need of finding more positive meaning in life.

The integral theory encourages readers to try out some of the logotherapy constructs discussed in this chapter. This can be done by reflecting on and recording your responses to the four existential-humanistic questions listed above. Interested readers are also encouraged to consider using this existential-humanistic exercise at different points in their lives as a way to assess their mental health and ongoing development over time.

Summary

This chapter builds on the information presented in the two preceding major theoretical forces in the mental health professions. It expands these discussions by focusing on issues related to existential-humanistic theories.

In Chapter 10, readers are provided information related to the principles, values, key constructs, and concrete intervention strategies that characterize the psychodynamic force in the mental health professions. The integral theory presented in this book draws the reader's attention to ways in which such psychodynamic concepts as the impact of early childhood and adolescent experiences on adult development, the power of the unconscious, and the use of defense mechanisms in response to people's anxiety can be explored from a psycho-political perspective.

Chapter 11 includes a detailed discussion of the impact of cognitive-behavioral theories (CBTs) on mental health professional training programs and clinical practices. In a similar manner, the new integral theory includes a description of ways that mental health professionals and community members can utilize principles, values, and intervention strategies from a cognitive-behavioral perspective to address the mental health crisis in our nation from a psycho-political perspective. Particular attention was directed to Dr. Albert Ellis's Rational-Emotive-Behavioral-Contextual theory (REBCT) as an effective way to address the perilous times we are situated as well as addressing our country's current mental health crisis.

Chapter 12 focuses on the third major theoretical force that continues to shape the mental health professions in many ways. Detailed information about the historic evolution, principles, values, and techniques driven by existential-humanistic theories are dissected in that chapter.

Discussion was also directed to important ways the new integral theory can be strengthened by utilizing various aspects of existential-humanistic theories to address the mental health crisis in our nation. This can be accomplished in ways that support the ongoing evolution of the multiracial/multicultural democracy in the United States.

Chapter 13 describes the fourth major force in the mental health professions referred to as multicultural counseling and social justice advocacy movements over the past 50 years. All of these theoretical forces have substantial support from the *integral theory of mental health and human development from a psycho-political perspective* that are discussed in detail throughout this book.

CHAPTER 13

MULTICULTURAL COUNSELING AND SOCIAL JUSTICE ADVOCACY THEORIES

Sometimes we are separated by differences, and sometimes we are united by common ideals of respect and compassion.

Paul Watson, environmental activist

The moral arc of the universe is long, but it bends towards justice.

Martin Luther King Jr.

Introduction

This chapter discusses issues related to the multicultural counseling and social justice advocacy movements as well as their relevance for the integral theory of mental health and human development from a psycho-political perspective. It is intentionally designed to accomplish four goals listed below.

First, it provides an overall introduction to the meaning of multicultural counseling theories and their relevance for the integral theory presented in this book.

Second, it describes the historic evolution of the multicultural counseling and therapy (MCTM) movement and the more recent social justice advocacy (SJAM) movement in our nation.

Third, it discusses the interface between mental health practices and social justice advocacy in the Age of Trump.

Fourth, this chapter introduces a pathway for the revitalization of the mental health professions in culturally and racially responsive ways. This pathway is described in greater detail in the final chapter of this book (See Chapter 15).

The Multicultural Counseling and Therapy Movement

The genesis of the multicultural counseling and therapy movement (MCTM) occurred in the late 1960s when several African American psychologists criticized the American Psychological Association (APA) for failing to support new ways of thinking about the mental health of Black persons in our society. Up until that point in time, the mental health professions were considered to be culturally encapsulated (Wrenn, 1962).

The early pioneers in the MCTM understood that the cultural encapsulation of the mental health professions contributed to the perpetuation of various forms of White supremacy and White racism as described in Chapter 2. Although the terms *anti-racism* and *social justice advocacy* were not commonly used in the 1960s, the meaning of these terms have become pivotal in the ongoing evolution of the MCTM and the social justice advocacy movement (SJAM).

The First Phase of the Evolution of the MCTM

There are numerous milestones that occurred during the first evolutionary phase of the MCTM from the late 1960s to the early 1980s. During that time multicultural counseling researchers directed attention to studying and describing the *between-group differences* commonly manifested among people in different racial/cultural/ethnic groups. This was an important step forward for the MCTM as it enabled mental health professionals as well as people in the general public to learn about such between-group differences and their relevance for living in a culturally diverse society.

The Second Phase of the Evolution of the MCTM

The second evolutionary phase of the MCTM is dated from approximately the late 1970s through the mid-1990s. Multicultural counseling researchers ushered in new knowledge during this evolutionary phase by studying and describing *within-group differences* manifested among people within the same racial/cultural/ethnic group. Commonly referred to as *multicultural identity development theories* as well as *racial identity development theories*, this expanding knowledgebase enhanced the ability of mental health professionals to operate in ways that reflect a more complex and accurate understanding of human development.

The integral theory embraces the above stated knowledgebase. It does so because an understanding of *between-group* and *within-group differences* is basic and essential when striving to promote democracy, mental health, human development, and social justice in our society.

These pillars of knowledge represent important advancements in the MCTM and the SJAM that are especially relevant in light of the unprecedented demographic changes occurring in our country. Among the racial/cultural identity development theories that have been developed and tested include those that focus on the identity development of White persons, African Americans, Asian Americans, and persons of Latino descent as well as multiracial persons.

The following section provides readers with more detailed information related to racial/cultural identity development theories. The work of Dr. Joseph Ponterotto and Dr. Paul Pedersen (1993) is highlighted in the following section with a detailed description of Ponterotto's stages of white racial consciousness and its relevance for the new integral theory presented throughout this book.

Before reviewing Ponterotto's stages of white consciousness, readers are encouraged to reflect on interactions you may have had with White persons in conversations related to White racism. It might be observations you may have experienced watching recorded television news reports, you tube videos, or other social media resources capturing White persons expressing their views of White racism and/or White supremacy. In doing so, see if the characteristics described at the different stages of Ponterotto's model fit any of your observations of White persons in these interactions. This activity is a concrete way to become more knowledgeable of Ponterotto's stages of White racial consciousness and their relevance for the ongoing evolution of the MCTM and the SJAM.

Ponterotto's Stages of White Racial Consciousness

Stage 1: Pre-Exposure

- Persons at this stage demonstrate little interest and give little thought to racial and/or multicultural issues.

- These individuals are very naïve about racial issues and privileges White people inherit in America.

- Persons at this stage believe that racism no longer exists or if it does exist it does so only to a limited degree.

- Perceptions of racism at this stage are old-fashioned and do not include notions of subtle or modern racism (e.g., overt and covert intentional and unintentional racism).

Stage 2: Exposure

- For many White people, operating at this stage begins when they are confronted with racial and/or multicultural issues.

- Persons at this stage begin to understand the existence of modern racism and individual, institutional, and cultural manifestations of this psycho-social cancer.

- Individuals at this stage acknowledge that White persons and minority-group members are treated differently (regardless of the person's economic status) and that minority racial group members face psychological, economic, social, educational, and housing challenges White people do not have to deal with.

- A growing sense of empowerment is felt among persons at Stage 2 as White people begin to acquire new knowledge related to White racism and White supremacy.

- White persons at this stage begin to experience disappointment, frustration, anger, hostility, and guilt over having been deceived for so long. For many White persons, these emotional reactions are grounded in their naïveté and acceptance of White racism without question, along with myths and stereotypes about racial minority group persons which are often perpetuated by the U.S. educational system and mental health professions.

- Individuals at this developmental stage begin to see how they themselves are subtly and/or complicitly racist.

Stage 3: Zealot-Defensive

- This stage of White racial consciousness begins in response to strong emergent feelings brought up at Stage 2. White persons commonly respond to Stage 2 factors in one of two ways.

- The Zealot Reaction – White persons operating at this stage become zealous about issues related to race, racism, and multiculturalism. Furthermore, many of these persons become pro-minority in their personal and political philosophy and behaviors.

- The Defensive Reaction – In contrast, other White persons manifesting characteristics associated with this developmental stage become very defensive and take the criticisms of the "White System" personally. They typically withdraw from discussions related to race, racism, and/or multicultural topics or express anger and frustration over such discussions.

Stage 4: Integration

- As persons, who are defensive about racial and/or multicultural issues are led to process and experience their feelings (disappointment, guilt, frustration, anger, defensiveness), they begin to demonstrate an increasing openness to learn about these issues.

- The intense feelings people operating at Stage 3 often experience begin to lessen at Stage 4 as individuals develop a more balanced and accurate perspective of race, racism, and multiculturalism.

- These persons now begin to accept the realities of modern racism, acknowledge their own subtle (and at times not-so-subtle) racism, and feel a growing sense of empowerment about eliminating racism in themselves and in their schools/universities/businesses and communities at-large.

- Persons at this stage feel good about themselves as members of the White cultural group and develop a renewed interest in their own racial background. Persons at this stage often manifest an increased curiosity about their own ethnic roots (e.g., their Italian, Polish, Irish heritage, etc.).

- Individuals operating from this stage typically manifest an increased appreciation of other cultures and a desire to learn more about these different groups.

- At the fourth stage of Ponterotto's White racial consciousness model, persons commonly demonstrate an increased level of interest in other identity commitments such as their own gender identity. They begin to think about the ways that these other personal identities impact their interactions with people in an increasingly diverse 21st-century society.

The integral theory of mental health and human development presented in this book affirms the ways that psycho-political factors can encourage and/or discourage White people's position on the four stages of Ponterotto's model. The new integral theory endorses the development and implementation of antiracist and social justice psychoeducational activities in our communities. The new integral theory reflects an awareness of the ways that a theoretical framework like Ponterotto's stages of white racial consciousness can be used to promote mental health and human development.

A Community/School/University Intervention

The following information explains how issues related to White supremacy and White racism can be addressed in community and/or educational settings. At a basic practical level of such community/educational interventions, mental health professionals and other persons interested in addressing these perilous times and the mental health crisis in our nation could be recruited to learn about the four stages of White racial consciousness. Based on this learning, the recruits could then be asked to work together to plan ways to develop psychoeducational meetings based on Ponterotto's model that fit the nuances of their communities.

Additional practical suggestions outlined by the new integral theory include making sure the initial group of interested persons, who agreed to learn about Ponterotto's framework, will also agree to work together to develop a plan to advertise future discussion group meetings that focus on the complex problem of racism in community and/or educational settings as spotlighted by Ponterotto's white racial consciousness theory.

Next, the recruits for this intervention would agree to be responsible for making copies of the four stages of White racial consciousness theory and distributed to other people who express interest in participating in group discussions of these important issues. At the initial group meeting, the recruits would explain that their role is to facilitate a discussion about the meaning and relevance of the four stages of White racial consciousness for the communities in which attendees are a part.

This is one of the practical and cost-effective ways the integral theory of mental health and human development could be implemented to stimulate positive changes in people's views about White supremacy and White racism. This suggested community/school/university intervention is most effective when it is facilitated by persons who possess *transformational leadership* knowledge and skills. More detailed information about transformational leadership is discussed later in this chapter.

The Third Phase of the MCTM

The third phase in the ongoing evolution of the MCTM was marked by multicultural advocates who asserted that problems associated with the cultural and racial encapsulation of the mental health professions has and, in many ways, continue to perpetuate cultural and racial biases. The perpetuation of such biases are manifested in the omission and commission of ways of thinking and operating in professional training programs, individual and community/ecological assessment processes, research methods, and mental health professionals' clinical practices. With these issues in mind, the pioneers in the MCTM highlighted the need to develop a set of multicultural counseling competencies for mental health professions in general and the counseling profession in particular.

Conversations about the need for multicultural competencies evolved during the 1970s. More structured discussions related to the need for cultural competencies in the mental health professions increased during the 1980s. Dr. Allen Ivey, a long-time pioneer in the MCTM, was one of the few White mental health professionals to promote productive structured discussions related to the need for multicultural counseling competencies in the mental health professions during the 1980s. The 1990s extended these discussions and became more organizationally political and action oriented.

The culmination of much scholarly reflection and collaborative discussions led by numerous pioneers in the MCTM as well as an increasing cadre of young mental health professionals of color during the 1980s and 1990s, resulted in the drafting of 31 multicultural competencies by leaders in the Association for Multicultural Counseling and Development (AMCD) (Sue, Arredondo, & McDavis, 1991).

The multicultural pioneers, who spearheaded, supported, and celebrated the 1991 publication of the 31 multicultural counseling competencies, continued to be met with resistance and hostility by numerous White mental health colleagues. In spite of these ongoing negative reactions, the unprecedented impact of the 1991 publication of the 31 multicultural competencies in two of the leading counseling journals greatly advanced the evolution of the MCTM.

These historic publications were authored by Derald Sue, Patricia Arredondo, and Rodney McDavis (1991) and simultaneously published in the *Journal of Counseling and Development* and the *Journal of Multicultural Counseling*. The unprecedented publication of the competencies in these two journals resulted in their becoming the most widely referenced multicultural articles in the counseling profession and a hallmark in the third phase of the MCTM's evolution.

In light of the continuing resistance and hostility exhibited by numerous White mental health educators, practitioners, and students, who persisted in supporting traditional, culturally biased theories and practices, led to the establishment of the National Institute for Multicultural Counseling (NIMC). The respected and influential founding members of NIMC persisted in effectively and publicly unpacking the various ways that institutional racism, White privilege, and White superiority contributed to the negative reactions which were directed toward the most outspoken and emboldened multicultural counseling competency advocates (D'Andrea, 2006, 2014; D'Andrea & Daniels, 2015).

Despite the continuing negative reactions directed towards the most outspoken advocates of the MCTM, these pioneers persisted by operating in principled ways as well as remaining disciplined and diligent in implementing a broad range of interventions designed to promote a growing multicultural counseling competency movement. These interventions included outreach, consultation, and organizational development efforts. The goal in implementing these professional/organizational change activities was to garner broad-based support for the multicultural counseling competencies in the mental health professions in general and in the counseling profession in particular. Specific outreach efforts were routinely implemented with individual faculty members and various mental health organizations and professional training programs during the late 1990s (D'Andrea, 2006).

Directing much time and energy with little success in gaining substantial organizational support from the American Counseling Association (ACA) during the 1990s, the NIMC leaders informed ACA officials that they planned to organize non-violent demonstrations at future ACA conferences until substantial organizational progress was made within ACA by formally supporting the evolution of the MCTM in general and the multicultural counseling competencies in particular (Arredondo & D'Andrea, 1997).

The above-stated action strategy was directly drawn from the non-violent principles and protest actions implemented by Dr. Martin Luther King Jr. and many other participants in the civil rights movement. The basic assumption underlying this NIMC strategy was the belief that the implementation of bold, public, and agitational organizational change efforts would result in a greater level of support by large mental health professional organizations like the ACA.

This assumption proved to be true as ACA leaders discussed the above stated demands presented by the NIMC. Meeting these demands was partly due to the NIMC leaders who understood an important principle articulated by Frederick Douglass more than a century earlier. Simply stated, this principle acknowledges that, "Power concedes nothing without demand. It never did and it never will" (Douglas, 1857). This principle remains a central value when implementing the new integral theory discussed in this book.

As stated early in this book, one of the important goals is to provide readers with information and suggestions they can use to address major challenges occurring in our society. Among these challenges include the following:

(1) addressing these perilous political times and their implications for our nation's mental health crisis,

(2) tackling the increasing problems caused by expanded forms of White supremacy and White racism,

(3) attending to the need to support the ongoing evolution of our nation's multiracial/multicultural democracy, and

(4) focusing on ways to promote the cultural competence of our nation as a whole in ways that complement the third phase of the MCTM and SJAM.

From the perspective of the integral theory of mental health and human development, it is important to highlight the fourth challenge briefly outlined above. Having mental health professionals make a commitment to embrace the integral theory's expressed need to foster the cultural competence of large numbers of people across the United States requires the implementation of innovative community-based projects that have been tested and found to be effective in addressing this need (D'Andrea, 2015). In doing so, supporters of the integral theory are able to help people navigate the unprecedented transformation in our country's demography in ways that enable them to experience a greater level of optimal mental health which facilitate their pursuit of happiness within a rapidly diversified 21st century society.

The new integral theory acknowledges how remnants of the cultural and racial encapsulation that characterized the mental health professions for decades continue in various ways in professional training programs, individual and community-wide mental health assessment services, and practitioners' clinical practices. Efforts to address these issues gained strength during the third phase of the ongoing evolution of these movements.

The integral theory compliments efforts by supporters of the MCTM and SJAM who engage in the above stated actions and ensure the ongoing third evolutionary phase of these movements. The integral theory does this by expanding the definition of White supremacy and White racism and introducing a new theory that expands readers' thinking about the scope and purview of the meaning of multiculturalism (See Chapter 2).

Continuing evolutionary accomplishments manifested during the 1990s to the present time by supporters of the MCTM and SJAM are designed to re-focus attention to the ways that remnants of traditional forms of culturally and racial encapsulation persist in many professional mental health training programs, clinical practices, individual and community assessment services, and research endeavors.

The Fourth Phase of the MCTM

Based on the knowledge underlying the integral theory of mental health and human development from a psycho-political perspective, it is clear that the MCTM faces important challenges in the fourth phase of its evolution. It is important to acknowledge that these challenges are complemented by a rapidly growing social justice advocacy movement (SJAM).

Among the challenges facing the ongoing evolution of the MCTM include directing attention to the impact of multiple identities on people's mental health and human development. The integral theory discussed throughout this book places a high value on assisting mental health professionals and people in the general public to understand what can be done to support people in realizing their untapped potential for optimal mental health.

An increased understanding of all of the above stated issues can lead mental health professionals and interested people in the general public to address our nation's mental health crisis, in part, by promoting the dignity and healthy development of all the people in our country who are impacted by multiple identities. Safe it is to say that this challenge is relevant for all of us since we all are, consciously and unconsciously, impacted by multiple identities.

The new integral theory of mental health and human development based on a psycho-political perspective reminds us of the importance of taking psycho-political factors into consideration when assessing the mental health of individuals as well as entire communities where people live, work, and play. This perspective has been validated by a growing research-supported knowledgebase that leads to important questions about the positive and negative impact of psycho-political factors on people's mental health.

Chapter 7 provides research-validated evidence that brings clarity and a deeper understanding to questions people in our society have about the perilous times in which we live. Specific attention is directed to research findings that explain the negative impact of Donald Trump and his leadership style, Trump's supporters, and particularly persons included in the Trump cult on the mental health of millions of people in the United States.

What Have We Learned from the Evolution of the MCTM?

This section directs the reader's attention to what we have learned from the ongoing evolution of the MCTM and the SJAM.

We learned that the unprecedented transformation in the demography of the United States is stirring many changes in our democratic society.

We learned that these demographic changes have a strong impact on people's mental health and human development.

We learned that the genesis of White supremacy and White racism has been maintained in our society since the colonial times to our contemporary societal situation.

We learned that the racial/cultural demographic changes occurring in our society will soon result in the U.S. becoming a minority majority nation.

We learned that increasing numbers of White people are experiencing depression, concern, frustration, anxiety, anger, and hostility as a result of the changing demographics and rising multiracial/multicultural democracy in our nation.

We learned that the crisis in the mental health system in the United States is, in part, due to the many toxic and divisive political dynamics increasingly exhibited during the Age of Trump.

We learned that our nation's mental health system is in need of substantial revitalization if it is to continue to be relevant and viable in our 21st century society.

We learned about the promise and pitfalls of a multiracial/multicultural democracy as it evolves in the United States.

We learned how everyone in our nation would benefit from developing cultural and racial competencies to live productive and effective lives in our rapidly changing multiracial/multicultural society.

We learned that increasing our knowledge about between-group and within-group identity development as well as the impact of the interface of multiple personal identities are all key in developing cultural and racial competence in our nation.

We learned that the promotion of social justice is directly linked to our individual and collective mental health and the sustaining of America's democracy.

However, we have not learned if this country will be successful in addressing these perilous times, realize its untapped potential to foster optimal mental health, and addressing the various forms of White supremacy and White racism that will continue to impair our collective will and courage to eradicate these toxic psycho-political dynamics in our society.

The continuing evolution of the MCTM is resulting in an increased activation and expansion of the social justice advocacy movement (SJAM) in the United States. Before discussing the connections between the MCTM and the SJAM, it is important to provide the reader with definitions of the meaning of social justice as used in this book.

Definitions of Social Justice

Several definitions of social justice and social justice advocacy have been put forth by a number of experts in the mental health professions. These definitions are presented below as the social justice advocacy movement represents the continuing evolution of the MCTM and a cornerstone of the integral theory of mental health and human development from a psycho-political perspective.

Toporek and Williams (2006) provide a working definition of social justice. This definition was put forth by the Social Justice and Ethics Social Action Group organized at the 2001 National Counseling Psychology Conference in Houston, Texas. This definition is stated as follows:

> Social justice is a concept that advocates engaging individuals as co-participants in decisions which directly affect their lives; it involves taking some action, and educating individuals in order to open possibilities, and to act with value and respect for individuals and their group identities, considering power differentials in all areas of counseling practices and research endeavors (Blustein, Elman, & Gerstein, 2001, p. 9).

Based on a review of the literature on social justice as it applies to the work mental health professionals do, Dr. Courtland Lee (2007) defined social justice in the following manner:

> Broadly defined, social justice involves promoting access and equity to ensure the full participation of all people in the life of our society, particularly for those who have been systematically excluded on the basis of race or ethnicity, gender, age, physical or mental disability, education, sexual orientation, socioeconomic status, or other characteristics of one's background or group membership. Social justice is based on a belief that all people have a right to equitable treatment, support for their human rights, and fair allocation of societal resources. Social justice places a focus on issues of oppression, privilege, and social inequities (p. xiv).

The integral theory of mental health and human development from a psycho-political perspective is in agreement with these definitions. In addition to incorporating several concepts presented in the above definitions, the meaning of *social justice* as used in the new integral theory reflects an even more expansive way of thinking about this vital concept. Thus, as used in this book, *social justice* refers to:

> The right of all people to equitable and fair treatment. This includes having equal access to opportunities and services that enable people to lead lives that are characterized by optimal health and ongoing development, the freedom to express their views without recrimination, and the wherewithal to pursue happiness as they and their cultural group defines it without denying other people of such rights in the process.

Implementing social justice advocacy interventions from the integral theory requires mental health professionals to be:

1. aware of their own assumptions as they relate to their meaning of social justice;

2. cognizant of the unearned privileges individuals in the dominant group experience simply by being a part of the dominant group;

3. knowledgeable of the adverse impact of unearned privileges among members of the dominant group in our society for both the perpetrators and victims of these injustices; and

4. committed to implementing a broad range of advocacy services intentionally designed to address environmental barriers and social injustices that impede the mental health and ongoing healthy development of large numbers of individuals, their families, and the communities that they are a part. From the perspective of the integral theory, this includes and is not limited to social justice advocates participating in various forms of organized, collective, non-violent resistance and civil disobedience in their communities.

Encouraging mental health practitioners to participate in organized, collective, non-violent acts of civil disobedience as a part of their social justice advocacy is likely to create dissonance and resistance among persons in the field. Nevertheless, it is indisputable that these types of social justice advocacy interventions have historically contributed to positive societal changes. This includes major societal changes stimulated by India's political liberation from Great Britain in 1947 (led by Mahatma Gandhi) and the civil rights movement of the 1960s led by Dr. Martin Luther King Jr.

The new integral theory supports the implementation of bold non-violent social justice advocacy initiatives at the local, state, and national levels of our society. Support for this principle is based on research findings from multiple disciplines. These research findings point to the positive impact of engaging in such social justice advocacy endeavors on people's mental health and their ongoing personal and collective development.

Many of these investigative findings are discussed and referenced throughout this book. From an integrally-informed perspective, additional suggestions for the types of social justice advocacy initiatives that are useful in fostering the mental health and ongoing development of our nation include the following actions: rallying support for women's reproductive rights; addressing the epidemic of gun violence by outlawing automatic weapons; supporting and participating in community-based anti-racist rallies and psychoeducational interventions; advocating for the life, liberty and pursuit of happiness among sexual minority persons; lobbying support for public health education initiatives related to the negative long-term impact of the global environmental crisis; developing and implementing respectful, humane and just immigration policies; and supporting national and international efforts aimed at the total deactivation of all nuclear and biological weapons on the planet.

The importance of advocating for the latter issue from a mental health perspective has gained attention as a result of Russian President Putin's recent threats to possibly use strategic nuclear weapons in the Ukraine War. The suggestion of having mental health professionals engaged in advocacy efforts aimed at deactivating and dismantling all nuclear and biological weapons is additionally supported by Noam Chomsky's (the internationally and nationally respected social justice and peace advocate) detailed analysis of this catastrophic issue in his recent public presentations and publications.

In addition to participating in protests, public rallies, and various forms of non-violent civil disobedience, social justice advocacy involves the use of numerous other intervention strategies. This includes mental health professionals, who work as educators in schools and universities where a range of social justice issues and health promotion topics can be explored; working as facilitators in group counseling settings where social justice issues are discussed; providing social justice consultation services with policymakers in different organizational, community, and educational settings; and lobbying support for social justice and mental health issues with elected officials at the local, state, and/or national levels to name a few (Lewis et al., 2011).

The brief descriptions of the above-stated recommendations need to be supplemented by a new kind of leadership in the mental health professions. This leadership is one in which MCTM and SJAM advocates demonstrate the knowledge, skills, and moral courage that characterize transformative leaders in their efforts to address our perilous times, support the ongoing evolution of our multiracial/multicultural democracy, and addressing the mental health crisis in the United States.

Transactional versus Transformational Leadership

Two leadership theories have received a great deal of attention over the past 30 years. They are referred to as *transactional* and *transformational leadership styles*. Both of these leadership styles have implications for the work mental health professionals do in general and are relevant for the implementation of the new integral theory in particular.

A growing body of research findings (many of which are discussed throughout this book) illuminate how social injustices adversely impact the mental health and ongoing development of millions of persons in the United States. These research findings represent a clarion call for mental health professionals to develop and implement effective leadership knowledge and skills to ameliorate social injustices known to impair mental health and adversely impact human development.

Transactional Leadership

Transactional leadership has and continues to be increasingly manifested in business, education, medical associations, counseling/psychology training programs, and mental health organizations. The primary purpose of transactional leaders is to maintain the core values and principles of the existing status quo in each of the areas listed above. These leaders reap benefits that serve as motivators for other persons to consider developing and implementing transactional leadership in their work settings.

Actively advocating for substantial systemic changes to promote social justice and mental health is typically not viewed in favorable terms by many transactional leaders in the mental health professions. Instead, more moderate reform proposals for organizational, professional, systemic, community, and educational changes are often supported and implemented by transactional leaders.

Transactional management is the dominant leadership style manifested among counselors, psychologists, and other allied mental health professionals in our society (D'Andrea, 2020). The interpersonal interactions that characterize transactional leaders and their subordinates can be described in the following phrase: "You scratch my back and I'll scratch your back."

Practical mutual reciprocity drives transactional leadership. In the mental health professions, transactional leaders are rewarded for maintaining the established goals, values, beliefs, and services of their chosen field. Such rewards include financial support, professional respect and validation, and increased power within the organizational settings where these leaders work.

The genesis and rise of the MCTM and SJAM's in the mental health professions have been fundamentally grounded in a rejection of any aspect of the status quo that perpetuates individual, organizational, institutional, and cultural injustices in our society. The pioneering leaders of the multicultural counseling and therapy movement aggressively described how culturally and racially biased theories, research findings, and psychological services perpetuate injustices that are validated in our socialization processes and manifested in our broad society. This includes and is not limited to the perpetuation of intentional and unintentional forms of White supremacy and White racism (See Chapter 2).

On one hand, transactional leaders in the mental health professions remain largely committed to maintaining the existing professional and societal status quo. In supporting these efforts, transactional leaders unintentionally perpetuate injustices that are discussed in a variety of ways throughout this book.

On the other hand, transformational leaders unabashedly articulate the need for substantial changes in the mental health professions. The goals of these transformational leaders include stimulating a greater level of cultural competence, racial respect, and cultural responsivity in their own ranks and social justice in all aspects of our society.

Leadership researchers point out that many people can become transactional leaders. The primary task in doing so is to demonstrate a commitment to the policies and procedures of the organization, agency, institution, and professional training program where one is situated. This results in a form of conformity where critical thinking is not a primary necessity. It is further asserted that transactional leadership is a dominant leadership style in our society.

For those persons interested in adopting new leadership character-istics, they are encouraged to do so by utilizing honest self-reflection to expand their current leadership perspective in bold and intentional ways. This can be done by developing new strategies that follow the principles, beliefs, and goals articulated by the MCTM pioneers and current supporters of the SJAM. The aim in doing so is to help foster the developmental changes necessary to realize one's untapped potential to manifest *transformational leadership* characteristics in our society in general and within the mental health professions in particular.

Transformational Leadership

Twenty-first century transformational leaders in the mental health professions are committed to working with other persons to achieve what has been referred to as the *grand transformational goal*. This goal is embedded as a central value driving the new integral theory presented in this book. More specifically, this goal is stated as follows: *Transformation-al leaders are committed to fostering and sustaining the healthy development of larger numbers of persons in diverse groups by integrating a much more expansive social justice advocacy perspective into the core of the mental health professions than has been done in the past.*

Transformational leaders in the mental health professions are not satisfied with ongoing discussions and the implementation of reform efforts that require minimal changes in traditional approaches to mental health. Such reform efforts, although well-intentioned, often uninten-tionally help to sustain an existing status quo that continues to dominate the mental health professions at the present time.

During the Age of Trump, when racist and culturally oppressive pol-icies and practices were routinely manifested by many (perhaps most) political operatives, mental health organizations like the American Counseling Association (ACA) typically addressed these harmful in-justices by developing and publishing position statements. These posi-tion statements were designed to repudiate toxic actions and injustices taken by Donald Trump and his supporters in general and persons in the Trump cult in particular (See Chapters 6 & 7).

When published position statements become the only or primary responses to social injustices, they unintentionally enable the perpetua-tion of ongoing complex and toxic forms of racial violence and injustice.

Transformational leaders know that greater actions need to be implemented requiring more fundamental changes in communities in general and professional mental health organizations in particular. Such position statements are consistent with the characteristics of transactional leadership and not in line with the multidimensional approach to social justice advocacy as exhibited by transformational leaders.

In an interesting analysis of the impact of publicly published social justice position statements, Dr. Ward Churchill, a former faculty member at the University of Colorado, who was terminated from his faculty position for his transformative leadership actions, referred to these position statements as *symbolic exercises*. While such *symbolic exercises* provide comfort to the sensitivities of many mental health professionals, they do little to address status quo factors that enable Trump and his supporters to continue to perpetuate various forms of White racism and cultural oppression in our society.

As a result, Trump and his supporters are able to continue to threaten our country's democratic principles of life, liberty, and the pursuit of happiness, especially among persons in marginalized and vulnerable racial/cultural groups. In contrast, transformational leaders would more likely follow the strategies employed by Dr. Martin Luther King Jr., working with other people to organize and implement acts of non-violent civil disobedience to more effectively address the pattern of authoritarian and fascist leadership manifested by Trump and supported by his loyal cult members.

Social Activisticism

Another distinguishing characteristic of transformational leaders is reflected among those persons who demonstrate a consistent commitment and the moral courage to withstand resistance and hostility manifested among stakeholders in the status quo. The manifestation of such reactionary resistance is referred to as *social activisticism*.

Social activisticism is an injustice commonly manifested by mental health professionals who resonate with transactional leadership perspectives, support the maintenance of the existing status quo, and respond negatively towards persons striving to realize the untapped potential to foster social justice in ways that lead to increased optimal mental health and support for our evolving multiracial/multicultural democratic society. Persons exhibiting *social activisticism* respond negatively and usually with hostility towards transformational leaders. This results in efforts by transactional leaders and their supporters to discredit and invalidate the professionalism, commitment, and courage exhibited by transformational leaders.

It is useful to keep in mind that Dr. Martin Luther King Jr. was subjected to social activisticism by a majority of Americans near the end of his life. At that time, survey results indicated that 63% of all Americans disapproved of Dr. King's non-violent civil disobedience approach to eradicating the racial and cultural injustices manifested in our nation.

Investigators have traced much of the negativity and hostility directed towards transformational leaders to their authentic, passionate, assertive, and courageous efforts to increase multicultural competence and social justice advocacy services in the mental health professions as well as in the workplaces where transformative agents are employed. These distinguishing leadership characteristics are grounded in a complex understanding of the ways that transformational leadership endeavors can serve as conduits in achieving the grand transformational goal for the mental health professions described above.

Promoting a Paradigm Shift

In essence, transformational leaders actively strive to promote a paradigm shift in our nation's failing mental health system. Such a paradigm shift complements and extends the principles and accomplishments that the pioneers and many current supporters of the multicultural counseling and social justice advocacy movements are committed to realize in the mental health professions.

This paradigm shift underlies much of the transformational leader's work as it represents a more comprehensive and integral approach to mental health and human development. As documented throughout this book, there are numerous factors unfolding in the United States that support the birth of this new paradigm shift. At the same time, increasing numbers of White people continue to perpetuate various forms of White racism and White supremacy by supporting and participating on the wrong side of the growing cultural and racial wars in our nation.

Promoting and Implementing the New Integral Theory

From an integral perspective, transformational leaders are further distinguished by their commitment to work with other professionals and interested people in the community where they live and work to promote mental health by implementing social justice advocacy services. One of the key goals to be achieved in undertaking these efforts is to foster a paradigm shift that stimulates a revitalization of community mental health. This paradigm shift can be facilitated by institutionalizing the integral theory in communities targeted for such changes. The following points are important to keep in mind when striving to accomplish this goal.

First, transformational leaders recognize the unique challenges mental health professionals face in the 21st century given the unprecedented demographic transformation currently occurring across our nation. As stated earlier, this demographic transformation is reflected in the fact that, while the United States has historically been comprised of a majority of persons coming from White, western European, English-speaking, and often Christian backgrounds, the current demographic transformation happening in our country is rapidly leading to our nation to be comprised of a majority of persons who come from non-White, non-western European, non-English speaking, and increasingly non-Christian backgrounds.

It is becoming increasingly clear that this national transformation requires much more than reforms in the way mental health professionals have traditionally addressed the needs of people's mental health and human development. Despite the predictable and continuing resistance manifested by mental health professional purists, transformational leaders, social justice advocates, and interested community members, are encouraged to continue to work together to support efforts to transform their community's and this nation's mental health system.

Second, to be clear, a new integral approach to mental health and human development from a psycho-political perspective includes the implementation of traditional remedial counseling services (i.e., individual therapy, small group counseling, family therapy, etc.). It is important to do so to meet the needs of millions of people in our nation identified as being in need of mental health services for psychological, emotional, and/or behavioral problems. The continued implementation of these traditional professional services will always be an important responsibility for mental health practitioners.

However, given our nation's current mental health crisis, we know that a majority of people identified as being in need of professional services do not receive such care (See Chapter 7). This research finding begs for the implementation of a paradigm shift in which traditional mental health services are complemented by an integration of multi-level prevention, psychoeducational, social justice advocacy, and systems change interventions. The effective delivery of these integrated components would need to be coordinated and implemented by well-trained, culturally competent practitioners committed to social justice advocacy, mental health, and human development; all aimed at addressing the perilous times we face as a nation.

Third, as detailed in Chapter 7, the National Institute of Mental Health (NIMH) publishes research findings that are particularly relevant for the vision many transformational leaders adhere. Briefly stated again, the NIMH findings indicate that more than 51 million people are in need of mental health services each year in the United States. This does not include persons who are at high risk for psychological-emotional-behavioral problems. Of the 51+ million persons currently in need of professional help only 44.8% of these persons (23 million persons) actually receive professional services for the psychological, emotional, and/or behavioral problems they face in their lives.

The fact that the current mental health system in the United States fails to provide services for 55.2% of the 28 million persons identified as being in need of professional help did not receive such help during the 2019 – 2021 years. Since these statistics are similar to the number of people in need of mental health services over the past several years, it is asserted that the continued failure of our national mental health system to meet the mental health needs of larger numbers of people than has been done in the past is a threat to the long-term viability and relevance of this human system. Recognizing the reality of this situation, transformational leaders understand the urgent need to address all of the factors outlined above by continuing their efforts to effectively institutionalize a new paradigm in the mental health professions in transformative ways. All of these points are discussed in greater detail in Chapter 15.

With this backdrop in mind, transformative leaders are challenged to use multifaceted organizational and community development change strategies that have been tested and found to be effective in realizing the untapped potential of our mental health system to achieve the grand goal described in the new integral theory of mental health and human development from a psycho-political perspective. This goal states that: *Transformational leaders are committed to fostering and sustaining the healthy development of larger numbers of persons in diverse groups by integrating a much more expansive social justice advocacy perspective into the core of the mental health professions than has been done in the past.*

Fourth, the probability of achieving this goal will be enhanced by implementing new mental health and human development interventions in the communities where counselors, psychologists, and other allied professionals live and work. This includes and is not limited to working with educators in our public schools, athletic coaches, business leaders, elected officials, members of religious communities, political activists, and medical professionals to name a few.

A brief and incomplete listing of specific interventions that would be helpful to incorporate when implementing the new integral theory of mental health and human development will need to result in major changes to our mental health system that support the ongoing evolution of our country's multiracial/multicultural democracy. This incomplete list includes life skills training, prevention efforts, political organizing, community development, empowerment amenities, anti-racist psycho-education efforts, and promoting community-based training for people interested in acquiring new multicultural and social justice advocacy competencies.

Success in these areas require mental health professionals to exhibit the courage of their convictions and the commitment to address the different forms of social activisticism transformational leaders continue to be subjected. In short, these leaders are challenged to demonstrate a genuine though precarious responsibility to operate as social justice advocacy change agents that simultaneously address our nation's mental health crisis while supporting the ongoing evolution of our country's multiracial/multicultural democracy. These latter points are crucial in effectively implementing the new integral theory of mental health and human development from a psycho-political perspective.

Fifth, the passion and dedication manifested by transformative leaders transcends traditional mental health training and clinical practices. These characteristics of transformative leadership reflect what Dr. Robert Lipton describes as a willingness among increasing numbers of mental health professionals to express what they are learning by witnessing the broad-based psychological, emotional, and behavioral impairments traversing across our nation. As reported in numerous research findings, the multidimensional phenomenon reflected in our nation's mental health crisis begs for mental health professionals and interested community members to work together to address the multiple factors contributing to our nation's mental health crisis (See Chapters 5, 6, & 15).

Finally, the new integral theory presented in this book asserts that the transformational leadership characteristics and endeavors described above are vital to ensure the long-term relevance and viability of the mental health professions in an increasingly multicultural/multiracial 21st-century society. In working to ensure this on-going viability and relevance, transformative leaders understand that their success largely depends on the degree to which they will successfully help to institutionalize a new paradigm in the mental health professions. It is hoped that the new integral theory can serve as a starting point in developing and maintaining the paradigm shift which is necessary to effectively address our nation's current mental health crisis in these perilous political times.

Summary

This chapter discusses issues related to the multicultural counseling/therapy and social justice advocacy movements as well as their relevance for the integral theory of mental health and human development from a psycho-political perspective. It is intentionally designed to accomplish the following goals.

First, it provides an overall introduction to the meaning of multicultural counseling theory and its relevance for the integral theory presented in this book.

Second, it describes the historic evolution of the multicultural counseling and therapy (MCTM) and social justice advocacy (SJAM) movements.

Third, it discusses the interface between mental health practices and social justice advocacy in the Age of Trump.

Fourth, this chapter introduces a pathway for the revitalization of the mental health professions in culturally and racially responsive ways. This pathway is highlighted in the discussion of transactional versus transformational leadership and described in greater detail in the final chapter of this book (See Chapter 15).

Fifth, this chapter proceeds to describe an unfortunate injustice referred to as *social activisticism*. This injustice serves as a pitfall that transformational leaders commonly encounter when using social justice advocacy strategies in calling for a paradigm shift in our nation's mental health system. As highlighted in this chapter, social justice activisticism is defined as an injustice commonly manifested by mental health professionals who resonate with transactional leadership perspectives that support the existing status quo, and respond negatively towards persons striving to realize the untapped potential to stimulate social justice in ways that lead to increased optimal mental health and support for our evolving multiracial/multicultural society.

The next chapter discusses the most recent theoretical force in the mental health professions. The discussion of the neuroscience force uncovers another aspect of the paradigm shift that is rapidly unfolding by increasing numbers of mental health professionals. This new force is comprised of essential factors that are linked to the emergence and relevance of neuroscience for the integral theory of mental health and human development from a psycho-political perspective.

CHAPTER 14

THE NEUROSCIENCE FORCE

From a neuroscience perspective the challenge of recovery from intergenerational trauma is to reestablish ownership of your body and your mind—of yourself. This means feeling free to know what you know and to feel what you feel without becoming overwhelmed, enraged, ashamed, or collapsed. For most people this involves (1) finding a way to become calm and focused, (2) learning to maintain that calm in response to images, thoughts, sounds, or physical sensations that remind you of the past, (3) finding a way to be fully alive in the present and engaged with the people around you, (4) not having to keep secrets from yourself, including secrets about the ways that you have managed to survive. Neuroscience research shows that the only way we can change the way we feel is by becoming aware of our inner experience and learning to befriend what is going inside ourselves.

Bessel van der Kolk, M.D.

There may be times when we are powerless to prevent injustice, but there must never be a time when we fail to protest.

Elie Wiesel, Nobel Prize for Peace awardee

Introduction

Mental health practitioners are becoming increasingly aware of the neuroscientific revolution that is unfolding in the fields of counseling, education, psychiatry, psychology, human services and social work. Although there is growing awareness of this exciting new force in the mental health professions, many practitioners lack the training that would enable them to more fully understand the relevance of neuroscience in addressing our national mental health crisis.

This chapter is designed to serve five goals briefly described below:

a. This chapter provides an overview of what neuroscience is;

b. Chapter 14 discusses how and why neuroscience is making a substantial impact on the work mental health professionals do;

c. It explains the relevance of this new force for the new integral theory of mental health and human development from a psycho-political perspective;

d. This chapter also clarifies the meaning of *developmental stagnation* (as briefly presented in Chapter 8) from a neurological perspective; and

e. This chapter discusses the relevance of neuroscience in the Age of Trump.

What is Neuroscience?

Neuroscience is defined as the study of the nervous system. Traditionally, neuroscience has been seen as a branch of biology. However, it is currently viewed as an interdisciplinary science that incorporates knowledge from many other disciplines such as psychology, computer science, mathematics, physics, philosophy, and medicine.

As a result of its interdisciplinary nature, the scope of neuroscience has broadened to include the study of the molecular, developmental, structural, functional, evolutionary, medical, and psychological aspects of the nervous system in general and brain functioning in particular. The research focus and techniques used by neuroscientists have also expanded enormously. This expansion is reflected in advancements made from biophysical and molecular studies of individual nerve cells to a broad range of new imaging techniques used to study different aspects of mental health and human development from a neurological perspective.

Each human brain is made up of billions of interconnected neurons wired together to form unique brain networks and pathways. We are born with a foundation of brain structures. Over time, these structures change based on our life experiences.

When people are involved in learning, some brain network connections become stronger and faster in certain parts of the brain. As Hebb's Law (1949) states, "Neurons that fire together wire together." Simply stated, this means the repeated stimulation of specific neurons and neural networks as a result of one's experiences in life can either strengthen existing brain networks or weaken unused neurons which is referred to as neural pruning. The adage, "use it or lose it," has a specific meaning when it comes to understanding the neurological nature of the brain.

Neuroplasticity

Neuroplasticity is the capacity for the brain to be shaped, molded, or altered by life experiences. It is also the ability of the brain to adapt or change over time by creating new neurons and building new brain networks (neural wiring).

Historically, scientists and persons in the general public believed that the brain stops growing after childhood. But current research shows that the brain is able to continue growing and changing throughout the lifespan, refining its architecture or shifting functions to different regions of the brain.

The importance of *neuroplasticity* cannot be overstated because it means that it is possible to change dysfunctional patterns of thinking, feeling, and behaving by developing new mindsets, new memories, new skills, and new abilities. As noted in research findings described in Chapters 5, 6, and 7, many people in our society have experienced negative cognitive, emotional, and behavioral outcomes that are tied to the neurological impact of Trump's leadership style and his explicit racist actions during his presidency.

Recent research findings verify that neuroplasticity is enhanced when people are engaged in repetitive behaviors such as practicing a musical instrument; being a part of enriched environments (such as enriched preschool/elementary/secondary school programs); and involved in new, novel, supportive, and challenging activities, including and not limited to becoming more politically engaged in one's community (i.e., via volunteering to help with national, state, or local elections and/or participating in counseling/psychotherapy) (Cozolino, 2002).

The points made in the above paragraphs have particular relevance for the integral theory of mental health and human development from a psycho-political perspective. To reiterate, researchers have emphasized the importance of people encountering new experiences that result in reorganizing their brains in positive ways.

With this knowledge in mind, mental health professionals would do well to work with other persons in their communities participating in various forms of political activism which are meaningful for large numbers of people who share such interests. Neurologically speaking, these experiences can and often do result in positive cognitive, emotional, and behavioral outcomes.

The Future Relevance and Viability of Our Nation's Mental Health System

Recommending that mental health professionals would do well to increase their political activism with other interested community members is likely to be seen a bold and radical strategy among some traditionally trained mental health professionals. However, this suggestion supports the idea of participating with other people in the communities where mental health professionals live and work to engage in new activities that stimulate the process of *neuroplasticity* from a psycho-political perspective.

The integral theory of mental health and human development places political activism as a centerpiece of this new theoretical framework. From a prevention perspective, mental health professionals would do well to be more strongly and frequently focused on how toxic psycho-political factors threaten many people's individual and collective mental health. The information presented in the new integral theory is intentionally aimed at enhancing readers' understanding of the negative neurological impact that occurs from Trump's leadership style and the emotional reactions by his most ardent supporters.

One of the potential barriers in incorporating political activities with the intention of stimulating mental health and human development (via positive neuroplasticity) predictably includes mental health professionals who have been trained in traditional programs. While many mental health training programs spotlight the importance of operating from a holistic perspective, many of the points made in this book point to the fact that psycho-political factors are generally excluded from being a part of such holistic training programs.

There was a time when people's religious beliefs and identities were not addressed in counseling and therapy. In the not-too-distant past, cultural and racial factors were avoided by practitioners who otherwise embraced the concept of operating in holistic ways. Over time, mental health professionals and their professional organizations came to realize the tremendous impact of religious beliefs and identities as well as learning more about research-based *between-group and, within-group differences* on people's mental health and their ongoing development. As these factors were incorporated into the consciousness of mental health practitioners and people in the general public, they have slowly been incorporated in mental health training programs and professional practices.

Given the profound and comprehensive manner in which political policies, actions, statutes, and laws impact people's mental health and human development, it is inexcusable as to why psycho-political factors have and continue to be systematically avoided in mental health training programs, individual and community assessment processes, and clinical practices. On a more optimistic perspective, it is possible that the psycho-political impact of the Age of Trump is helping mental health professionals recognize that their relevance and viability in our 21st century society will be compromised unless they operate from a truly holistic perspective by addressing religious, cultural, racial, and psycho-political factors in their work. It is hoped that mental health professionals will incorporate theoretical models like the integral theory of mental health and human development from a psycho-political perspective before they suffer in terms of their increasing irrelevance and compromised viability in our nation's mental health system.

Epigenetics

Another important neuroscience concept relates to the definition of *epigenetics*. In the past, mental health professionals and persons in the general public believed that genetics had a primary and automatic function in human development. However, neuroscientific research findings have found that genetic variables do not work automatically as people undergo changes across the lifespan. The belief that genetic factors operate automatically is being replaced with a more accurate understanding of the impact of *epigenetics* in activating or deactivating people's genetic potential as it relates to one's mental health and on-going human development.

Clearly, our genes play an important role in our health, but so do our behaviors and environmental experiences. What a person eats, how physically active people are, even people's sleep habits are some of the factors that contribute to the activation or deactivation of people's genetic potentials.

The suffix *epi* is a Greek derivative that means *above*. Thus, the term *epigenetics* is the study of the ways that variables operating *above genetics,* including people's behaviors and environmental experiences, cause biological and neurological changes that effect the way their genes work. Unlike the long-held belief that genetic changes work automatically and are not reversible, epigenetic changes (changes in one's behaviors and environment) overpass automatic genetic changes and are reversible.

The term *gene expression* refers to another inaccurate belief that has been thought to occur when proteins are created from genetic activation. While genetic changes can alter which protein is made that results in gene expression, epigenetic changes affect gene expression by turning genes "on" and/or "off." Since your environment and behaviors (such as diet, exercise, sleep routine, and one's reaction or inaction to the impact of psycho-political factors) can result in epigenetic changes, it is easy to see the connection between people's genetic expression, their behaviors, and environmental experiences.

Brain Parts and Networks

Neuroscience tells us that there are seven main networks consisting of different brain parts. These networks are listed below with descriptive words related to their focus and function. These include:

- The default mode network.
- The salience network.
- The limbic system network.
- The dorsal attention network.
- The central prefrontal executive network.
- The visual system network.

Two brain networks have repeatedly been identified as having much relevance for mental health professionals in general and for the integral theory of mental health and human development from a psycho-political perspective in particular. This includes the neurological connections routinely manifested between the limbic system and the prefrontal executive network.

Given space limitations, the remaining sections of this chapter focus on five common neurological patterns manifested in the electro-chemical interactions between the prefrontal network and the limbic system. The new integral theory hypotheses that these important electro-chemical interactions between the limbic system and prefrontal network have had a substantial impact on Trump supporters' cognitions, emotionality, and behaviors during the Age of Trump. Much of this impact has been discussed in detail in Chapters 5, 6, and 7.

Healthy Brain Functioning

Mental health professionals and interested persons in the general public will continue to have access to information related to neuroscience and brain functioning in both the professional journals and through related posts on social media. Many mental health professionals and people in the general public have benefited from learning about such advances in neuroscience. Becoming knowledgeable of these neuroscientific advances simultaneously stimulates increased understanding of the interactions that occur between our brain functioning, people's mental health, and ongoing human development.

A question that people often ask when thinking about the above-stated issues is: "What is positive and healthy brain functioning?" Gratefully, there are numerous publications by neuroscientists which provide thoughtful responses to that question. These neuroscientific publications add to the increasing resources available to mental health professionals and persons in the general public who are interested in learning about the interconnections that are manifested in people's brain functioning with implications for their mental health and their ongoing development.

If you are like me, you probably get overwhelmed at times with the tsunami of important neurological information that is constantly available in new publications. The seemingly constant flow of information related to neuroscience is creating a sea change in the thinking of many mental health professionals and interested people in the general public regarding the interconnections that are manifested in people's brain functioning and manifested in their mental health and their ongoing human development. With that in mind, information that is presented in the next section of this book is intentionally designed to help answer the above question by explaining what *positive and healthy brain functioning* means from a neurological perspective.

First, I draw from the many contributions that Dr. Daniel Siegel made in describing positive and healthy brain functioning in his numerous publications. For readers who are interested in learning more about positive and healthy brain functioning, you are encouraged to secure a copy of Dr. Siegel's (2012) book entitled, *Pocket Guide to Interpersonal Neurobiology: An Integrative Handbook of the Mind.*

As briefly mentioned earlier, Dr. Siegel describes two primary neurological factors that are important characteristics of positive and healthy brain functioning. The first neurological factor addressed by Dr. Siegel is the importance for the human brain to realize its innate potential to develop and sustain distinct, healthy, and fully functioning brain parts. This process begins in utero and accelerates during infancy, childhood and adolescence, stabilizing in adulthood.

The second major neurological factor that is useful in defining positive and healthy brain functioning is the process of what Siegel (2012) describes as the *integration of the distinct brain networks* via *enhanced neural connectivity*. Siegel emphasizes the importance of both of the above factors for positive and healthy brain functioning to occur. From the perspective of the new integral theory presented in this book, the *neurological integration process* is a key factor that impacts the way people think, feel, behave and construct meaning of their lives for better or for worse.

Overactivation and Deactivation of Neural Networks

Overactivation of a brain network is a common occurrence in human life. It should not be automatically viewed as a neurological deficit depending on the intensity and time duration of the brain network overactivation.

Similarly, deactivation/lower activation of a brain network is also a common occurrence in human development. However, brain network deactivation should not be automatically viewed as a neurological deficit depending on the intensity and time duration of such a deactivation of a particular brain network.

The Relevance of Neuroscience in the Age of Trump: A Psycho-Political Perspective

Writing for the *Scientific American* magazine, Douglas Fields (2020) refers to several concepts related to neuroscience in an article entitled, "Neuroscience and Psychology Suggest No Surprise Victory for Trump this Time." In Fields's article, he discusses how helpful it was for him to draw from neuroscientific research findings to accurately predict the outcomes of the 2016 and 2020 presidential elections. The reader's attention is directed to those neurological concepts as they apply to Fields's psycho-political-neurological analysis and are relevant for the new integral theory described in this book.

Fields accurately predicted the outcomes of the 2016 and 2020 presidential elections by using several neuroscientific research findings related to brain functioning. In analyzing the psychology of these election results, Fields distinguishes between the function of the prefrontal lobe (which operates from reason) and the limbic system (particularly the amygdala and hippocampus) which are primarily associated with emotional reactions and threat detection circuitry as well as human fear and anxiety circuitry.

In the lead up to the 2016 election, Trump repeatedly utilized campaign strategies that appealed to the brain's threat detection circuitry, emotion-based decision-making processes, and the activation of fear often in racialized terms. Fields used this neuroscientific analysis to correctly predict Trump's 2016 election victory despite polling results that had him losing the election by 16 percentage points.

Fields further describes his rationale in predicting that Trump would lose the 2020 election. In doing so, he summarized his neurological analysis by concluding the Trump's 2020 inflammatory campaign speeches are less likely to activate the same decision-making circuits in people's brains as occurred in 2016.

The following statements are taken directly from Fields's article. They provide details aimed at increasing the reader's understanding of the relevance of neuroscience when one directs attention to the psycho-political-neurological differences that occurred in the 2016 and 2020 presidential election campaigns. As Fields stated in his article:

> In order to instill fear among the persons who voted in the 2020 election, Trump regularly made the following fear-based comments at his political rallies leading up to the November 2020 election:

> "Biden wants to surrender our country to the violent left-wing mob… If Biden wins, very simply, China wins. If Biden wins, the mob wins. If Biden wins, the rioters, anarchists, arsonists and flag burners, they win."

> These inflammatory comments were made by Trump at his Wisconsin campaign rally on September 17, 2020, as he offered new threats to our nation as he did in his 2016 misinformation about the rapist and drug trafficking immigrants, both of which lost their potency in the 2020 campaign.

> As Trump invoked threats of anarchy and street violence, any tangible rise in violence at his 2016 political assemblies benefited the Trump strategy to generate fear in many people's brain-functioning. Some supporters reacted by brandishing firearms at Trump's public political rallies.

> In the 2016 campaign, Trump egged his supporters on to commit violence, suggesting that an assassination of Hillary Clinton by

gun rights advocates could be used to prevent her from picking Supreme Court Justices. In the summer of 2020, then-President Donald Trump inflamed the presidential campaign atmosphere by having large anti-Trump protests surrounded by calling to the scene military and unidentified federal security agents, even as local officials objected to this action.

Trump continued to make bombastic statements throughout the 2020 campaign. In his own words he stated, "I am your wall between the American dream and chaos," he told an audience in Minnesota. When asked by the debate moderator, Chris Wallace, whether Trump was willing to condemn White supremacists and paramilitary groups, he would not do so. Instead, Trump barked out what sounded like strategic instructions to the right-wing Proud Boys, widely regarded as an extremist hate group, by stating: "Proud Boys—stand back, and stand by."

But such fear-driven appeals persuaded fewer 2020 voters. This is because people overcome fear in two ways: by reason and by experience. Inhibitory neural pathways of the prefrontal cortex to the limbic system enable reason to quash fear especially if the articulated dangers are not grounded in fact. The type of street violence Trump rails against in 2020 was not the norm during the Obama and Biden years. Nor was the fear that Biden would allegedly turn the United States into a socialist state, an issue in the 2020 election. On the contrary, Biden defeated the self-described "democratic socialist" candidate Bernie Sanders in the democrat presidential primaries.

A neuroscience-based perspective also illuminates Trump's constant interruptions and insults during the first presidential debate in 2020, steamrolling over the moderator's futile efforts to have a reasoned pairing of facts and positions. The structure of a debate is designed to engage participants in a deliberative reasoning in the brain's prefrontal lobe. However, Trump hijacked the debate format by intentionally inflaming increased emotionality in the limbic system which did not serve him well in the 2020 election.

Trump's dismissal of experts, be they military generals, career public servants, scientists, or even his own political appointees, is necessary for him to sustain the subcortical decision-making in voters' minds that won him the 2016 election and sustained his support throughout his presidential term. The fact-based decision-making that scientists rely upon is the polar opposite of people's emotion-based decision-making.

Fields further notes that "it is clear that Trump does not address factual evidence. He dismisses or suppresses it even for the events that are apparent to many, including global warming, foreign intervention in U.S. elections, the trivial headcount at his inauguration, and even the projected path of a destructive hurricane. Instead, alternative facts or fabrications are substituted for reality."

"These conclusions are based on neurological findings related to the brain's neural networks. Such conclusions also help to explain the Trump administration's unprecedented erosion of government institutions with missions intended to protect the public (ranging from the Center for Disease Control to the FBI). These diversions also distract attention from the real, controllable threats, such as the coronavirus pandemic, that have undermined Trump's political and economic objectives."

According to Fields, "reason cannot always overcome fear, as PTSD demonstrates; but the brain's second mechanism of neutralizing its fear circuitry experience can do so. Repeated exposure to the fearful situation where the outcome is safe will rewire the brain's subcortical circuitry. However, for many people, credibility has been eroded by Trump's outlandish assertions, like suggesting injections of bleach to cure COVID-19 or infusing a plant toxin touted by a pillow salesman, while scientific experts in attendance at such meetings grimace and bite their lips."

Neurological and Developmental Stagnation

There are many people in our society who continue to inaccurately believe that people's psychological development ceases to expand further after a certain age. Some people have told me they believe people really do not change much after they are 40 years old. I believe these persons are referring to the lack of psychological changes, as many (perhaps most) people are aware of the physical changes that are evident after 40 years of age.

Published research findings indicate that many (perhaps most) people's cognitive, psychological, emotional and behavioral abilities are not substantially altered after a person is in her or his late 20s. After reading about the fluidity and changeableness in neuroplasticity described above, the reader might be led to ask, "Why does human development commonly stagnate at less complex developmental stages for an extended (maybe lifelong) period of time than might be expected?" The new integral theory raises a reasonable hypothesis to explain how *developmental stagnation* occurs from a neurological perspective.

There are a couple points, which are substantiated by neuroscientific research findings that reflect what can be considered to be an innate propensity for brain network wiring and development. During infancy, this innate propensity is unconscious. Nevertheless, these early and unconscious neurological patterns are fundamentally important in human development (See Chapter 10).

The biochemical patterns that result from specific ways of thinking, feeling, and behaving are grounded in our society's socialization process. The integral theory suggests that this socialization process results in less than the best (more complex) neurological reactions and a potential barrier in many people's ability to realize their untapped potential for optimal brain functioning (See Chapter 8).

Our socialization process stimulates a repetition of the same brain functioning reactions that not only result in conscious and unconscious ways of constructing meaning of one's environmental experiences as well as one's purpose in life, but also fosters the grooming of patterned neurological/bio-chemical/brain-functioning reactions in the process. Consequently, the term *neurological stagnation* refers to repetitive brain functioning processes described above. These repeated neurological/biochemical reactions that occur over an extended period of time during the socialization process are barriers to the sort of neurological conditions necessary in promoting openness for new learning, new patterned neurological reactions, and new changes in one's life.

Perhaps more pertinent to the above stated question is the recognition that a combination of environmental dynamics and people's sense of personal responsibility result in many (perhaps most) of the same brain functioning and neurological reactions that occur on a daily basis throughout people's lives. One of the important hypotheses presented by the integral theory calls for researchers to study how the constant repetition of the socialization process results in repeated neurological reactions that strengthen a certain type of neural network wiring while simultaneously impairing motivation for realizing new ways of thinking, feeling, and behaving. Thus, the term, *neurological stagnation,* is thought to be a subcomponent of what is referred to as *developmental stagnation* (See Chapter 8).

Summary

This chapter opens by acknowledging the revolutionary changes occurring in the mental health professions as a result of substantial advances in neuroscience and their relevance for people's mental health and ongoing development. This acknowledgement begins by defining what neuroscience is and discussing key terms related to research advancements in this area. Among the terms and concepts discussed include describing the meaning of neuroplasticity, epigenetics, and the function of the seven main brain networks neuroscientists have described.

The question that focuses on the meaning of *positive and healthy brain functioning* is also addressed in this chapter as well as the relevance of this concept for the work mental health professionals do in the field. Attention is further directed to research findings reported by Dr. Dan Siegel on the mental health of people experiencing overactivation or deactivation of various brain networks.

The neurological analysis Douglas Fields utilized in explaining the different brain-functioning factors manifested in the 2016 versus the 2020 presidential elections demonstrate the practical use of neuroscientific research findings in understanding the perilous political times in which we are situated.

Chapter 15, the final chapter in this book, is aimed at synthesizing many of the ideas, terms, concepts, and suggestions/recommendations discussed in the preceding chapters. By using community counseling and community psychology theories as a basis for this synthesis, it is hoped that readers will experience increased faith in the ability of *We the People* to support the ongoing evolution of our multiracial/multicultural democracy during these perilous times and, do so, by revitalizing the mental health professions as we strive to address our nation's mental health crisis.

It is further hoped that the information presented in the final chapter will result in readers exercising a new commitment to move beyond the many lies fueling these perilous times in ways that enable people to realize their untapped potential for optimal mental health, peace, and justice.

Lastly, persons reading this book need to understand that the position of the author is not to ask individuals to do 100% more on ten different things as we move beyond the lies perpetrated by Donald Trump, his supporters, and the Trump cult. Rather, I hope inspired readers will commit to doing 5% more on one thing to move us, as a nation, beyond the lies that underlie these perilous times and contribute to effectively addressing the mental health crisis in the United States.

CHAPTER 15

REVITALIZING THE MENTAL HEALTH PROFESSIONS

Social justice is never a solo endeavor, it is conceived and lived in community. A community considers itself to be just when it becomes a place in which each person is valued, where differences are recognized as assets, where children and youth can look up to their seniors as role models in the process of character development, where women's abilities are recognized and encouraged, where the elderly and those who live with any kind of limitations can be ensured of respectful care, and where abundance means that everyone has all that is needed to live a good and meaningful life.

A community in which social justice reins will be characterized by decreased levels of competition, abuses of power, fears and anxieties, and violence. A community of justice will be able to tap into the force and talents of the collective to appropriately respond to poverty, natural disasters, and in the visual weaknesses that are part of human life. Such communities possess resiliency and the ability to bounce back in times of adversity!

Dr. Regine Uwibereyeho King, survivor of the 1994
genocide against the Tutsi people in Rwanda

I am no longer accepting the things I cannot change. I am changing the things I cannot accept.

Angela Y. Davis, educator and social justice advocate

Introduction

The final chapter of this book is designed to assist readers in synthesizing many of the facts, terms/concepts, suggestions and recommendations discussed in the preceding chapters. To facilitate this process, the new integral theory of mental health and human development from a psycho-political perspective is linked to community counseling and community psychology theories. The relevance of this linkage in moving beyond the lies that continue to be perpetuated by Donald Trump, his supporters, and the Trump cult is detailed later in this chapter.

It is important to reiterate that I have intentionally avoided replicating what I refer to as the *Rudy Guiliani Syndrome*, named after former President Trump's attorney, who asserted that he had lots of theories about the 2020 presidential election results, but no evidence to validate these theories. History will show that Guiliani's asserted theories turned out to be nothing more than political lies aimed at replacing American democracy with an authoritarian and fascist government lead by Donald Trump. From the psycho-political perspective presented in the new integral theory, these lies continue to have a serious negative impact on many people's mental health and in stimulating mistrust in our country's election processes; a cornerstone of our democracy.

The reactions many people have to the misinformation repeatedly stated by Guiliani, Trump, and Trump's supporters have and continue to contribute to the deterioration of mental health and human development in the United States (See Chapters 6 & 9). For all of these reasons, I have intentionally avoided presenting mere opinions throughout this book. Instead, I have consistently referenced the results of more than 100 research publications to validate numerous psychological theories, terms, concepts, and suggestions/recommendations in the preceding chapters.

Additional information related to the important concept of *optimal mental health* is presented later in this chapter. This is done with intentional overtures for the reader's consideration of the potential benefits that might be derived by infusing the political teachings of Dr. Martin Luther King Jr. into the new integral theory. It is predicted that the benefits derived in doing so could stimulate readers' neurological, psychological, emotional, and behavioral domains as a result of thinking in new and more expansive ways about mental health and human development from Dr. King's political philosophy and psychology.

The integral theory of mental health and human development from a psycho-political perspective represents a call for a paradigm shift in our collective thinking about mental health. This collective thinking extends beyond what continues to be a dominant view of mental health problems as being disturbances that are strictly individual incidents. As noted in Chapter 9, experts like Erich Fromm (1955) and Robert Lifton (2017) call into question whether our society is, itself, sane and the ways in which a lack of sanity in our society is the source of people's mental health problems.

Not only is it reasonable, but the new integral theory asserts that it is vital for mental health professionals and other interested people in our society to address the following questions: To what degree is the *malignant normality* that Lifton describes present in our nation? A related question that would be useful to explore further is: What actions can mental health professionals and other interested people in our communities take to address the malignant normality occurring in our society?

Factors Contributing to Mass Psychological Disturbance

In defining a *mass psychological disturbance,* it is important to gather evidence that describes specific factors/conditions which result in the manifestation of this unique and detrimental disturbance. One way I have done this is by gathering information from various surveys that serve two purposes:

(1) The first evidence gathered for this study includes surveys that consistently indicate a majority of people in the United States express the belief that this nation is the greatest country in the world.

(2) The second evidence involves comparing reliable data that identifies the actual ranking of the United States on numerous surveys commonly used in social and political science studies with

responses made by people in the United States who state that they believe our nation is still the greatest in the world.

The following information summarizes my research findings that are used to compare the actual rankings of the United States on various social, economic, health care, and quality of life survey items with the majority of Americans who believe the United States remains the greatest country in the world.

A majority of people surveyed in August 2021 stated that they believe the United States is the greatest country in the world because of the freedom it guaranties its citizens. It is important to add that of the 207 sovereign states in the world, 180 support similar freedoms. Consequently, the United States should not in reality be viewed as a nation with a monopoly on freedoms.

The new integral theory of mental health and human development from a psycho-political perspective suggests that there are additional important conclusions to be drawn from these research findings. First, a majority of all the persons polled in August 2021 indicated that they believe the United States is still the greatest country in the world for many reasons; many of which are inaccurate beliefs. The research findings reported in this section of Chapter 15 were similar to the results of previous surveys conducted during the 1950s. However, during that era, the United States was actually ranked either 1st or 2nd in the world on similar social-educational-health-care categories.

A summary of research findings generated in the August 2021 YouGov survey indicated that the U.S. ranks 7th in literacy rates, 27th in mathematics ratings, 22nd in science, 49th in life expectancy, 178th in infant mortality, 3rd in median family income, 4th in the labor force, and 17th in the world for quality of life.

There are two categories that our nation does rank #1 in the world. This includes the number of incarcerated citizens per capita and military defense spending, where we spend more than the next 26 countries combined.

Despite the top ranking given by a majority of persons who participated in the above-stated survey results, the statistical outcome of this study provides compelling evidence that such a rating among the majority of survey participants is not reality-based. From a psycho-political perspective, this finding contributes to the perpetuation of the multidimensional mass psychological disturbance that continues in the United States.

It is important to restate the following three points so that the reader can get a clearer understanding of the implications of the survey results presented above. First, given the low overall rankings on the various categories used to define the greatest nation in the world, it is clear that our nation is not now the greatest country on the planet.

Second, in the 1950s, the United States was consistently rated as the greatest country, ranking either #1 or #2 on the above listed social-economic-healthcare-quality of life variables.

Third, with our nation's historically high-ranking decades ago in mind, the integral theory of mental health and human development asserts that *we the people* can develop and implement new politically-based interventions and social justice advocacy-based initiatives aimed at addressing our nation's mental health crisis while simultaneously increasing the low ratings on survey items that represent positive aspects of our nation. These services, initiatives, and interventions can be integrated into our schools, universities, businesses, and at-large communities to regain our collective greatness in the above-stated categories and revitalize the mental health professions in the process.

Throughout this book attention has been repeatedly directed to the ways in which the negative, comprehensive, and persistent impact of White racism and White supremacy in our society continue to contribute to the threats to our democracy, the elevated mental health problems in our society, and an undermining of our past high rankings used as criteria to measure a country's greatness. With all of these points in mind, mental health professionals, community organizers, and political activists are strongly encouraged to address these psycho-social-moral-unjust cancers as we work together in building a great nation.

Again, from the perspective of the new integral theory presented in this book, it is asserted that the first step in solving any problem is recognizing that there is one. Given the above-stated research findings, it is clear that America is not the greatest country in the world anymore. The new integral theory also asserts that, as a united nation, we can regain our status as a great country. It is further emphasized that mental health professionals can play important roles achieving this goal if they so choose.

The following section begins a detailed discussion of the types of strategies mental health professionals and interested persons in the general public are encouraged to utilize by linking community counseling, psychology, and social justice advocacy theories along with the new integral theory presented throughout this book. As has been the case throughout this book, the reader's attention will now be directed to definitions of key terms/concepts used in the following sections of this chapter.

The Community Counseling Theory (CCT)

Definition of Terms/Concepts

The psychotherapist, Stephanie Gilbert, says that the term *community* can be defined in many ways, but when simplified down to its most important element, community is all about connection. According to Gilbert, "*Community* is not just an entity or a group of people, it's a feeling. It's feeling connected to others, feeling accepted for who you are and feeling supported. These kinds of connections can help us feel wanted and loved." Dr. Martin Luther King Jr. referred to such communities as *Beloved Communities*.

One of the reasons why *community* is important for people's mental health is because we are social beings and are not meant to live in isolation. *Community* is critical for us to thrive, especially for someone with mental health problems who is already experiencing symptoms of loneliness and isolation. *Community* provides many elements that are critical to mental health. The following factors are particularly important to address in fostering mental health and human development from a community mental health perspective.

Belonging

If you have ever felt like you don't fit in, you know it can be a lonely experience. *Community* provides a sense of belonging–a group you identify as being a part. This is different from conforming to fit into a group. A true sense of belonging includes the ability for each of us to feel that we are part of a *community* as our true selves. There is nothing you have to change in order to be a part of a *healthy community*. Instead, you are embraced and appreciated for your unique qualities. These are characteristics included in Dr. Martin Luther King Jr.'s description of a *beloved community*.

Support

A simple question to ask in defining support is simply stated as follows, "Who do you turn to when you need something?" Having someone you can call when you need to talk or need help with something can help you through difficult situations that might feel insurmountable when you are alone. Knowing that there are people who support you can help you feel cared for, safe, and can benefit your outlook on life.

Purpose

In community with others, people fill different roles. This can be a friend who enjoys cooking and can be counted on to bring a hot meal to another person in the community who is experiencing stressful challenges in her or his life. A healthy community is where people know someone they can call when they need to talk about their struggles. These roles can give people a sense of purpose through bettering other people's lives. Having a purpose by helping others helps give positive meaning to life.

Natural Helpers

The meaning of the concept of *natural helpers* is central in understanding how many community members are helpful in making connections with other persons experiencing stresses that are detrimental to people's optimal mental health. As stated earlier, natural helpers are not professionally trained therapists. Rather, they are effective listeners who can and often do help friends and other community members explore their own psychological, emotional, and behavioral concerns by talking with them in various settings.

As outlined by Dr. Judy Lewis and her colleagues in their book entitled, Community Counseling: A Multicultural-Social Justice Perspective (2011), the authors discuss in greater detail many community members who function as *natural helpers*. These persons play important roles in helping other people realize their untapped potential for optimal mental health and ongoing human development. This includes but is not limited to family members, teachers, neighbors, members of different religious communities, athletic coaches at all levels of sport activities, bartenders, hair stylists, uber and taxi drivers, law enforcement professionals, elected officials, medical doctors/nurses and other related professionals, peer counselors in school settings, community organizers, and political activists to name a few.

During Jimmy Carter's presidential term in the 1970s, he established the White House Committee on Mental Health, which was led by his wife, Rosalynn Carter. The reported findings of that committee are relevant for the CCT. Among the findings reported by this committee was an acknowledgment of the specific skills which are routinely demonstrated by natural helpers that are relevant in promoting mental health and ongoing human development.

The White House Committee's report highlighted persons in three different fields that were particularly effective in supporting other community members during stressful times. This includes taxi drivers, hair stylists/barbers, and bartenders. Specific counseling skills were noted to be routinely manifested by these natural helpers that were helpful in addressing human crises as well the use of what mental health professionals refer to as prevention efforts as these natural helpers helped community members at-risk for mental health problems talk about their life stresses in ways that could lead to positive outcomes.

For example, the 1970s White House Committee on Mental Health found barbers and hairstylists to be effective listeners who maintain the confidentiality of their conversations when their customers discuss challenges they face in their daily lives. From a neurological perspective, we have learned that massaging a person's scalp helps to stimulate the release of dopamine and serotonin. These are pleasure promoting and relaxing neurotransmitters. When the brain releases these neurotransmitters, people commonly experience enhanced pleasurable relaxation that can be a precursor to enable customers to more freely discuss issues they might not normally talk about in other settings.

The final report from the 1970s White House Committee on Mental Health further noted that taxi drivers often demonstrate the effective use of crisis counseling skills with customers who are experiencing heightened stress and seek transportation for various reasons. This might include persons seeking transportation to remove themselves from domestic violence situations as well as people in need of someone to safely drive them home because they are inebriated.

As someone who has had contact with numerous bartenders in my life, I have come to understand the role they can play as natural helpers in our society. In the 1970s, the White House Committee on Mental Health acknowledged some of the similar observations I have had with these natural helpers.

Gene Delibero, an expert certified bartender explicitly addresses these points in his article entitled, "Customer Experience: It's Why You Love Your Bartender." As Delibero states:

> Great bartenders are excellent listeners. They listen to your stories and opinions. Sometimes they offer their own anecdotes, but only if they *truly* pertain to what *your* interests are. They do this for every customer, but they make you feel like their special attention is only for you.

> Great bartenders get to know who you are, what you like to drink, and why. They look you in the eye. They don't interrupt your conversation with the person next to you to ask if you want another drink–they just point to your waning beverage and catch your eye, waiting for your nod. They've got your back. They *know* you.

> Let's face it… great bartenders anticipate your needs, read your body language, and pay attention to your interactions with other customers. And great bartenders make great tips. Funny thing is that customers are more than willing to pay for those excellent customer service experiences, over and over again.

The latter statement highlights the point that bartenders' customers are more than willing to pay for excellent customer service experiences. This gratitude is similar to the reason many (perhaps most) clients pay mental health professionals for providing excellent customer services in counseling and psychotherapy.

This statement is not intended to be frivolous. Rather, it is intended to spotlight the role and function bartenders, taxi drivers, hairstylists/barbers, and millions of other community members play as natural helpers by making positive, empathic, and respectful connections with people in their communities resulting in positive aspects of their mental health.

The CCT recognizes that there are millions of natural helpers that live, work, study, and play in communities across the United States. The integral theory emphasizes the importance of incorporating new mental health and human development initiatives to address our nation's mental health crisis from a psycho-political perspective.

The goals of such innovative efforts could include addressing the perilous times in which we currently face as a nation, supporting the ongoing evolution of our multiracial/multicultural democracy, and fostering the realization of our untapped collective potential to stimulate optimal mental health across our country. These are some of the conditions and efforts that are necessary in revitalizing our mental health professions. These issues are addressed in greater detail later in a section of this chapter that describes the *indirect community service domain in the CCT theory*.

The Genesis and Evolution of the CCT

The CCT was developed in 1977 (Lewis & Lewis, 1977). Since its inception, this theory has been tested, refined, and expanded (Lewis, Lewis, Daniels, & D'Andrea, 1998, 2003, 2011). This research-based theoretical model marks a shift toward a new multi-service, culturally responsive, social justice-oriented helping paradigm. Although this new paradigm and its evolutionary offshoots are not yet fully realized in the mental health professions, they have much relevance in addressing our nation's mental health crisis. This untapped benefit will necessitate structural changes in mental health professional training programs, individual and community assessment processes, and clinical practices.

The CCT provides practitioners with practical guidelines by describing a broad range of services intentionally aimed at addressing our nation's mental health crisis. The essence of the CCT and its relevance in transforming our nation's mental health system is its emphasis on the need to implement an integrative, non-fragmented, and truly holistic approach to mental health (Ivey et al., 2012). In short, the CCT represents a helping framework that encourages new ways of thinking about mental health practitioners' and natural helpers' purpose and purview in the 21st century (Lewis et al).

The CCT is built on coherent and research-supported assumptions that guide the work mental health practitioners do along with other community stakeholders. These assumptions include the following:

1. People's environments may nurture, sustain, or impair healthy human development.

2. The goal of mental health care is to facilitate and sustain the healthy development of individuals, communities, and society at-large.

3. A multifaceted, multisystem approach to mental health is more efficient and sustaining than a single-service approach.

4. Attention to the multidimensional nature of mental health and human development is central in the planning and delivery of comprehensive mental health services in the 21st century. This includes increasing benefits to be derived from advances made in neuroscientific research findings (See Chapter 14).

Addressing these assumptions as part of a national project to increase the efficacy of our country's mental health system are key considerations for promoting systemic changes. The CCT outlines comprehensive and cost-efficient services that represent realistic and necessary interventions to address our nation's mental health crisis. Such interventions would be particularly useful in moving beyond the fragmentation of interventions which characterizes the current mental health system in our society.

Defining Optimal Mental Health

The definition of *optimal mental health* as used in this book is drawn from suggestions made by numerous mental health practitioners and their professional organizations. In addition to terms drawn from the integral theory of mental health and human development, concepts that fit the notion of "strong mental health" (National Alliance on Mental Illness [NAMI], 2019; Rosenbaum & Newby, 2020) and "positive psychology" (Seligman, 2002) are outlined below.

In discussing the meaning of *strong mental health*, Rosenbaum and Newby make the following points:

It is important to note that mental health and mental illness are not simply two sides of the same coin. Mental health, just like physical health, exists on a spectrum from poor to optimal. Like our physical health, some days we naturally feel stronger and more energetic than others. Similarly, some days our mental health is worse than others, and that too, is a natural part of being human. We may feel tired, grumpy, sad, angry, anxious, depressed, stressed, or even happy at any point in time. These are all normal human emotions with an innate potential to develop into *optimal mental health*.

Optimal mental health is a combination of feeling good and functioning well. Among the important components of optimal mental health include the following:

- Developing the skill of self-reflection which is useful in consciously thinking about the person one is. This involves investing time reflecting on the thoughts one has during the day, the feelings that are linked to these daily thoughts, and consideration as to how one might change her or his behaviors as a result of routinely engaging in self-reflection;

- Developing the capacity for intentional emotional regulation. This aspect of optimal mental health is important to develop and implement in different family interactions, among neighbors and friends, at school, in people's work settings, and at community, athletic, social, and/or entertainment events. The lack of emotional regulation is a hallmark in Donald Trump's political rallies and routinely failed to be manifested during his one-term presidency from 2016–2020;

- Having positive relationships that include people you care for and they care for you;

- Developing a genuine purpose in life;

- Experiencing a sense of accomplishment which involves doing things that give people a sense of personal competence;

- Developing the ability to cope with the stresses of life and keeping up to date on political issues and actions that impact the mental health of millions of people in the United States;

- Feeling generally positive about one's life knowing that there are times when life in general and the perilous political times we are currently experiencing can result in periodic negative thoughts and feelings about the future;

- Operating from a sense of self-esteem that involves generally feeling positive about oneself; and

- Feeling energetic with vitality from a psychological, emotional, physical and mental health perspective.

The integral theory presented in this book embraces the important work that Dr. Martin Seligman has done in introducing his theory of positive psychology (Seligman, 2002). Seligman's work complements and expands the above list of characteristics that define optimal mental health.

The new integral theory resonates with Seligman's detailed instructions as to how people can renew their personal, psychological, emotional and behavioral strengths, and personal virtues to realize one's untapped potential for optimal mental health. Seligman's work is also cutting edge in the ways he details the relevance of experiencing work and personal satisfaction in life as well as his description of love and raising children as they can help people to more fully realize their potential for optimal mental health.

Drawing Optimal Mental Health Concepts from Martin Luther King Jr.

The word *psychology* is derived from two Greek words, 'psyche', denoting the soul or spirit and 'logos', meaning to study. The mental health professions have drifted from the *soul* when discussing issues related to psychology, mental health, and human development to more scientific-based concepts, research methods, and empirically supported professional practices.

I have been a student of the life and legacy of Dr. Martin Luther King Jr. since the 1960s as a high school student and then as an undergraduate student at Fairfield University. More recently, I have increased my understanding of the importance of the unspoken word regarding Dr. King's political philosophy and psychology and their relevance for the mental health challenges we face at the present time. With this understanding in mind, I make an effort to put into words the relevance of Dr. King's political philosophy and psychology as it relates to addressing our nation's mental health crisis, an expanded definition of optimal mental health, and the relevance of Dr. King's teachings for the new integral theory presented in this book.

The following points begin an exploration of terms and concepts that are foundational in Dr. King's political philosophy and psychology. I begin this exploration by highlighting the words of Coretta Scott King in her Forward of Dr. King's book entitled *Strength to Love* (1963).

> I believe this book best explains the central element of Martin Luther King Jr.'s philosophy of nonviolence and his belief in a divine, loving presence that binds all life. This belief was the force behind all of my husband's quests to eliminate social evil and what he referred to when he preached of 'the interrelated structure of reality.'

Current findings in quantum physics result in very sophisticated and complex explanations of the interrelated structure of reality. Dr. King explains this important concept in ways that all of us can understand. As he stated:

> All people are caught in an inescapable network of mutuality, tied in a single garment of destiny. Whatever affects one directly affects all indirectly. I can never be what I ought to be until you are what you ought to be, and you can never be what you ought to be until I am what I ought to be.

The integral theory of mental health and human development from a psycho-political perspective acknowledges that the above statements are key political components of Dr. King's philosophy. Given the perilous times that mark our current situation, providing mental health and psychoeducational interventions intentionally designed to foster the essence of the above quotation is much needed in a world that has become pathologically absorbed in various forms of hate and violence. The current epidemic of gun violence, which has now become one of the leading causes of death for children in the United States, is an indicator of the need to incorporate Dr. King's thoughts about violence in our society in ways that foster optimal mental health.

Coretta Scott King further points out that Dr. King's first pastoral position was as Minister of the Dexter Avenue Baptist Church in Montgomery, Alabama. It was in that position that Dr. King actively combined theology with social-political change strategies. In doing so, she refers to the following words in a sermon Dr. King presented to his parishioners related to the Montgomery Improvement Association project.

> The basic conflict here in Montgomery is not really over the buses. Yet we believe that, if the method we use in dealing with equality in the buses cannot eliminate injustice within ourselves, we shall at the same time be attacking the basis of injustice—man's hostility to man. This can only be done when we challenge the white community to re-examine its assumptions as we are now prepared to re-examine ours.

One of the factors that contributes to realizing optimal mental health involves a person's commitment to routinely implement self-reflection that directs attention to the types of thoughts, feelings, and behaviors that emerge from our nation's socialization process. A repeated theme throughout this book and the primary cause of these perilous times is linked to the adverse impact of various forms of White supremacy and White racism for both the victims and the perpetrators of these inter-related psycho-political cancers.

The above quotation by Dr. King underscores the importance of eliminating all injustices–and particularly racial injustices–that are hallmarks of the new integral theory presented throughout this book. It remains to be seen how this aspect of Dr. King's political philosophy and psychology can be pragmatically implemented in our communities as well as in mental health training programs and mental health practitioners' clinical practices.

Clearly, it is important to maintain ongoing discussions about these important challenges as they relate to our country's mental health in general and the relevance of the integral theory of mental health and human development when addressing this nation's mental health crisis. Readers interested in participating in an ongoing exploration of ways to implement the integral theory by incorporating Dr. King's political philosophy into our mental health system are invited to participate in a special meeting in New Orleans, Louisiana during April 2024. More details about this event are provided at the end of this chapter.

The final sections of this chapter direct the reader's attention to a discussion of the types of community-based interventions that the new integral theory endorses to address our nation's mental health crisis. This involves describing four intervention domains that are foundational in the CCT and complementary of the new integral theory of mental health and human development discussed throughout this book.

Four Intervention Domains of the CCT

The CCT includes four intervention domains that are aimed at fostering and sustaining the mental health and ongoing human development of larger numbers of persons in diverse populations than mental health practitioners have been able to achieve in the past. Collectively, these intervention domains represent pathways to facilitate the realization of people's untapped individual and collective empowerment to deal with the current perilous times by supporting the ongoing evolution of our nation's multiracial/multicultural democracy. These intervention domains include direct client services, direct community services, indirect client services, and indirect community services.

Direct Client Services

Direct client services include the ongoing implementation of individual, small group, marriage/couples and family counseling/therapy services. A newly emerging direct client service of particular attention and support is referred to as neuropsychotherapy (Grawe, 2007).

Neuropsychotherapy starts with the utilization of functional magnetic imaging (fMRIs) as a scientific assessment of the neurological basis for many persons' mental health problems. The increased understanding of the intimate connections that exist among people's psychological, emotional, and behavior problems and their brain functioning begs for increased support for this data-driven approach to mental health.

Calls for broad-based accessibility of fMRIs among persons in the general public already experiencing mental health problems as well as those individuals identified as being at-risk for such problems would be an important step in democratizing neuropsychotherapy in our 21st century society. The cost in supporting such an important direct client service could be addressed by the reestablishment and expansion of the

1963 Community Mental Health Center Act as mentioned earlier in this book.

Direct Community Services

Many mental health professionals provide direct community services that are crucial in promoting mental health and human development. These services include psychoeducational interventions intentionally aimed at increasing the knowledge and skills necessary for larger numbers of people from diverse groups and backgrounds to experience healthy, effective, and happy lives (Lewis et al.).

Direct community services also involve support groups for persons who, although not currently manifesting mental health problems, are at-risk for such difficulties in the future. A partial list of these persons includes people feeling overwhelmed with their parenting responsibilities; students manifesting a broad range of challenges at all levels of our nation's education system; veterans, persons in LGBTQ communities, immigrants/refugees, persons with disabilities, and poor/unemployed persons to name a few (Dubus, 2009). Rather than operating from a reactive disposition by providing individual counseling and psychotherapy services among persons already manifesting mental health problems, direct community services involve prevention, psychoeducation, and life skills training to nurture the untapped empowerment potential of persons in at-risk groups.

Unfortunately, the preventive nature of direct community services continues to play second fiddle to the ongoing overuse of individual counseling and psychotherapy services with clients already manifesting life problems. Research findings provide compelling reasons why psychoeducation, life skills training, prevention groups, and related community-based interventions result in positive benefits for larger numbers of persons in diverse client populations in cost efficient ways than has been done in the past (Raczynski, Waldo, Schwartz, & Horne, 2013).

The possibilities in developing and implementing direct community services are endless. As noted in the proposed goal for the transformation of our mental health system, one of the challenges practitioners face relates to their implementation of programs, techniques, and concepts intentionally designed to support and sustain the mental health among larger numbers of persons from a broad and diverse range of groups and backgrounds than has been done in our past (Motlova, Balon, Beresin, Brenner, Coverdale, Guerrero, Louie, & Roberts, 2017).

Indirect Client Services

The CCT emphasizes the importance of building on the vital contributions millions of *natural helpers* make in fostering and sustaining the healthy development of large numbers of persons from diverse groups and backgrounds in our society. As noted earlier in this chapter, an incomplete listing of these natural helpers includes parents, extended family members, teachers, athletic coaches, persons in religious communities, peers, barbers/beauty salon service providers, taxi/uber drivers, and community human service volunteers to name a few.

All of these persons provide the guidance and support necessary to foster and sustain the well-being of millions of people across the lifespan who would not otherwise have access to such important human development experiences. One of the best ways to build on the untapped potential of natural helpers is for mental health practitioners to develop and implement ongoing, non-fragmented, developmentally integrated, and culturally responsive paraprofessional training opportunities with these persons. It is recommended that such training opportunities lead to the certification of natural helpers as paraprofessionals across our country.

Financial support is necessary to ensure the success of these efforts. Numerous researchers have noted that the utilization of such natural helpers predictably increases the relevance, viability, and effectiveness of our nation's mental health system (Brotman et al.). As previously noted, funding for these CCT services can, in part, be realized as part of increasing calls for reestablishing and expanding the 1963 Community Mental Health Act.

Indirect Community Services

From a community counseling and psychology perspective, it is critical to implement various indirect community services to be successful in forging the changes necessary to increase the untapped efficacy of our nation's mental health system. Indirect community services include social justice advocacy and ecological change strategies that support the rights and empowerment of groups of persons adversely impacted by injustices in various forms resulting in the disempowerment of large numbers of people in our society (Ivey et al.).

One of the theoretical frameworks holding much utility in understanding the impact of ecological systems on human development is Bronfenbrenner's theory of human development (Bronfenbrenner (1974, 1977, 1995, 2000). As noted earlier, much of the knowledge used by many mental health professionals focuses on variables associated in what Bronfenbrenner describes as clients' microsystems. Less attention is directed to the positive and negative impact of macrosystems on large numbers of people in our country (D'Andrea, 2019).

The microsystem is the first level in Bronfenbrenner's ecological systems theory of human development. It is comprised of variables having a direct impact on people's immediate environment. This includes the impact of family members, teachers, coworkers, and friends to name a few. Research findings highlight the impact that relationships at the microsystem have on people's mental health (Bronfenbrenner, 1995).

Of particular relevance for this chapter is the attention Bronfenbrenner directs to the impact systemic and cultural variables have on the health and well-being of all people in our society. This includes the impact of a person's socioeconomic status, access to healthcare resources, and education status as well as the impact of structural injustices including those linked to systemic racism, sexism/heterosexism, ableism, ageism, religious/spiritual discrimination, and immigration/refugee status (Daniels & D'Andrea, 2009). All of these dynamics fall within the realm of macrosystems.

The overemphasis mental health practitioners place on addressing microsystem factors in their professional practices contribute to the failure of our mental health system to foster and sustain the mental health and ongoing human development of a majority of people in need of such services. The failure to address macrosystem factors that undermine the healthy development of large numbers of people in our society results in fragmented, incomplete and, inaccurate assessments of people's environmental strengths and needs (D'Andrea, 2020).

Over the past 20 years, increasing attention has been directed to the role mental health practitioners can play in fostering the healthy development of persons from diverse groups and backgrounds by ameliorating social injustices perpetuated in different ways in our country's macrosystems. Though controversial for some, research findings unveil the connections between social injustices and mental health. These findings provide empirical support for the use of indirect community services that result in macrosystem changes to increase the efficacy of our country's failing mental health system (Hage & Romano, 2013).

Again, drawing from Bronfenbrenner's ecological theory, the outcome of implementing truly holistic client assessments, treatment planning, and helping interventions requires an integral team approach. At the risk of being repetitive, support in achieving these goals can come from the reestablishment and expansion of the 1963 Community Mental Health Center Act. This historic public health legislation is a formula for successfully increasing the relevance, viability, and efficacy of our nation's current mental health system.

Summary

This chapter summarizes a number of points highlighted in the preceding chapters. It also synthesizes the meaning of important concepts and recommendations from previous chapters with new, research-based information presented in this final chapter.

Earlier in this chapter, the reader's attention is directed to what researchers refer to as the *mass psychological disturbances* occurring in our society. This mass psychological disturbance continues to be manifested in the United States. Among the multiple sources of evidence used to validate this point is the fact that Donald Trump received 74,000,000 votes by his supporters in the 2020 presidential election as well as being the front runner for the Republican Party's nominee for the 2024 presidential elections. This pattern of support continues despite more than 34,000 documented lies Trump has and continues to articulate in his false conspiracies and related misinformation via social media networks and during his political rallies.

Specific points spotlighted in this chapter include emphasizing the need to revitalize our nation's mental health professions to effectively address the current crisis in the United States. From the perspective of the new integral theory presented in this book, it is suggested that these interrelated goals require mental health professionals to infuse psycho-political issues into their assessment and service delivery strategies.

These actions represent intentional efforts to foster the optimal mental health of larger numbers of persons in diverse racial and cultural groups than has been done in the past. They also represent a more intellectually honest demonstration of mental health professionals' commitment to operate from a truly holistic approach to mental health and human development.

This chapter defines the term *community* in an effort to link community counseling and psychology theories to the new integral theory. This definition illuminates the important impact of *belonging, support,* and *natural helpers* in promoting people's mental health and ongoing human development.

The next section of this chapter adds definitions of *optimal mental health*. It does so by drawing from relevant publications by mental health experts including Dr. Martin Seligman's positive psychology theory. These additional definitions are aimed at increasing the reader's thinking about new ways to address this nation's mental health crisis.

The new integral theory of mental health and human development also draws from Dr. Martin Luther King Jr.'s political philosophy to expand the definition of optimal mental health. It is predicted that linking Dr. King's political philosophy to new ways of thinking about mental health and human development will be controversial among some (perhaps many) mental health professionals.

Nevertheless, the integral theory acknowledges the important advancements mental health professionals can experience by thinking out of the box to consider the unique benefits to be derived by linking Dr. King's political psychology in inclusive ways to effectively address our nation's mental health crisis. More specifically, the successful recommendation to draw Dr. King's teaching about human development into the mainstream of the mental health professions requires new, formal, and institutionalized inclusion into professional training programs, revised professional ethical standards, new psychological assessment strategies, clinical practices, community development initiatives, and persistent social justice advocacy.

The final section of this chapter provides a description of the four service domains that comprise the community counseling theory; all of which complement the new integral theory of mental health and human development. This includes the direct client, indirect client, direct community, and indirect community service domains.

At the end of Chapter 15, it is acknowledged that much more discussion needs to occur when planning to employ the community counseling theory in conjunction with the new integral theory of mental health and human development in community settings. The author of this book will be convening a special meeting for interested readers to attend and participate in this continuing discussion, planning, and action. This gathering will be held in New Orleans, Louisiana in April 2024. Additional details will be provided when individuals interested in participating in this meeting contact Dr. Michael D'Andrea, President of the Social Justice Creations Nonprofit Organization via email at: michaeldandrea1@gmail.com.

REFERENCES

Adler, A. (1959). *Individual psychology.* Paterson, NJ: Littlefield, Adams, & Company.

Adler, A. (1963). *The problem child.* New York: Putnam.

Adler, A. (1969). *Understanding human nature.* New York: Fawcett Crest.

Aldarondo, E. (Ed.). (2007). *Advancing social justice through clinical practice.* Mahwah, NJ: Erlbaum.

Amen, D. (1998). *Change your brain; change your life: The breakthrough program for conquering anxiety, depression, obsessiveness, anger, and impulsiveness.* New York: Random House.

Americans Counseling Association. (2003). *Multicultural counseling competencies.* Alexandria, VA: Author.

Americans Psychiatric Association. (2000). *Diagnostic and statistical manual of mental disorders* (4th ed., text revision). Arlington, VA: Author.

Americans Psychological Association. (2003). *Guidelines on multicultural education, training, research, practice, and organizational change for psychologists.* Washington, DC: Author.

Andersen, T. (1993). See and hear: And be seen and heard. In S. Friedman (Ed.), *The new language of change* (pp. 54–68). New York: Guilford.

Arredondo, P., & D'Andrea, M. (2000, May). Census 2000: Implications for counselors and educators. *Counseling Today, 42,* 12.

Arredondo, P., Toporek, R., Brown, S. P., Jones, J., Locke, D. C., Sanchez, J., et al. (1996). Operationalization of the multicultural counseling competencies. *Journal of Multicultural Counseling and Development, 24,* 42–78.

Aubrey (1986). The professionalization of counseling. In M. D. Lewis, R. L. Hayes, & J. A. Lewis (Eds.), *An introduction to the counseling profession* (pp. 1–35). Itasca, IL: Peacock.

Bandura, A. (1962). *Social learning and imitation.* Lincoln: University of Nebraska Press.

Bandura, A. (1975). *Social learning and personality development.* Newark, NJ: Holt, Rinehart, & Winston.

Bandura, A. (1976). Effecting change through participant modeling. In J. Krumboltz & C. Thoresen (Eds.), *Counseling methods* (pp. 248–264). Troy, MO: Holt, Rinehart, & Winston.

Bandura, A. (1982). Self-efficacy: Mechanism in human agency. *Americans Psychologist, 37,* 122–147.

Bandura, A. (1997). *Self-efficacy: The exercise of control.* New York: Cambridge University Press.

Bowlby, J. (1969). *Attachment.* New York: Basic.

Cole, Nicki Lisa, Ph.D. "How Emile Durkheim Made His Mark on Sociology." ThoughtCo, Aug. 27, 2020, thoughtco.com/emile-durkheim-relevance-to-sociology-today-3026482.

Comstock, D. (Ed.). (2005). *Diversity and development: Critical contexts that shape our lives and relationships.* Belmont, CA: Brooks/Cole-Thomson Learning.

D'Andrea, M. (2005a). *Promoting multicultural competence and social justice.* Workshop presented to students, faculty members, and administrators at George Mason University as part of a national tour sponsored by the National Institute for Multicultural Competence.

D'Andrea, M. (2005b, January). *Reclaiming "positive psychology" from a multicultural perspective: Combating new forms of ethnocentrism and racism in psychology.* Unpublished paper presented at the national Multicultural Summit, Hollywood, CA.

D'Andrea, M. (2006). In liberty and justice for all: A comprehensive approach to ameliorating the complex problems of White racism and White superiority in the United States. In M. Constantine & D. W. Sue (Eds.), *Addressing racism: Facilitating cultural competence in mental health and educational settings* (pp. 251–270). Hoboken, NJ: Wiley.

D'Andrea, M., Arredondo, P., & Daniels, J. (2005, March). Multicultural advocacy and community service. *Counseling Today, 47,* 40–41.

D'Andrea, M., & Daniels, J. (2009). Promoting multiculturalism, democracy, and social justice in organizational settings: A case study. In J. G. Ponterotto, J. M. Casas, L. A. Suzuki, L. A., & C. M. Alexander (Eds.), *The handbook of multicultural counseling* (3rd ed.). Thousand Oaks, CA: Sage.

D'Andrea, M., & Daniels, J. (2009). *Strategies to prevent cultural-racial prejudice.* In C. F. Salazar (Ed.). *Group work experts share their favorite multicultural activities: A guide to diversity-competent choosing, planning, conducting, and processing* (pp. 129-131). Alexandria, VA: Association for Specialists in Group Work.

Daniels, J., & D'Andrea, M. (2009). *Using the RESPECTFUL counseling model to foster multicultural competence in group settings.* In C. F. Salazar (Ed.). *Group work experts share their favorite multicultural activities: A guide to diversity-competent choosing, planning, conducting, and processing* (pp. 238 – 246). Alexandria, VA: Association for Specialists in Group Work.

D'Andrea, M. (2006). Addressing racism: Facilitating cultural competence in mental health and educational settings, In M. Constantine and D. W. Sue (Eds.), (pp. 112 – 135). New York: Wiley.

D'Andrea, M., Daniels, J., Arredondo, P., Ivey, A. E., Ivey, M. B. Locke, D. C., et al. (2001). Fostering organizational changes to realize the revolutionary potential of the multicultural movement: An updated case study. In J. G. Ponterotto, J. M. Casas, L. A. Suzuki, & C. M. Alexander (Eds.), *Handbook of multicultural counseling* (2nd ed., pp. 222–253). Thousand Oaks, CA: Sage.

Duran, E. (2006). *Healing the soul wound: Counseling with Americans Indians and other native peoples.* New York: Teachers College Press.

Duran, E. & Duran, B. (1995). *Native Americans postcolonial psychology.* Albany: State University of New York.

Fanone, M. & Shiffman, J. *Hold the line: The insurrection and one cop's battle for AmEricha's soul.* Atria Books: New York.

Ellis, A. (1958). *Sex without guilt.* Secaucus, NJ: Lyle Stuart.

Ellis, A. (1971). *Growth through reason.* Palo Alto, CA: Science & Behavior.

Ellis, A. (1975). *Growth through reason: Verbatim cases in rational-emotive therapy.* Palo Alto, CA: Wilshire Book Company.

Ellis, A. (1983). The origins of rational-emotive therapy (RET). *Voices, 18,* 29–33.

Ellis, A. (1994). *Reason and emotion in psychotherapy.* New York: Birch Lane.

Ellis, A. (1995). Changing rational-emotive therapy to rational-emotive behavior therapy. *Journal of Rational-Emotive and Cognitive-Behavior Therapy, 13,* 85–90.

Ellis, A. (2000). A continuation of the dialogue on issues in counseling in the postmodern era. *Journal of Mental Health Counseling, 22,* 97–106.

Fields, D.R (2020). Neuroscience and psychology suggest no surprise victory for Trump this time. *Scientific Americans,* October 18, 2020.

Frankl, V. E. (1959). *Man's search for meaning.* New York: Pocket Books.

Frankl, V. E. (1969). *The will to meaning.* New York: New Americans Library.

Frankl, V. E. (1970). Forerunner of existential psychiatry. *Journal of Individual Psychology, 26,* 38.

Frankl, V. E. (1984). *Man's search for meaning* (Rev. ed.). New York: Washington Square Press/Pocket Books.

Freud, A. (1982). *Psychoanalytic psychology of normal development: 1970–80.* London: Hogarth.

Freud, S. (1964). Negation. In S. Freud (Ed.), *On metapsychology* (pp. 435–442). London: Penguin.

Freud, S. (1966). *A general introduction to psychoanalysis.* New York: Norton.

Gilligan, C. (1982). *In a different voice.* Cambridge, MA: Harvard University Press.

Ivey, A. E. (1986). *Developmental therapy: Theory into practice.* San Francisco: Jossey-Bass.

Ivey, A. E. (1991, September). *Developmental therapy and media therapy: An update.* Presentation to Veterans Administration Conference, Orlando, FL.

Ivey, A. E. (1993). *Developmental counseling and therapy: A review of the 1971–73 microtraining/media therapy psychoeducational project with psychiatric inpatients.* Paper presented at the Veterans Administration Conference, Orlando, FL.

Jung, C. G. (1964). *Man and his symbols.* New York: Doubleday.

Jung, C. G. (1971). *The portable Jung.* New York: Penguin.

King, M. L., Jr. (1986). The drum major instinct. In J. M. Washington (Ed.), *A testament of hope: The essential writing of Martin Luther King, Jr.* (pp. 259–267). San Francisco: HarperCollins.

Kimmel, M. (2018). *Healing from hate: How young men get into—and out of—Violent extremism* (e-book ed.). University of California Press.

Lee, B. X. (2000). Profile of a nation: Trump's mind, AmEricha's soul. A World Mental Health Coalition Book.

Lewis, J., Lewis, M., Daniels, J., & D'Andrea, M. (2011). *Community counseling: A multicultural social justice perspective* (4th ed.). Pacific Grove, CA: Brooks/Cole

Lewis, J. A., & Lewis, M. D. (1977). *Community counseling: A human services approach.* New York: Wiley.

Lewis, J. A., Lewis, M. D., Daniels, J. A., & D'Andrea, M. J. (1998). *Community counseling: Empowerment strategies for a diverse society* (2nd ed.). Pacific Grove, CA: Brooks/Cole-Thomson Learning.

Lewis, J. A., Lewis, M. D., Daniels, J. A., & D'Andrea, M. J. (2003). *Community counseling: Empowerment strategies for a diverse society* (3rd ed.). Pacific Grove, CA: Brooks/Cole-Thomson Learning.

Lewis, J. A., Lewis, M. D., Daniels, J. A., & D'Andrea, M. J. (2011). *Community counseling: Empowerment strategies for a diverse society* (4th ed.). Pacific Grove, CA: Brooks/Cole-Thomson Learning.

Loevinger, J. (1986). *Paradigms of personality.* New York: Freeman.

Maslow, A. (1971). *The farther reaches of human nature.* New York: Viking.

Maslow, A. H. (1970). Holistic emphasis. *Journal of Individual Psychology, 26,* 39.

Quiñones-Rosado, R. (2007). *Consciousness-in-action: Toward an integral psychology of liberation and transformation.* Caguas, Puerto Rico: Ilé.

Seligman, M. E. P. (2002a). *Authentic happiness: Using the new positive psychology to realize your potential for lasting fulfillment.* New York: Free Press.

Seligman, M. E. P. (2002b). *Positive psychology.* Washington, DC: Americans Psychological Association. Available online at http://www.apa .org/releases/positivepsy.html

Siegel, D. J. (2007). *The mindful brain: Reflection and attunement in the cultivation of well-being.* New York: Norton.

Sue, D. W., Arredondo, P., & McDavis, R. J. (1992). Multicultural counseling competencies and standards: A call to the profession. *Journal of Counseling and Development, 70,* 477–486.

Sue, D. W., & Sue, D. (2015). *Counseling the culturally diverse: Theory and practice* (6th ed.). New York: Wiley.

Thorndike, E. L. (1911). *Animal intelligence.* New York: McMillan.

Wilber, K. (2000). *Integral psychology: Consciousness, spirit, psychology, therapy.* Boston: Shabhala.

Wolpe, J. (1982). *The practice of behavior therapy* (3rd ed.). New York: Pergamon.

Wolpe, J., & Lazarus, A. (1966). *Behavior therapy techniques.* Elmsford, NY: Pergamon.

Zukav, G. (1989). *The seat of the soul.* A Fireside Book. New York.

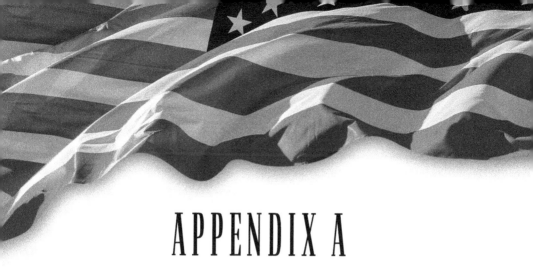

APPENDIX A

Multicultural Competencies for a Multiracial/ Multicultural Democracy

The following multicultural competencies are adapted from a list developed by multicultural counseling and psychology experts in the mental health professions (Sue, Arredondo, & McDavis, 1992; Sue et al., 1998).

There are three major multicultural competency domains that are important for all people in our society to develop to effectively support the ongoing evolution of our fragile multiracial/multicultural democracy. These three major competency domains include multicultural awareness, multicultural knowledge, and multicultural skills. These competencies are described below.

Awareness of One's Own Racial/Cultural Assumptions, Values, and Biases

Awareness Competencies:

1. Culturally competent persons have moved from being culturally unaware to being aware and sensitive to their own cultural heritage and valuing and respecting differences in others.

2. Culturally competent persons are aware of how their own cultural background and experiences, attitudes, values, and biases

influence their thinking about and reactions to racially and culturally different people.

3. Culturally competent persons recognize the limits of their racial and cultural competence.

4. Culturally competent persons are comfortable with differences that exist between themselves and racially/culturally different people in terms of race, ethnicity, culture, values, and beliefs.

Knowledge Competencies

5. Culturally competent persons are knowledgeable of their own racial and cultural heritage. They also understand how this knowledge personally affects their definitions and biases of normality-abnormality.

6. Culturally competent persons possess knowledge about the ways that various forms of oppression, racism, discrimination, and stereotyping affect themselves personally. This allows culturally competent persons to acknowledge their own racist attitudes, beliefs, and feelings. The definition of the four quadrants of White racism detailed in Chapter 2 is helpful to utilize in developing this cultural competence. Although this standard applies to all groups, for White people it may mean that they understand how they have directly or indirectly benefited from individual, institutional, and cultural racism.

7. Culturally competent persons possess knowledge about their interpersonal impact on others. They are aware of communication style differences. They also understand how their own interpersonal style may clash with or facilitate multicultural interactions with persons from different racial/cultural groups.

Skill Competencies

8. Culturally competent persons seek out educational experiences to enrich their understanding and effectiveness in working with racially/culturally different populations.

9. Culturally competent persons seek to understand themselves as racial-cultural beings and actively strive to develop an anti-racist identity.

Understanding the Worldview of Racially and Culturally Different People

Awareness Competencies

10. Culturally competent persons are aware of their negative emotional reactions toward other racial and cultural groups.

11. Culturally competent persons are aware of the stereotypes and preconceived notions they may hold toward other racial/cultural groups.

Knowledge Competencies

12. Culturally competent persons are knowledgeable of the different worldviews people in racially/culturally diverse groups operate from in their lives. They are knowledgeable of the life experiences, cultural heritage, and historical background of racially and culturally different people in their community.

13. Culturally competent persons are knowledgeable of the ways race and culture may affect personality development, career/vocational choices, and different ways of thinking about healthy human development. This includes differences among racially and culturally different groups that value collectivistic versus individualistic views of the world and healthy human development.

14. Culturally competent persons are knowledgeable of political influences that impinge upon the lives of racially and culturally different people. Immigration issues, poverty, racism, stereotyping, and powerlessness all leave psychological scars among many people in marginalized groups.

Skill Competencies

15. Culturally competent persons make an effort to familiarize themselves with information describing the mental health and psychological problems that commonly occur among people in various cultural and racial groups.

16. Culturally competent persons become actively involved with people in diverse cultural-racial groups (via community events, social, and political functions, celebrations, friendships, neighborhood groups, and so forth).

Developing Mutually Respectful Connections with Persons in Diverse Populations

Awareness Competencies

17. Culturally competent persons are aware of and respect other people's religious and/or spiritual beliefs and values.

18. Culturally competent persons respect indigenous helping practices and minority communities' help-giving networks.

19. Culturally competent persons value bilingualism and do not view another language as an impediment to developing positive connections with other people (monolingualism may be the culprit).

Knowledge Competencies

20. Culturally competent persons are knowledgeable of institutional barriers that prevent minorities from realizing their untapped potential for healthy human development and optimal mental health across the lifespan.

21. Culturally competent persons have knowledge of minority family structures, hierarchies, values, and beliefs. They also possess an understanding of the community characteristics and resources that may be useful in supporting culturally diverse families to realize their untapped potential for healthy human development and optimal mental health.

22. Culturally competent persons are aware of discriminatory and racist practices occurring at the individual, social, political, and community levels that adversely impact the psychological welfare and physical health of people in oppressed and marginalized racial/cultural groups.

23. Culturally competent persons are knowledgeable of numerous models of minority and majority identity development. Two points discussed earlier in this book related to this cultural competence are briefly reiterated below.

First, multiple theories of racial/ethnic identity development have been created that describe the different manifestations of a racial/ethnic identity consciousness among persons in diverse racial/cultural groups in our multicultural 21st-century society.

Second, mental health professionals generally agree that effective and respectful multiracial/multicultural interpersonal interactions can be enhanced when they meet people in racially/culturally diverse groups where these individuals are operating psychologically, cognitively, emotionally, behaviorally, and in terms of such persons racial/cultural identity development. These important issues are discussed in greater detail in Chapter 14.

Skill Competencies

24. Culturally competent persons are able to exercise institutional, political, community, and social justice advocacy skills on behalf of people negatively impacted by societal toxins that impair healthy human development.

25. Culturally competent persons strive to eliminate biases, prejudices, and discriminatory practices. They are cognizant of racially/culturally diverse individuals psycho-political experiences. They also continually attempt to develop greater sensitivity to issues of oppression, sexism, and racism, especially as they affect racially and culturally diverse people's lives.

Sources: Adapted from Sue, D. W., Arredondo, P., & McDavis, R. J. (1992). Multicultural counseling competencies and standards: A call to the profession. *Journal of Counseling and Development, 70*, 477- 486 and Sue et al. (1998) *Multicultural counseling competencies: Individual and organizational development.* Thousand Oaks, CA: Sage.

Printed in the USA
CPSIA information can be obtained
at www.ICGtesting.com
LVHW071733260424
778546LV00011B/144